D1446573

The
Confederate
Belle

The
Confederate
Belle

Giselle Roberts

University of Missouri Press
Columbia and London

Copyright © 2003 by
The Curators of the University of Missouri
University of Missouri Press, Columbia, Missouri 65201
Printed and bound in the United States of America
All rights reserved
5 4 3 2 1   07 06 05 04 03

Library of Congress Cataloging-in-Publication Data

Roberts, Giselle, 1974–
  The Confederate belle / Giselle Roberts.
    p. cm.
Includes bibliographical references and index.
  ISBN 0-8262-1464-9 (alk. paper)
  1. United States—History—Civil War, 1861–1865—Women. 2. United
States—History—Civil War, 1861–1865—Social aspects. 3.
Mississippi—History—Civil War, 1861–1865—Women. 4.
Mississippi—History—Civil War, 1861–1865—Social aspects. 5.
Louisiana—History—Civil War, 1861–1865—Women. 6.
Louisiana—History—Civil War, 1861–1865—Social aspects. 7. White
women—Confederate States of America—Social conditions. 8. Elite
(Social sciences)—Confederates States of America—History. 9.
Confederate States of America—Social conditions. 10. Southern
States—Social conditions—19th century. I. Title.
  E628 .R63 2003
  973.7'082'0975—dc21

                                                    2003000204

∞™ This paper meets the requirements of the
American National Standard for Permanence of Paper
for Printed Library Materials, Z39.48, 1984.

Designer: Stephanie Foley
Typesetter: Foley Design
Printer and binder: Thomson-Shore, Inc.
Typeface: Goudy

For my parents, Ron and Tricia Myers
And for Glenn, with love

Contents

Acknowledgments

It gives me great pleasure to acknowledge all those who have offered me advice, support, and encouragement during the writing of this book. Researching and writing southern history from Australia involves many additional challenges, the greatest one being geographical distance. The Internet and a host of enthusiastic and knowledgeable archivists have made the world seem a much smaller place to me indeed. I am grateful to all the librarians who offered me their advice and support and gave most generously of their time in an effort to help me locate all the materials I required. I would like to extend special thanks to Anne Webster and all the staff at the Mississippi Department of Archives and History for making my husband and me feel so welcome during our trip to Jackson in the summer of 1998. I would also like to thank Elizabeth Dunn, research services librarian at the Special Collections Library at Duke University, for her advice on all matters of research, writing, and publishing. Her professional expertise and friendship mean a great deal to me.

At the University of Missouri Press, Beverly Jarrett's professionalism and support have made the publication process both exciting and enjoyable. I thank her for believing in this book. Jane Lago and the other members of the staff also welcomed me from the beginning and have patiently answered a multitude of questions. I greatly appreciate their enthusiasm and advice. Special thanks to Julie Schorfheide for editing the manuscript for publication.

LaTrobe University's commitment to American Studies fostered my interest in Southern history, which was reinforced by three exceptional historians and mentors: William Breen, John Salmond, and Warren Ellem. Over the last ten years they have listened to my ideas (and frustrations), read drafts, and provided me with advice and encouragement. My respect for their scholarly work is only equalled by my respect for them as individuals. I am profoundly grateful. I would also like to thank Charles

East, Laura Edwards, and Charles Joyner for taking an interest in my work and for so kindly offering their advice and support, which helped me sharpen my focus and consider new and interesting viewpoints.

I owe a great deal to my family and friends, who have shared in the highs and lows of this journey with me. Jenny Alexander and Erin Gook have been more than friends; they have been kindred spirits. They read my articles, requested regular updates on the project, and, most important, helped me through the difficult times. I will always treasure their friendship. Fran, William, and Marie Fenamore of New York welcomed me into their lives so many years ago and have become my American family. I feel blessed to know them—and love them. I would also like to thank my grandmother, Patricia Shanks, who, through her own example, taught me to love books and encouraged me in my dream to some day write one. My sister, Nerissa, did what only the best sisters can do by arriving on my doorstep at the most appropriate times with a box of chocolates, which are certain to make anyone feel better after a long day of reading or writing.

Since the day I arrived home with a copy of Sarah Morgan's diary, my parents, Ron and Tricia Myers, have encouraged my research into the world of the Southern belle. They have read drafts, offered suggestions, scanned photographs, and watched as my research evolved into a book. Their unconditional love and support have been my lifeline. I can never repay the debt, only gratefully acknowledge their contribution by dedicating this book to them, with love.

And finally, I would like to thank my husband, Glenn, whose patience, generosity, and good humor have made me appreciate life, and enjoy living it. While our cats, Abby and Katie, assumed their faithful positions at either side of my computer, Glenn gave me the time and space to write on weekends and during holidays. He is my best friend and greatest supporter, and I am thankful for every day of our life together.

Parts of chapter 4 have appeared in *Louisiana History* 43 (spring 2002): 189-214.

Parts of chapter 5 have appeared in the *Journal of Mississippi History* 42 (summer 2000): 97-122.

I would like to thank all those institutions and individuals who granted me permission to use images for this book. Special thanks to Morgan Potts Goldbarth for allowing me to use a previously unpublished carte de visite of Sarah Morgan, to Charles East for allowing me to use a carte de visite of Church Street, Baton Rouge, and to

Alice Dale Cohan for her permission to use the portrait photograph of Clara Solomon.

I have preserved the inconsistencies in the nineteenth century diaries and letters used in this book. These include variations in spelling and punctuation, unenclosed quotes, and inconsistencies in capitalization. I have, however, substituted *and* for *&*. Spelling mistakes have not been corrected, and where the mistake is only a minor one, I have refrained from using the editorial convention "[*sic*]."

The
Confederate
Belle

Introduction

It is hard to write a book about the Southern belle without mentioning Scarlett O'Hara. Margaret Mitchell's imposing character with her raven locks, penetrating green eyes, "magnolia white skin," and seventeen-inch waist has come to dominate our popular understanding of the belle and the American Civil War of which she was a part. Ironically, Scarlett was anything but the embodiment of the quintessential belle ideal. Clad in a green-trimmed muslin dress that stole the heart of more than one eligible Southern gentleman, Scarlett's ability to assume the physical guise of an accomplished young lady did little to mask her complexity or her passion. Quick witted, charming, cunning, and determined, Scarlett demonstrated a tenacity to use anything, including the war itself, to snare her beloved Ashley away from the meek and mild Melanie Wilkes. She possessed neither the piety nor gentility required of elite Southern ladies, and assumed the sacrificial air of the patriotic woman only to further her own personal ambitions. While this lavishly dressed, charismatic young "heroine" has become synonymous with the Southern belle, Scarlett O'Hara was actually the antithesis of the exalted feminine ideal.[1]

Perhaps Scarlett's stranglehold on representations of young Southern womanhood can partly be attributed to a relative lack of scholarship in this area. Anne Firor Scott, Catherine Clinton, Elizabeth Fox-Genovese, Drew Gilpin Faust, and Marli Weiner have published an impressive body of work on the plantation mistress, but surprisingly, the Southern belle has not been examined in detail.[2] Similarly, Civil War historians are yet to examine the lives of young, elite, white, Southern women, whose wartime experiences have often been dismissed because of their strong association with the romance and fanfare of war. Other studies have used the diaries and letters of young women, but distorted the experience of the belle by incorporating it into larger analyses of elite

1

Confederate womanhood in which women of all age groups are represented as having common ideals and wartime experiences. While historians have defined women according to their race, class, and gender, they have often failed to draw upon age as a category of analysis. Age, however, had a powerful impact on a Confederate woman's understanding and experience of war. A mistress, for example, encountered a set of practical and emotional challenges that were vastly different from that of her mother or her daughter. These varied wartime experiences would ultimately shape the ways in which women of all ages confronted the changed social landscape in the postwar period.

It is the purpose of this book to draw upon the category of age to examine the lives of young, elite, white women in Confederate Mississippi and Louisiana. In doing so, this work also seeks to make a contribution to the historiography that has sought to unravel the long-term social and cultural effects wrought by war, in particular, the extent to which the conflict became a "watershed" for Southern women. An earlier generation of historians argued that the Civil War "provided a springboard" from which women leaped into a world "heretofore reserved for men." Recent scholarship has revised this interpretation, and suggests that the wartime experiences of elite Southern women led them to "invent new selves designed in large measure to resist change" rather than embrace it. While these historians have often emphasized the ways in which postwar life fostered women's involvement in the social reform movement, they conclude that "everything had changed, and nothing had changed." In the postbellum South, ladies may have entered the "public arena," but they continued to cling to the preexisting racial and class hierarchy as they looked for ways to assert their elite status in a world without wealth or slaves.[3]

Historians have regarded the reasons why Southern women clung to old ideals as self-explanatory: Their race, class, and gender afforded them a privileged position they were unwilling to relinquish, especially after they had encountered the many hardships associated with four long years of war. This is indeed true. Yet there was also another powerful ideology at work that ensured their commitment to the old order, and that was Southern honor.

Scholars are yet to examine the importance of Southern honor in shaping the wartime lives of Confederate women. In the antebellum South, men and women lived—and sometimes died—by the code of honor; but they never defined the abstract and elusive concept with any precision, perhaps because its meaning was so inextricably linked to an individual's status and to the context of specific events, people, and places. Honor, and the importance of protecting it, was bound up in the web of Southern social relations and, more specifically, in that "set of beliefs in which a person has exactly as much worth as others confer upon" them. Bertram Wyatt-Brown argues that Southern honor was made up of three components: the inner conviction of self-worth, the claim of self-assessment before the public, and the assessment of self-worth by the public. It was internalized within the self through the family unit and externalized through the judgment of this honor by the community. While race, class, and gender determined one's position in the social hierarchy, honor was the mechanism through which individuals or families affirmed or enhanced their status and gentility. Honor was embraced by planters and yeomen alike but was most fully expressed by the Southern elite, who used it as a means of controlling social relations and asserting their power and influence.[4]

Not surprisingly, class, age, and gender influenced the ways in which Southerners expressed their honor. Southern men and women, for example, were socialized in different forms of honor. Elite men affirmed their honor through business and politics. Honor was also reflected in a gentleman's elegant home and family and in his domination over his slaves. If any one of these relationships was called into question or the family unit suffered an insult, an elite male was compelled to defend honor by an act of courage. He frequently did so by entering into a duel with his accuser. This violent form of dispute resolution asserted individual character and defined class boundaries, which were essential to the maintenance of a rigid social hierarchy.[5]

Of course, not all men stood at fifteen paces with guns drawn in an effort to maintain their honor. As Edward Ayers has noted, a man's class position influenced his understanding of what constituted "public opinion" and how the insult would be avenged. "To many poor men [public opinion] meant the respect of a few drinking friends; to local luminaries it meant the judgment of nearby planters and professional men; to politicians it meant the verdict of the press." The context and the people involved set out a course of action to deal with harmful slander: Elite men dueled; poor men often fought in taverns or on the streets. All, however, were compelled to defend their honor or risk losing their status and self-worth in the eyes of the community.[6]

Elite women were also educated in the principles of Southern honor. While historians contend that men possessed individual honor, which could be established and affirmed through business, politics, or duels, many have argued that women's honor was merely a reflection of the honor of the head of household. Wyatt-Brown argues that female honor embodied a "multitude of negatives" and was underscored by the ability of Southern women to exercise "restraint and abstinence." A woman's submission, deference, religious piety, and sexual purity, then, highlighted the honor of the head of household.[7]

Because female honor was used to enhance the honor of male kin, many historians agree that women did not possess honor, "only virtue," because "the ultimate protection of honor lay in physical courage, an attribute not considered to be within woman's sphere."[8] This interpretation not only maligns but also dismisses women's different, yet equally important, contribution to family honor. Just as Southern men upheld their honor in different ways according to their class position, gender also shaped the ways in which honor was expressed and understood. Women may not have been able to physically defend their honor, but they did possess it. Ladies expressed their honor by embodying the Southern feminine ideal. Their appearance, accomplishments, social ties, and roles as wife, mother, sister, daughter, and mistress affirmed their gentility and self-worth, which in turn affirmed the status of the family unit. Women had the ability to destroy family honor through sexual indiscretion, or enhance it by marriage to a social equal. Family honor was not just a direct reflection of male honor. Rather, it was a form of collective honor, where the family unit reaped the rewards (in different ways) for each member's individual and gender-proscribed affirmation of honor.

Historians are yet to explore adequately either the significance of honor to the socialization of antebellum Southern women or the ways in which it was embraced by Confederate women during the Civil War.[9] By centering the analysis on young Southern women, our understanding of the belle's role in antebellum society, and the part honor played, is deepened and reconfigured. This understanding of honor allows us to see young women not merely as social ornaments or a reflection of their male kin, but as individuals capable of shaping their family's status through their appearance and accomplishments and, ultimately, by marriage. It also deepens and reconfigures our understanding of young women's contribution to the Confederate War, which was, in large part, shaped by their commitment to family honor. In wartime, young ladies extended their role in society in the name of family honor. With their men gone to war, they also assumed the responsibility of upholding honor in communities grappling with the effects of Federal occupation.

Young women's important contribution to family honor rendered them active and valued participants in the culture of honor, not just symbolic or passive figures who helped affirm the status of their male kin.

This book will use the categories of age and honor as a prism through which to explore the different wartime experiences of young, elite, white Confederate women. In the plantation culture of the antebellum South, these young ladies, or belles, had been trained to embody the finest aspects of Southern gentility, and to extend—or even enhance—family honor by marrying well. A belle represented elite femininity and actively asserted it by pursuing her "natural" role as a wife and mother.

During the war, patriotic womanhood superseded the antebellum feminine ideal. It demanded that Confederate women sacrifice everything for their beloved cause: to give up their men, their homes, their fine dresses, and their social occasions to ensure the establishment of a new nation and the preservation of elite ideas about race, class, and gender. As men folk answered their call to arms, Southern matrons had to redefine their role as mistresses and wives. While their task was challenging, and at times overwhelming, most matrons were able to adapt their antebellum roles and responsibilities to embrace the patriotic ideal. The management skills they had acquired through years of supervising slaves and running households were now used to organize sewing societies or benefits to raise money for the Confederacy. The countless hours they had devoted to maintaining their family's genteel attire or assisting with the production of slave clothing were, in wartime, extended to include soldier's uniforms, socks, gloves, and knapsacks. A matron's interest and involvement in antebellum politics nurtured a strong and articulate sense of nationalist feeling among many elite women. As the ravages of war began to encroach on the Southern home front, these women understood the shortages, the loss of slaves, and the presence of Federal soldiers in terms of their life experience as mistresses, wives, and mothers.

Elite young ladies also used their life experience to understand, and adapt to, the wartime world around them. Their experience, however, was a very different one, primarily because of their age, which influenced their participation in domestic and community affairs. Unlike their mothers, belles did not have comprehensive training in household management; in many cases, they had been relegated to the periphery of antebellum domestic life. Aside from needlework, darning, and embroidery, young women had little knowledge of the heavy-duty sewing and knitting often completed by the mistress. Unlike their mothers, most belles were not particularly interested in politics, preferring instead to devote their time to visiting, music, reading, society, and beaux. And after being encouraged to embody Southern gentility, young women perceived the shortages, the loss of slaves, and the other repercussions of Federal occupation as an assault on their honor, status, and gentility. After being prepared for a delightful "bellehood," young women were forced to reassess their traditional rite of passage into womanhood, to compromise their understanding of femininity at a pivotal time in their lives. They found themselves caught between antebellum traditions of honor and gentility, a binary patriotic feminine ideal, and wartime reality.

Young ladies did not simply sacrifice their antebellum socialization for patriotic womanhood. Instead they drew upon their conceptual framework of Southern honor to shape their understanding of themselves as young Confederate women. They regarded the sewing and knitting they completed for the soldiers and their role on fundraising committees as honorable activities that affirmed status and self-worth. Without balls and parties, belles participated in benefits, concerts, and tableaux as an alternative way to exhibit their accomplishments. They justified the hours spent patching and remodeling old clothing as necessary to maintain their gentility and "keep up appearances." And finally, young ladies used honor to legitimize their treatment of Federal soldiers and to absolve the shame they felt over the loss of their slaves. By drawing upon this powerful concept, Confederate belles ensured the basic preservation of elite ideology. They also preserved something of their own understanding of self.

Young women's commitment to honor, however, did not always result in a seamless transition from antebellum ideals to wartime reality. Family honor, like the families themselves, had to adapt to the challenging contingencies of war. Young women were often forced to expand their role in the family and the household in order to meet the new patriotic requirements of family honor. In the latter stages of the conflict, they were compelled to defend family honor, an office previously performed by male kin. The competing and often contradictory ideologies of genteel honor and sacrificial patriotism were never far from the surface, and this ever-present tension forced young ladies to confront fissures in the mold of the Southern feminine ideal. Still, it largely prevented a further questioning of the social hierarchy, which had always used race, class, and gender to affirm the dominance of the elite white male.

A number of factors define the scope and nature of this study. First, this book provides an analysis of the lives of young women in Confederate Mississippi and Louisiana. I have chosen to examine these two states for three reasons. The rich primary material that exists within this region is the first. Second, Mississippi and Louisiana provide a good example of the cultural dominance of planter ideology in the late antebellum period and the ways in which it was repeatedly challenged and unraveled during the course of the war. Planter ideology, which was founded on elite ideas about race, class, and gender, formed the cornerstone of the antebellum Southern hierarchy. Planter ideology invested complete dominance in the elite white patriarch, who in turn governed politics, business, family relationships, and the household. At the other end of the scale, it placed African Americans in positions of legal, economic, and social inferiority and, with few exceptions, consigned them to slavery. Most Southerners fell somewhere in between. A white yeoman farmer was given rights and privileges in accordance with his race and gender but was restricted by his class position. Elite white women were elevated socially by their race and class, but this power was tempered by their gender. Planter ideology reinforced this hierarchy by drawing upon the notion of reciprocal obligations between husbands and wives, parents and children, and masters and slaves, to cast the elite male in the role of the benevolent provider who protected his subordinates in return for their deference and obedience. It underpinned Southern culture and remained largely unchallenged until the upheaval generated by the Civil War.[10]

Inevitably, planter ideology adapted to the different geographic, economic, and cultural conditions present in Mississippi and Louisiana, which were both relatively new states at the outbreak of war. Carved out of the Louisiana Purchase of 1803, the state of Louisiana was admitted to the Union in 1812 and was followed in 1817 by Mississippi. In the 1820s and 1830s, many aspiring seaboard planters and small farmers fell prey to the lure of western wealth and prosperity and migrated with the hope of finding their fortunes in the Mississippi region. Despite the long and influential role of Creole society in Louisiana, a strong Anglo planter culture developed alongside it, founding itself on the traditions of the Southeast. The tropical climate and the rich, fertile soil proved ideal for the staple crops of cotton and sugar, and by the late antebellum period, log cabins and frontier wilderness had, in many cases, made way for the grand pillared plantation homes reminiscent of genteel life on the Southern seaboard.

Nottoway, one of the largest and most opulent plantation homes in the South, stood as testimony to the wealth, prosperity, and dominance of the Mississippi region's Anglo elite. Situated on Louisiana's River Road, Nottoway was built by John Hampton Randolph in 1859 and became the crown jewel of his thousand-acre sugar plantation. Designed by renowned New Orleans architect Henry Howard, the imposing structure—a combination of Greek Revival and Italianate styles—comprised sixty-five rooms and included a magnificent white ballroom, wide balconies, more than four thousand yards of plastering, Italian black marble mantels, and an elegant dining room featuring a seventeen-foot American Empire table.

The grace and grandeur of Randolph's estate was reproduced up and down the river from Vicksburg to New Orleans. Just south of Nottoway, John Smith Preston, the son-in-law of General Wade Hampton, built Houmas House—another pillared Greek Revival mansion surrounded by majestic oaks and ten thousand acres of working land. Farther up the river, Englishman Daniel Turnbull, a descendant of George Washington, built Rosedown, an elegant home flanked by Greek Revival wings and a formal garden designed by an esteemed French landscape artist. In 1850, Dr. Haller Nutt chose a picturesque location just outside Natchez to build Longwood, a unique, octagonal mansion with ornate ironwork, wide balconies, Italian marble mantles, and a punkah to ensure that genteel Southern dining was attainable all year.[11]

Planters and elite professionals also built elegant homes in prominent river towns such as Baton Rouge or Natchez. Sarah Morgan's parents, Judge Thomas Gibbes Morgan and Sarah Hunt Fowler Morgan, purchased a handsome double story home on Church Street in Baton Rouge, with spacious rooms, servants' quarters, and wide galleries that provided some relief from the oppressive Louisiana summers. In Natchez, the social capital of Mississippi, elite residents embraced Greek Revival architecture, wide balconies, elegant gardens, and genteel town living. In Louisiana, New Orleans emerged as a thriving business center, shipping the cotton grown on estates such as Nottoway to mills in the North, Britain, and continental Europe. By 1860, New Orleans was the only Southern locale to be ranked among the fifteen most-populated cities in the United States.[12]

Like their established counterparts, Mississippi and Louisiana were founded on the exploitation of slave labor. Planters and yeoman farmers alike relied on slaves to cultivate their staple crops, and the rural and urban elite drew upon slave ownership to assert their gentility and status. On the eve of the Civil War, half of Louisiana's population was made up of slaves, while in Mississippi, slaves outnumbered the white population.[13] The entire plantation system was dominated by the Mississippi River, in terms of both the landscape and the economy. The river was responsible for the pattern of settlement, and the biggest plantations in the region converged along its banks. The river also provided planters with "commercial significance" as they used its vast, muddy waters for the transportation of crops and goods.[14]

The development of a plantation system of agriculture also culminated in the emergence of a planter class reminiscent of those in the established eastern region. This class adhered to the basic notions of honor, slavery, and patriarchy, with one important difference. Unlike the older Southern states, which linked family lineage to gentility, the development of the Mississippi region as a land of promise and fortune led to an emphasis on "wealth and professional success, rather than kinship in and of itself," as the determinants of social status.[15] Consequently, special attention was given to the exhibition of wealth and gentility through the physical appearance of family, home, and possessions. The belle's ability to embody and extend her family's social position placed her at the forefront of this struggle to attain power and prestige.

The young ladies in this study came from the Anglo slaveholding families of the region, which in 1860 comprised approximately 31 percent of the population in Louisiana and 49 percent of the population in Mississippi. Those families belonging to the planter class (which has been broadly defined as those families owning twenty slaves or more) comprised 5.5 percent of the total white population in Louisiana and 9.37 percent in Mississippi. Many of the young women in this study were members of the planter class. Others, who belonged to urban professional families or did not own twenty or more slaves, often identified with and were accepted as members of this class. I have used the term *elite* to describe this group of urban or rural, upper- or upper-middle-class young women who were the daughters of planters or professionals.[16]

Finally, I have focused my study on Mississippi and Louisiana because of the wartime conditions in these states. With the outbreak of war, the young ladies in this region were among the first to encounter patterns of Northern invasion and occupation. By 1862, Union general Benjamin Butler had taken control of New Orleans and the Federal army had captured strategic points along the Mississippi River. By mid-1863, Baton Rouge, Natchez, Vicksburg, and Port Hudson had surrendered to the

Union army. Throughout this period, large areas in both states were occupied by Federal troops.

The wartime conditions in Mississippi and Louisiana had a profound impact on young women, who, with their mothers and sisters, were left to defend the home front. Women of all ages soon became accustomed to surprise raids by Union soldiers and the subsequent loss of food and provisions. Many were forced to become refugees. The Federal blockade of all Southern ports further increased the hardships of these women as they struggled to find food, accommodation, and hope in an isolated region. As members of this wartime community, the young ladies of Mississippi and Louisiana experienced the full impact of the war much earlier than women in most other parts of the Confederacy. They watched their understanding of planter ideology unravel before them. Consequently, their diaries reveal an acute pattern of crisis and change.

Race, age, and class also define the limits of this study. All the young Southern women were white, and most ranged in age from fifteen to twenty-five when they composed their extant journals or letters. While this age group includes adolescents and adults, a woman's role in her family and household was largely determined by her marital status. This role remained constant until marriage, or until a time when a young lady's family regarded her as a spinster.

This group of young women were often described by themselves, or by others, as "belles." This term has a dual meaning. *Belle* was often used as a label for all young, elite, white women who had made their formal debut into society. *Belle* also referred to a stylization of young womanhood that embodied the finest aspects of the Southern feminine ideal. The "belle ideal" was an exalted representation of gentility, piety, physical beauty, and accomplishment, a precursor to the more matron-ly representations of the Southern wife, mistress, and mother. During the Civil War, Confederate belles were those young women who were compelled to surrender their social debut for a role as sacrificial patriots of the Southern cause. To avoid any confusion in the use of this term, I have used "belle ideal" when referring to the stylization of young womanhood.

The Confederate belles in this study shared a heritage that was shaped by their race, class, gender, and age; yet there were many other factors that rendered their wartime experiences complex and diverse. Their lives were profoundly affected by the absence or presence of male kin and extended family networks, their family's pre-war wealth, the occupations of male kin, the extent of slave ownership, the managerial capabilities of female kin, their socialization, patriotism, and individual personality. Regional difference was another key variable. Planter women, for example, confronted a set of wartime challenges that were in contrast to those of their elite urban counterparts. Regional differences also determined the impact of the Federal presence on women's lives. Some ladies stood constantly in the line of battle, while others seldom saw a Union soldier. Some women endured life in occupied cities such as New Orleans, while others experienced a mix of all these conditions because of their mobility or refugee status. I provide a discussion of these factors wherever possible. I have, however, decided to center my analysis on the lives and the stories of these young women—how their wartime experiences differed from those encountered by older women, what unique coping strategies they employed, and how their perception of themselves as belles changed as a result of the war—rather than providing a comparative analysis of young women in different geographical locations. While this study draws upon more than one hundred manuscript collections and published diaries, the narrative also centers on a select group of young ladies who reflect the commonalties, the diversity, and the inherent struggle that characterized the wartime experience of the Confederate belle. Further references to additional primary material and the wider historiographical debates relating to my analysis can be found in the endnotes.[17]

Finally, this book draws heavily from the diaries of the period. In the antebellum South, parents often encouraged their daughters to take up diary writing as a way to foster gentility and self-improvement. Education and leisure time also facilitated the development of this pastime, and during the Civil War era, young ladies emerged as prolific writers, busily working at daily chronicles of their tumultuous lives.

The diaries left by young women are as unique as the women themselves. Some were kept as records to be read by teachers and parents, others were secret places that allowed young women to explore their most intimate thoughts and feelings. Kate Foster's diary began as a wartime history for her nieces and nephews and evolved into a very personal account of her grief and depression. Sarah Lois Wadley's diary was introspective throughout the war. As she grew older, her "private" diary became a "public" family record of births, deaths, and marriages. Clara Solomon and Sarah Morgan wrote in their diaries as if they were dear and trusted friends. Sallie McRae merely jotted down her daily household chores. Each diarist had different motivations for writing her story, and the purpose and audience profoundly shaped the construction, inclusion, and exclusion of people, places, and events. Mood, memory, and socialization also influenced what a young lady chose to write about, or what she chose to exclude. Even in the "private" realms of a diary, nineteenth-century mores overwhelmingly prevented adolescent girls from engaging in a discussion about their changing bodies. Similarly, women's socialization in the principles of self-sacrifice also made some young ladies acutely aware of the "self-absorbing" function of diary writing, which influenced what they wrote about and the time they devoted to "journalizing." Despite these constraints, diaries provide a vivid and engaging self-representation of elite women and form a rich basis for the study of young womanhood.

This book also draws upon the correspondence written by parents, children, siblings, and friends. This material is also subject to a number of constraints. Letters, unlike many diaries, are intended for another living person and are shaped and filtered with this audience in mind. They can be more formally bound by etiquette and convention, and sometimes produce a "self consciousness which may be entirely absent from the pages of a diary."[18] Family letters, however, remain of great importance to the historian, and to this study. While diaries present only one side of family relationships, letters provide a multifaceted glimpse into familial expectations and responsibilities. They give us an "outside view," providing insight into other constructions of young womanhood and exposing the tensions between public representations of the self and the personal turmoil so often expressed in diaries.

The use of family correspondence in this study has been limited by the available material. Many of the relevant letter collections were small and fragmented, containing, for example, ten letters written by a father to his daughter away at boarding school. Some letters mentioned the wartime behavior of female kin but were "inadmissible" if a woman's age could not be determined. Only one collection in this study contained a diary written by a young lady along with a selection of family correspondence. Although the limitations on the volume and content of this material narrow our "outside view" of young women, they do not obliterate it. I have located a number of small yet rich collections of correspondence in which fathers, mothers, siblings, and friends provide another perspective on the wartime experiences of young women. Much of this material appears in the main text.

This study also draws upon the memoirs written by Southern women decades after Confederate defeat. Many of these accounts were written in the late nineteenth century at the height of the Southern memorial movement and were heavily influenced by the rhetoric of the Lost Cause. Women's memoirs were also constrained by organizations such as the United Daughters of the Confederacy, which provided writers with guidelines to promote the development of a "collective memory" of the Confederate War. As a literary genre, memoirs are influenced by mood and memory and are often susceptible to inaccuracies. With these theoretical constraints in mind, I have used this evidence only to supplement the other primary material found in diaries or letters.

All primary material comes with its own set of complex theoretical issues, yet diaries, letters, and memoirs help to uncover the wartime lives and experiences of young ladies in Confederate Mississippi and Louisiana, as well as a society grappling with the antebellum legacies of slavery, patriarchy, and honor. Throughout the conflict, young women's unique wartime path was filled with irreconcilable ideals: antebellum ideals, patriotic demands, and wartime reality. Young ladies used honor in an attempt to reconcile these ideals to become belles of the Confederate South.[19]

CHAPTER ONE

"When I Am Grown"

The Southern Belle in Mississippi and Louisiana

> I only can anticipate that eventful epoque in my life, the "coming out."
> I shall laugh and dance and flirt, haha, am I not going to have a nice
> time. I will have beaux, plenty of them (that is if I can get some) and
> go to parties and lead a very pleasant life.
>
> *Lemuella Brickell, February 10, 1859*

In 1859, fourteen-year-old Lemuella Brickell longed to become a
Southern belle: to enjoy that brief yet important "epoch" in her life
between completing her education and getting married. From her home
in Yazoo County, Mississippi, Lemuella dreamed of the days when she
would be able to put the drudgery of school work behind her and relish
the delights of her formal debut into society. She eagerly anticipated the
balls, parties, suitors, visiting, and leisure-filled days when she would
have "nothing to do but read, talk and go along in a 'harum scarum' sort
of way." Still, there was more to becoming an accomplished young lady
than just coming of age. Lemuella knew that the celebrated "belle ideal"—
the most exalted stylization of elite young womanhood—embodied the
finest representation of gentility. Belles were beautiful yet pious. They
were thoroughly educated in the classics, French, history, and philosophy and could converse on an array of interesting topics. They were fine
singers, graceful dancers, and accomplished musicians. Most of all, they
were captivating; they gained the admiring glances of women and stole
the hearts of eligible men.[1]

In Mississippi and Louisiana, the glamorous life of the Southern
belle was idolized by elite schoolgirls who longed for the day when they
could lower their hemlines, tie up their hair, and enter society with
grace, poise, and a swag of admiring suitors. Like Lemuella Brickell,

15

thirteen-year-old Mary Bertron fantasized about becoming a belle. Only weeks after her return to boarding school in February 1851, Mary pleaded with her mother to permit her to enter society the following fall. "Well dear child, you wish to come home as an accomplished young lady," replied her mother. "Now Ma thinks that would be too soon to make your debut into society."[2]

As Mary eagerly anticipated balls and beaux, her mother recognized the importance of her daughter's "social achievements" to the status of the family unit. In the developing states of the Mississippi region, membership to the elite may have been defined in terms of wealth rather than family lineage, but money alone did not ensure aspiring planters or professionals a place at the top of the Southern hierarchy. Instead, a family's social success depended on their ability to use their wealth to exhibit gentility. A fine home became the cornerstone in this quest for status and prestige. While frontier life still lingered in parts of Mississippi and Louisiana in the late antebellum period, this strong connection between gentility and elite culture had fostered the development of a plantation landscape quite reminiscent of that in the East. By 1860, stately pillared mansions with imported furnishings and carefully manicured gardens lined the banks of the Mississippi River. In river towns such as Baton Rouge and Natchez, elegant urban townhouses were often inhabited by planter families or wealthy professionals.

While a fine home became a prerequisite of status, the quest to affirm gentility and define social boundaries encompassed all aspects of elite life. A family's ownership of slaves, their ability to stage and attend lavish social occasions, their acceptance by other elite families, their clothing, manners, and leisure activities, all influenced their overall social standing. Each family member also had a role to play to ensure that family honor and gentility were upheld and publicly affirmed. Elite men contributed the wealth and prestige generated by their business and political interests. Mistresses contributed to family honor by exemplifying the ideal wife, mistress, and mother, and by fostering the development of a social network that was nurtured though activities such as visiting, attending church, and participating in events such as balls or parties.

Elite parents also looked to their daughters to further the family's social ambitions. While the belle has often been dismissed as a passive participant in the culture of honor—either as a glittering bauble on her father's arm or as the justification for her brother's engagement in the code of honor—the young Southern lady actually played a vital role in upholding and enhancing her family's reputation. A belle's appearance, her accomplishments, her ability to sing, dance, and play the piano, were all deemed evidence of her family's wealth and gentility. These attributes furnished a belle with the tools to enhance her family's honor and prestige through a favorable marital alliance. Marriage could potentially link elite professional families with planter families, or modestly affluent planter families with wealthier ones. It could lift a young woman and her kin into higher social circles, perhaps even facilitating the development of other personal and business allegiances. At the same time, marriage allowed a young lady to fulfill her "natural" destiny as a wife and mother.

There were few alternatives to marriage and children. The life of an "old maid" was hardly the crowning achievement of a successful bellehood, and some young women worried that they would fail to attract a suitor who would ensure them financial security and social respectability. While dreaming of a "pleasant life" filled with parties and leisure, Lemuella Brickell grew increasingly anxious that the frivolities of bellehood may all be for naught. "I hope I will not be an old maid," she wrote, with a hint of revulsion at the thought. She was not alone. After a rousing family sing-along in their parlor in New Orleans, Clara and Alice Solomon retired to the sofa to calculate the likelihood of their becoming "old maids." As they "mused upon the *impossibility* of any's getting married, considering the limited circle of our acquaintances," Clara consoled herself with the thought that out of the six Solomon girls, "*all* could not be 'old maids.'"[3]

The stigma attached to single life pointed to the harsh realities that confronted women alone in a patriarchal world. Unlike many of their Northern counterparts, single Southern women were not set up in households of their own and provided an allowance by family members. Instead, they were often ferried from family to family, as nursemaids to reproductive kin.[4] In many ways, they were considered failures. Single women did not extend family honor though marriage, nor did they fulfill their "natural" role to become mothers. Instead, the dreaded label "spinster" hounded them in life and death. When Maria Chambers, the sister-in-law of Mississippi governor Gerard Chittoque Brandon, died, her headstone did not mark her achievements, associations, or family ties. Rather, it was more concerned with her inability to embody the Southern feminine ideal. Under her name it simply stated, "Never Married."[5]

The undesirability of single life was compounded by the limited employment opportunities for elite women. A lady could bake or sew at home if financial circumstances compelled her to do so, but employment outside the household was undertaken only out of dire necessity, not choice. Young ladies who were single, orphaned, or without financial support were often forced into teaching, which was widely regarded as the only respectable profession for women. Educating children was not a task for the faint-hearted, and for many young women it was both a challenge and a burden. "No body can know how tired I am," wrote one governess from her post at Selma plantation in Washington, Mississippi, "neither can any, but those who labour at the pleasant task of 'teaching the young idea.'" Months later she recoiled from the drudgery and challenges of her position, and longed for the weekends when she could enjoy a brief respite from the schoolroom. "Oh how tired I am of this kind of life," she sighed. "Any thing and every thing is better than this living death."[6]

Expressions of discontent were common. Employed as a teacher of French at the Columbus Female Institute, twenty-seven-year-old Caroline Seabury had initially left New York in search of a "brighter future, of contented usefulness." In only a few short years she knew all too well the monotonous life of a "Yankee teacher" in Mississippi. "The dull round of daily duties in teaching is I hope faithfully gone through," Caroline commented in 1859, "but how little of my real self goes into that. It is merely machine work, fast becoming intolerably irksome—and just for dollars and cents."[7]

With these limited and unpalatable alternatives, it is not surprising that the elite young women of Mississippi and Louisiana devoted their attentions to beaux and marriage. While belles often dreamed of dashing suitors, a daughter's martial prospects were taken seriously by the Southern family wishing to affirm their status and honor. Elite parents devised mental lists of appropriate suitors, carefully considering a gentleman's background, education, religion, wealth, character, and compatibility with their daughter. Romantic love was also regarded as a solid foundation for a successful marriage.[8]

Young women drew upon similar criteria when daydreaming of the "perfect husband." Sarah Morgan's standards were so high that even her brother conceded she would probably never marry. "I need some one I would delight to acknowledge as the model of all goodness and intellect on earth," she proclaimed, "some one to look up to, and admire unfeignedly, some one to lead me upward, and teach me to be worthy of his regard." Sarah looked for intelligence, which she considered to be "a chief qualification in man," amiability, " . . . for I am satisfied that no home is a happy one where it is not an inmate," and social finesse. "He must be a man of the world," she remarked. "Of course he must be entitled to it by birth and education; I could marry no other than a gentleman." Even after losing her brother, Henry, to the infamous code of honor, Sarah still revered bravery and placed it high on her list of necessary criteria. "He must be brave as man can be," she declared, "brave to madness, even. I would hate him if I saw him flinch for an instant while standing at the mouth of a loaded canon. Let him die, if necessary; but as to a coward—! Merci! je n'en veux pas! [Thanks! I don't want any of it!] I am no coward; it does not run in our blood; so how could I respect a man who was one?" Dismissing physical appearance and money as neither desirable nor important, Sarah vowed that if she ever met this brave and intelligent gentleman, then "I will tumble heels over head in love, and get married forthwith, even if I had to do the courting!"[9]

Lemuella Brickell placed more faith in financial compatibility. After a spirited discussion with her friend on the "vulgarity" of "marrying persons for money," Lemuella assured "Miss Wilson" that practicality was just as important as love. "I said that I saw no 'fun' (to use a vulgar expression) or no use to marry a poor man, just because you perhaps may like him better than a rich one," she wrote. "If you are poor yourself, you certainly do not better your condition in life by uniting yourself for life to a poor man." Instead, Lemuella hoped that if she ever got married, "he may be a real gentleman and also *rich*." Sophie Collins dreamed of suitors who were both handsome and gallant. After attending a theatrical production in April 1858, she fell in love at "first sight" with a gentleman milling in the crowd. "He is very much like Dr. Kirkpatrick," she related in a letter to her sister, Mary, "only much handsomer, and more manly looking." A year later, Sophie dismissed the advances of a wealthy Louisiana sugar planter because he was "very ugly." "His nose is about a yard long, and turns up," she exclaimed in disgust. "It looks like it is hunting for something all the time."[10]

While belles like Sarah, Lemuella, and Sophie imagined detailed portraits of their beau ideal, attracting an appropriate suitor required years of training. A young lady's ability to exhibit gentility in society and extend family honor through marriage rested on her family's ability to provide her with the appropriate education. Academic training was a vital component, yet parents also furnished their daughters with religious and domestic instruction. They were responsible for refining a young lady's temperament, manners, fashion sense, and social graces. Preparation for society, courtship, and, ultimately, marriage were important concerns for the elite families of Mississippi and Louisiana.

"Feminine Training"

A young lady's preparation for womanhood began when she was a child. Under the tutelage of her mother and a collection of aunts, older sisters, neighbors, and friends, girls were educated on their place within the family and the complex web of social relations. While race and class elevated elite women above slaves and a large portion of the white population, gender limited their authority within the family, household, and community. They were bound to respect the head of household, whose position as master, husband, and father reinforced his power and authority. Young women such as Sarah Morgan revered this quality in a man and looked for it in a husband. "My lord and master must be . . . the one that, after God, I shall most venerate and respect," she declared. "Woe be to me, if I could feel superior to him for an instant!"[11]

Elite women were also required to observe their place within the system of reciprocity, a system that governed relations between masters and slaves, husbands and wives, and parents and children. Ideally, wives, children, and slaves sacrificed their independence and obeyed the head of household. For this, they received protection. In the case of women and children, protection was central to Victorian ideology and Southern honor. Women deferred to male kin and, in return, received protection and advice "on any matter pertaining to the greater world beyond the household." A lady's purity was also central to the code of honor, and a woman could disgrace her entire family by traveling alone or diverging from the accepted forms of social etiquette that governed relations between men and women. Consequently, Southern men went to great lengths to protect female kin. Gentlemen escorted ladies when visiting or traveling. Their honor was protected. Women, therefore, relinquished their independence for "acceptance, respectability and security" for themselves and the family unit.[12]

The cultivation of women's position within the social hierarchy was ensured through a combination of Enlightenment and religious thought, which argued that women's "natural" piety and gentleness made them perfect moral guides for their husbands and children. The lady was perceived as an "angel of the house," who, through her devotion to God and her family, elevated the moral temperament of the household. She provided support and spiritual guidance to her male kin and, by doing so, set the "moral temperament" of the nation. "A hundred times we have seen weak men show real public virtue, because they had at their sides women who supported them . . . by fortifying their feelings of duty, and by directing their ambition," declared the *Godey's Lady's Book*. "We do not hesitate to say that women give to every nation a moral temperament, which shows itself in politics."[13]

If it was women's duty to spur their men onto public greatness, it was also their responsibility to guard them from temptations such as drinking, gambling, or "deviant" women. Popular advice columns explained that this was achieved by providing a happy, inviting, and entertaining home for male kin, a "haven from the outside world" that would subdue their temptations to "wander." "It is well for the women of the household to remember that the pleasant evenings at home are strong antidotes to the practice of looking for enjoyment abroad, and seeking pleasure in by and forbidden places," instructed one Louisiana newspaper. "Happy are those who find in the home circle the diversion they need. A lively game, an interesting book read aloud . . . a new song to be practiced, will make an evening pass pleasantly."[14]

With this important role to uphold, it is no wonder that young women's religious instruction was given priority. From the time they were children, elite girls attended Sunday school and accompanied their mothers to church. At home, they studied the Bible, and often documented their spiritual development in their diaries. Religious instruction gave parents the opportunity to teach their daughters the virtues of discipline and restraint, while church membership provided young women with the opportunity to interact within a larger social network and to make an active contribution to the development of community values and interests. Young ladies frequently taught Bible class or Sunday school. They attended church picnics, concerts, and fairs. They also assisted with charitable endeavors for the sick or the poor. Most important, they cultivated piety while expanding their social connections and exhibiting their genteel accomplishments.

The sense of freedom and purpose generated by these activities was tempered by religious instruction that reinforced planter ideology and women's subordinate place within it. From their pulpits across the South, ministers encouraged young ladies to become virtuous women through their observance of piety, submission, resignation, and deference. The development of the Christian woman, they argued, facilitated the development of the ideal Southern lady—and ladies knew their place. Just like slaves, women were instructed that their salvation depended upon their ability to recognize their rightful position within the Southern landscape and to cheerfully and obediently fulfill the requirements of their designated role.[15]

Many young ladies found themselves in a daily spiritual struggle, battling vice in a desperate attempt to fulfill the Southern feminine ideal. In Noxubee County, Mississippi, Maria Dyer Davies used her diary to scrutinize her spiritual development. On regular occasions, she beseeched the Lord to assist her to become a better Christian, and, therefore, a better woman. "I feel that I need more religion," she wrote anxiously in 1853. "May God be merciful to me. God help me for I am weak and helpless." Without parents to instruct or guide her, Maria was often frustrated by her sister's well-meaning attempts to "mother" her. After venting her anger, she deplored her unchristian and unladylike behavior. "I feel that I am a monster," she cried, "an unworthy creature. . . . Oh God . . . have pity upon me . . . and help me to have those kindly sympathies and that sincere affection—that God only gives—and which he loves."[16]

Maria may have regarded herself as a "monster," but she saw that as no reason to abandon her role as a spiritual guide to others. After yet another argument with her sister, Maria prayed to God to "bless my dear sister here and may she be a better Christian." Berating her sibling on the importance of religious observance, Maria was shocked when Frances "said just now she believed I loved to scare her with hell and such things." "If I have spoken harshly or of unpleasant things, twas because I felt concerned for her soul," she retorted defensively. Although she was a "little hurt" by Frances's sharp comments, Maria continued to pray for her own salvation and that of her kin. By doing so, her spirituality affirmed her place within her family, household, and community and nurtured the development of qualities that lay at the heart of the Southern feminine ideal.[17]

EDUCATING THE BELLE

While religious instruction was considered vital to a young lady's preparation for womanhood, piety was a virtue, not an accomplishment. In the antebellum South, elite parents wanted to furnish their daughters with the best opportunities to allow them to fulfill their designated role as young ladies, and later, as wives and mothers. They believed that rigorous academic training provided the means to achieve this highly desired end. By the 1850s, most elite parents subjected their children to years of schooling with the expectation that the attainment of intellectual, musical, and artistic skills would enhance a young woman's

gentility while also fostering her sense of self-fulfillment. Parents anticipated that their daughter's accomplishments would impress potential
suitors and would later provide her with the requisite skills to establish
an intellectually and morally uplifting home environment for her husband and children.[18]

In Mississippi and Louisiana, young ladies were educated through a
combination of home tutoring and attendance at local neighborhood
schools, female academies, and boarding schools. In Louisiana, the most
prestigious academies were located in New Orleans, which by the late
antebellum period had developed into a bustling commercial center
attracting elite professionals and a large middle class. In Mississippi,
boarding schools dotted the rural landscape, and by 1860 there were at
least fifteen private female institutions, including the Elizabeth Female
Academy in Washington, Holly Springs Female Institute, Columbus
Female Institute, and the Carrollton Female Academy. A number of
schools were also established in Natchez, where teachers instructed the
daughters of some of the wealthiest cotton planters in the entire South.[19]

By the 1850s, many young ladies in Mississippi and Louisiana received
training in an array of intellectual, social, and artistic pursuits. Unlike
Northern society, which became hostile to the idea of educating women
who might use their knowledge to enter the paid workforce, elite Southerners embraced education as a way to elevate gentility and celebrate
refinement. At Mount Hermon Female Institute in Clinton, Mississippi,
Eudora Hobbs received academic training typical for a young lady of
her class. In 1857, she studied subjects including spelling, reading, writing, geography, history, arithmetic, English grammar, and music. Other
subjects available at the institute included botany, science of familiar
things, natural philosophy, logic, rhetoric, chemistry, political economy,
algebra, French, Latin, Greek, composition, and "ornamental branch-
es." In New Orleans, Laura Hyde Moss studied natural philosophy,
French, rhetoric, and essay writing. Her father also encouraged her
intellectual pursuits and provided her with supplementary books and
periodicals to read in her spare time.[20]

A young lady's education was also motivated by society's recognition
of the need to furnish women with the appropriate skills to allow them
to fulfill their moral obligation to the household. Southern parents
believed that education would produce an accomplished young lady
who would later become an accomplished wife and mother. Female
academies, therefore, not only instructed young girls in the classics, language, and rhetoric, they also provided an education in femininity. They

cultivated piety by encouraging Bible study and attendance at church. They educated young girls to become graceful hostesses by permitting students to receive guests in the college parlor. They also encouraged the feminine ideal through academic devices such as essay writing. While attending Pine Ridge Female High School, Leonora Bisland wrote compositions on a variety of set topics including "Grace," "Patience," "Self Control," and "Sympathy." Pine Ridge Female High School and other academies instructed under the precept that the successful education of young ladies assured the cultivation of a moral and genteel society.[21]

The highly structured nature of school life also furnished students with training in discipline and submission. The typical school year consisted of two sessions, one from August to January, the other from February to July. School life was demanding, and a strict timetable governed all activities, including leisure time. "System was in everything," commented Eliza Lucy Irion on her life at Corona College in Corinth, Mississippi. "No hurry. No fuss. There was a bell for rising; a bell for breakfast; a bell for prayers; a bell for study hour; a bell for recreation; a bell for supper; a bell for prayers (evening); a bell for retiring. All we had to do was to obey the numerous bells instantly." Cornelia Thornton related to her aunt a similar school routine. "We get up early in the morning and study two hours before breakfast, after breakfast school takes in at eight and lets out at twelve, we go in school again at half past one and are then let out at four for the rest of the day." The regimented days of the elite schoolgirl ensured a young woman's application to the important task of becoming an obedient, disciplined, and respectful Southern lady.[22]

"Apply Yourself to Your Studies"

A young woman's education was motivated by a set of interrelated objectives. Academic training taxed the financial and emotional reserves of the family, yet it provided girls with the opportunity to become accomplished young ladies. In turn, these young ladies provided the family unit with the best opportunity of enhancing its gentility and extending its honor and status through marriage.

For many young women, formal education involved boarding school. With hundreds of miles, even states, between them and their families, some girls struggled to adapt. "I cry every night because I cannot see you," wrote a distressed Louisiana Gibson to her father, Tobias. "O I want to see you so bad. Please come and see me. . . . Write as soon as you get this letter. I feel like kissing your hand a thousand times. . . . I am crying now." Also away at boarding school, Emma Shannon informed her mother that she kept "in pretty good spirits . . . when I get to writing or reading, and forget where I am." Still she admitted, "when I first awake in the morning and think I am at home, the awakening to the reality that thousands of miles separate me from home and friends, is actually terrible."[23]

While many parents also grieved the separation, they used their correspondence to remind their daughters that the procedure constituted a "disagreeable necessity" that was vital to their development as genteel young ladies. After outlaying significant amounts of money for board and tuition, elite Southerners urged their children to make the best of their opportunities and apply themselves to their educational pursuits. "I do hope, my dear Eudora, that you will apply yourself to your studies and be a good girl and try always to be at the head of your class," Mississippian planter Howell Hobbs advised his daughter, who had enrolled as a student at the prestigious Salem Female Academy in North Carolina. "Conduct yourself always with the utmost prudence, and respect and kindness to your teachers and school mates, so that when you come home, I may have the very exquisite pleasure of having an accomplished and intelligent daughter to introduce into Society." In particular, Hobbs stressed his desire for Eudora to master both music and French. "I want you to be a good performer on the guitar and *piano* both when you come home," he added.[24]

H. Browse Trist had similar motivations for sending his daughters, Lola and Mary Wilhelmine, to school in New Orleans. A wealthy sugar planter from Ascension Parish, Trist was aware that Lola's and Mary's "heads would be turned like other little heads by the operas, balls, parties [and] visits which will be the order of the day during the winter." He encouraged his girls to "enjoy these things . . . but . . . dismiss them from your thoughts the next day and go resolutely back to your books." Like Howell Hobbs, Trist also expected his daughters to improve their skills in drawing and music. "I don't know whether you have been going on with your drawing," he wrote with concern in 1853. "If not I must get a drawing master for you."[25]

The importance of a good education was of no consolation to Ellen Howe as she battled feelings of homesickness in July 1851. While she tried to apply herself to the rigors of school life in Aberdeen, Ellen's thoughts often wandered back to her parents, Julia and Chiliab Smith

Howe, and to Deerfield, the family's plantation in Okolona, Mississippi. "How long it seems to my heart since I left you," she wrote four days after her arrival at boarding school. "My spirit yearns for home. I am tired of the heat and dust and noise and I long for the silent and still and beautiful prairies and woods, but most of all, for you mother and Father."[26]

Julia and Chiliab also missed their eldest daughter. "We speak of you very often, particularly in the evening when we are drinking tea in the portico and enjoying the pleasant twilight," commented Julia. "We all feel constantly that something is wanting." Julia acknowledged that it was "natural" for Ellen to feel "home-sick for a time." Still, she reminded her daughter of the importance of her academic studies to her future and the "happiness" of the family unit. "Remember my dear daughter that the separation for the present is necessary," she commented, "and will ultimately add to our happiness as well as your own, if you do your duty and improve your opportunities as we trust you will."[27]

Despite Julia's motherly advice, a steady stream of homesick letters continued to arrive throughout July. By August, Chiliab was concerned that Ellen's continued longing for home would impede her ability to "make [her]self an accomplished woman." "You have now pretty near exhausted the subject of homesickness, and your feelings consequent thereon," he wrote tersely. "If you are ever thinking of home, and its quiet pleasures, you cannot fix your mind upon your studies and if you cannot subdue these feelings, it will be only a waste of time and money for you to continue at school." "We all love you, my daughter," he added, "and our great desire is to render you happy, and our happiness depends a great deal upon you."[28]

By late 1851, Ellen had grown accustomed to school life in Aberdeen. Aware that her educational success was linked to family honor and her prospects of marriage, she subdued her feelings of homesickness and endeavored to make her parents proud. Education reinforced Ellen's and her family's gentility and linked her academic success to family honor. Upon her graduation, she would be permitted to extend that honor through courtship and marriage.

Elizabeth Irion did not endure the rigors of boarding school, yet like Ellen Howe, she was keenly aware of its importance to the fulfillment of the Southern feminine ideal. The daughter of McKinny F. and Lucinda Gray Irion, fifteen-year-old Elizabeth was thrust into the position of guardian and mistress after her mother's death in 1846. Besieged by a host of new responsibilities, Elizabeth struggled to rear her five brothers and sisters without the education and refinements that she had always considered essential to motherhood. As she managed domestic affairs, Elizabeth grew increasingly "uneasy about the children," whom she felt were "not being raised right or agreeable to their situation." "I must try to fulfill my duties in the sphere in which I am placed," Elizabeth wrote in her diary, "even though I am not so accomplished or well read as I should wish to be."[29]

With only "ten short months" of schooling to her credit, Sarah Morgan also lamented what she regarded as her "shocking ignorance and pitiful inferiority." Unlike Elizabeth—whose personal loss had deprived her of the opportunity for further education—Sarah came from a family of judges, doctors, and lawyers and enjoyed the privileges and financial security that came from being a member of Baton Rouge's professional elite. While the reasons behind her limited education are unknown (but may have stemmed from her Northern-born father's attitudes towards women's education), she too felt intellectually deficient and connected these feelings of inadequacy to her self-worth as a young lady. "Answer for yourself," Sarah wrote in her diary. "With the exception of ten short months at school where you learned nothing except Arithmetic, you have been your own teacher, your own schollar, all your life, after you were taught by your mother the elements of reading and writing." "Give an account of your charge," she cried. "What do you know? Nothing! except that I am a fool! and I buried my face in the sheet. I did not like even the darkness to see me in my humiliation."[30] Deprived of the opportunity to obtain a comprehensive and genteel education, Elizabeth and Sarah were nevertheless painfully aware of its importance to their development as young women and to their fulfillment of the Southern feminine ideal.

"SWEEPING AND DUSTING": DOMESTIC EDUCATION

While a young lady could often discuss the literary merits of Shakespeare or Scott, conduct a genteel conversation in French, or play a complicated piece on the piano, it was likely that she did not have the skills to supervise slaves, cook a meal, or manage the household during a family emergency. Young ladies were trained to become attractive wives and potential mothers; domestic accomplishments would come later.[31]

In antebellum Mississippi and Louisiana, young women did not play an important role in the rigorous domestic regime. A young lady's presence within this realm, however, socialized her on her place within the larger Southern hierarchy. Standing at the "center of cultural understanding," the household reflected status according to race, class, gender, and age and set out reciprocal obligations between masters and slaves, husbands and wives, and parents and children. It defined the tasks and responsibilities allotted to different members of the household and regulated the expression of power through this organizational structure.[32]

The elite male stood at the helm of the entire operation and was responsible for providing the income to maintain his household and dependents. On a plantation, he also controlled business affairs, including planting and cultivating a staple crop, consulting with the overseer, maintaining buildings and fences, and monitoring his most important asset, his slaves. In his role as head of household, the ideal elite male exemplified the paternal patriarch, who asserted his dominance and position in a paternalist or fatherly way.[33]

The mistress, who was his subordinate, took charge of the daily operation of the household. She supervised and instructed slaves, tended to the sick (both black and white), ordered or prepared dinner, monitored food supplies, entertained guests, and maintained a happy and inviting home for her husband and children. The duties of the plantation mistress extended to the slave community and included supervising or assisting in the production of slave clothing, the distribution of food, and the maintenance of the smokehouse and vegetable patch. While the mistress's duties were onerous, they were largely supervisory, and it was the slaves who cooked dinner, dusted furniture, laid down or took up carpets, polished silver, washed, ironed, and cleaned.[34]

Young ladies in urban and rural households grew up with an understanding of domestic obligations and frequently looked to their mothers as the embodiment of the ideal mistress. Mississippian Annie Jacobs recalled that her mother was "a splendid manager." "She not only managed her great household, but was consulted about plantation affairs," she remarked. Kate Stone described her mother, Amanda, as a celebrated belle who had become the quintessential Southern lady. "[Mamma] was married before she was sixteen, before she had left school, but she had been out enough to reject ten lovers before she met papa," Kate wrote proudly. "She was and is a beautiful woman of most attractive manner and a brilliant conversationalist with a great power of attracting love, the first and greatest gift that can be bestowed on anyone. She has the most cheerful, brightest spirit and is a brave resourceful woman." Mary Carson Warfield also regarded her mother as the true embodiment of the Southern feminine ideal. "Her husband and six children claimed her first loving care, but with many Negro slaves to serve her, her days were passed in serving," she wrote. "She felt her responsibility as mistress of all those poor, ignorant, loving humble souls. I can see her now visiting the sick, carrying delicacies or comforts of some kind, stopping at the day nursery to inquire into and look after the welfare of the babies and small children whose mothers were at work in the field." In accordance with her role, Warfield's mother was a kind and attentive mother and a benevolent mistress to her slaves.[35]

An understanding of the role and responsibilities of the mistress, however, was quite different from the reality. In antebellum Mississippi and Louisiana, the presence of slaves, combined with an emphasis on a young woman's gentility, meant that belles only participated at the fringes of the domestic landscape. They engaged in embroidery and other forms of decorative needlework, arranged flowers, assisted in making preserves and cakes, and took charge of their rooms and clothing. They accompanied their mothers on rounds of visiting and planned and attended parties, picnics, or balls. Some parents may have stressed the need for "good housekeeping," but very few furnished their daughters with a comprehensive education in domesticity or the skills to manage a household with slaves.[36]

As she enjoyed a life filled with visiting, reading, and embroidery, it is no wonder that Kate Stone did all she could to escape the drudgeries of housekeeping. While her mother, Amanda, assumed the managerial role of the plantation mistress, Kate chose not to involve herself with domestic concerns. When the carpets were taken up in expectation of a hot Louisiana summer, she "retired to the fastness of [her] room with a new novel and a plate of candy and was oblivious to discomfort until Frank [one of the family's domestic slaves] came to say dinner was ready and 'the house shorely do look sweet and cool.'"[37]

Other young ladies also shunned any involvement in household affairs. The daughter of John Anthony Quitman, cotton planter and governor of Mississippi, Annie Rosalie Quitman's girlhood was spent at Monmouth, the family's elegant home just outside Natchez. While Rosalie attended church, took walks with her father, and wrote long letters to her absent sisters, her role within the household was minimal. She accompanied her mother on visits to town or to her grandmothers and helped to make a cake to celebrate the homecoming of her sister Louisa. But for the most part, Rosalie's life was occupied with new books, needlework, and pottering in the greenhouse. On one rare occasion when her mother was unable to attend to domestic duties, she "kept house." This, however, was unusual. For Rosalie Quitman, a regular "day passed in reading and embroidery" and other pleasant pursuits.[38]

Sarah Lois Wadley led a similar life in Monroe, Louisiana. After a lengthy Northern tour in the summer of 1859, she settled down to a life of cultural improvement. Sarah invested considerable time and effort in her school work and took regular walks for exercise. Most days, however, were devoted to more leisurely pursuits. "Between sewing (of which I do not do a great quantity) practicing, reading, and painting, my days fly away very fast indeed," she admitted. It was only when Sarah's mother gave birth to another child that the household duties were delegated to her. "I am housekeeper now," she wrote in April 1860, "and have much to occupy me." Later in the year, Sarah commented on the exhaustion she had felt after "sweeping and dusting." "I am so easily fatigued, perhaps if I took more exercise of this kind I might be stronger," she concluded.[39]

Lemuella Brickell and Sarah Morgan were also ill-equipped to handle even the simplest domestic tasks. In February 1861, Lemuella was thoroughly bored with her leisurely life as a Southern belle. "I am grown now," she wrote in her diary. "O what a world it is; if I live this idle life much longer I will go mad." Still, she was not interested in acquainting herself with the finer points of domesticity. "I am almost eighteen and I can't make any kind of garment by myself," she declared, showing no desire to learn. In Baton Rouge, Sarah Morgan was "unable to walk" after she helped to lay the carpet in her bedroom. Neither responsible for domestic tasks nor trained to manage the household, young ladies were, like their mothers before them, less than prepared for the considerable duties they would undertake upon marriage.[40]

"Frills, Furbelows, and Romance"

While a young woman's understanding of and participation in the antebellum domestic landscape was limited, her instruction on the finer points of fashion was given paramount importance. Clothing and appearance signified that a girl had become a young lady as hemlines were lowered and hair was raised. A fashionable yet elegant wardrobe also became a sign of gentility. Whether visiting friends or attending a ball, a belle became a physical representation of her family's elite status.[41]

Preparing for the day when they too would become accomplished young ladies, elite schoolgirls exhibited a keen interest in fashion. Even within the confines of a female academy, clothing helped students attain status within the school community. Away at boarding school, Eliza Lucy Irion was delighted that her clothing was far superior to that of her peers. "I dress as fine (and you know how fine that is) as any girl in school, and my hat is as nice as any of their hats or bonnets," she exclaimed in 1858. "The girls don't dress fine at all down here, and all my clothes are made so nicely that none of them look any nicer than I do." Lonely and exhausted from the unremitting pattern of study at a Philadelphia boarding school, Emma Shannon was more enthusiastic about having her "hair curled" than she was by any of her academic achievements.[42]

Some young schoolgirls thought more about fashion than their educational pursuits, prompting many academies to ban frivolous items, which they considered subversive to the development of good Christian women. At Elizabeth Female Academy, "extravagant and fantastic dresses, jewelry of every description, artificial flowers, hats, artificial curls, feathers, paintings and superflous decorations [were] peremptorily prohibited." Upon her arrival at boarding school in Aberdeen, Laura Howe was somewhat perturbed when her rather simple bonnet was stripped of all its accessories. "The girls are not allowed to wear fine bonnets," she wrote her mother. "Mrs Nash made me take out both the flowers and border of mine, before I wore it." At institutions where such rules did not exist, some mothers worried about their daughters' consuming interest in fashion. Julia Howe instructed her daughter, Ellen, to keep herself "neat in every respect," but warned of the frivolity and impropriety of lavish dress. "I have no wish that you should dress finely or gaily even if others do," she instructed, adding, "a girl of your age ought to be thinking of other things."[43]

Yet once they were belles, young women were encouraged to dress "finely and gaily." Inappropriate for school attire, elegant clothing formed an important component of a belle's formal induction into elite society. While social mores prevented a young lady from initiating a conversation with a man, her appearance helped her attract the attention of eligible suitors. Beauty was equated with gentility, and for many adolescent girls struggling to attain the belle ideal, it was also connected to self-worth. As a result, young ladies scrutinized their clothing, searched for ways to improve their looks, and compared their fashionable wardrobes to those of their peers. After receiving news that her father had produced a bountiful cotton crop, schoolgirl Florence Chapman wrote to her parents about the urgency of getting her teeth fixed. "I am afraid that you will put it off too long, until they cannot be fixed," she wrote anxiously. "Aunt Fillis says that we made more cotton this year than we ever did. Tell Pa if he did make so much cotton that he ought to do me a favor if he ever intend to, to have my teeth fixed. Tell him it is the best thing he can do for me."[44]

Lemuella Brickell was obsessed with what she considered her "ugliness" and declared that she knew all too well that "ugly people are not liked." In Vicksburg, Mississippi, Mary Shannon was quick to engage in a little sisterly competition about appearances. After receiving a letter from Emma, Mary was perfectly shocked to read that her sister had gained weight. "Emma it's horrible the way you increase in weight," she wrote, "a short fat woman is awful, there will be quite a contrast between you and me when you come back, for I get taller and thinner every day." In a society that restricted women's social behavior, belles focused upon their appearance as a means of self-representation. Ultimately, their elegance would aid them in their search for a marriage partner.[45]

This "search" began with a young lady's entrance into society, which, in Mississippi and Louisiana, encompassed both the formal and more casual aspects of genteel life. Elite society marked social boundaries, generated ties with families of similar status, and provided young women with the opportunity to exhibit their gentility and accomplishments. Society included balls, parties, dances, church activities, picnics, political social events, and fish fries. It embodied leisure and culture, formality and fun. While the belle's role was an important one, many young women recalled this short "epoch" in their lives as a time of excitement and anticipation. In 1862, Sarah Morgan reflected on her life the year before: "the guests at home, the visits abroad; the buggy rides, the walks, the dances every night; the merry, kind voices that came from laughing lips, the bright eyes that then sparkled with pleasure." Kate Stone also lived an antebellum life filled with "songs, music and games," while Annie Jeter Carmouche recalled her days as a belle in the late 1850s as times filled with "dances and card parties . . . and delightful evenings [spent] with a social few."[46]

Not every young lady was lucky enough to live in a community buzzing with social activities and eligible men. Consequently, some elite families chose to enhance their daughter's prospects by sending her to stay with relatives in thriving social centers like Natchez or New Orleans. After her graduation, Sophie Collins spent much of her time staying with family and friends throughout Mississippi and Louisiana. Writing home to her mother and her younger sister, Mary, Sophie described the balls and parties she had attended and the informal but "delightful" evenings she had spent "talking, playing on the piano, and playing cards and cheating." Noting the flurry of activity that surrounded an upcoming ball in October 1857, Sophie proudly informed her sister that she was "already engaged three sets, one with Mr Tucker, Mr Airey and Fred Airey." "I expect to be the belle," she wrote with delight.[47]

A young lady was most likely to meet her husband at these social gatherings: at the ball of a local planter, at a church picnic, or even within the confines of the household. Often a brother's schoolmate or a friend's brother was a likely candidate. If romance was to blossom, Southern parents thoroughly assessed a gentleman's eligibility before encouraging the courtship. If he was deemed an appropriate suitor, a young lady was permitted to receive chaperoned visits or enter into a correspondence with her beau. Belles were able to exert some control over the courtship process; they could refuse a marriage proposal or take their pick of eligible gentlemen. By doing so, they enjoyed a brief yet important exertion of power over their lives and their destiny.[48]

The ideal and anticipated outcome of the courtship process was marriage, which had the potential to reinforce or extend family honor. Elite families assessed the success of a daughter's marriage on a number of criteria. Most regarded the couple's romantic, religious, political, and moral compatibility as essential. The code of family honor rendered a woman's ability to marry within or above her status as another key determinant. If a young lady from an elite urban family, for example, married a gentleman from a planter family, she extended family honor. Upon taking her place within a new and prestigious social circle, the bride also enhanced the status of her kin by connecting them (through marriage) to the highest echelons of the Southern hierarchy.

Marriage also symbolized a transitional phase in a woman's life as she laid aside the pursuits of her girlhood to undertake her role as wife, mistress, and, later, mother. Many young ladies struggled to adapt, indicating how little they had actually participated in domestic affairs. One day a leisured carefree belle interested in music and fashion, the next she could be a wife and mistress, burdened with the responsibilities of home and family, including the management of a household and the supervision of slaves. This transition was particularly difficult for Southern women, who frequently married at a younger age than their Northern counterparts and entered married life "still firmly identified with the role of daughter."[49]

On her sister's wedding day in June 1858, Annie Rosalie Quitman reflected on the immensity of the event. "Our dear sister has given her consent," she wrote, "and tonight she resigns her maidenhood for the more sedate position of a matron." As she watched her accomplished sister wed a handsome elite gentleman, Rosalie prayed that she too would meet the same fate. In antebellum Mississippi, her education, training, and social graces would have ensured this anticipated outcome. Rosalie, however, was being prepared for a world that would soon be lost forever. Three years later, her eligible gentlemen would don uniforms of gray and march off to defend their homeland. She, and the other young ladies of Mississippi and Louisiana, would be left to carve out a new role for themselves as belles of the Confederate South.[50]

CHAPTER TWO

The Trumpet of War Is Sounding

Young Ladies Respond to the Cause

We are now out of the Union with the North and I hope to stay so.

Howell C. Hobbs to his daughter, Eudora, February 8, 1861

In late 1860, fourteen-year-old Eudora Hobbs eagerly anticipated her life as a Southern belle. The daughter of Mississippian planter Howell C. Hobbs, Eudora had been sent away to one of the finest boarding schools in Salem, North Carolina. There, she diligently applied herself to her studies in an effort to return home with the academic and ornamental skills that would allow her to make her formal debut into fashionable Jackson society. "I wish you to study hard and be a good girl," Howell instructed Eudora. "It will afford me great pleasure to hear that you are applying yourself to your studies and that you are making yourself agreeable to your teachers."[1]

As Eudora honed her reading, writing, and musical skills, the world she was being prepared for was changing rapidly. Aware that his daughter remained largely isolated from events outside the school room, the topical flavor of Howell's letters shifted in late 1860 from pronouncements about the virtues of genteel womanhood to an informed commentary on the political storm that had erupted in Mississippi after the election of Abraham Lincoln. "We are having some excitement holding meetings &c and making speeches and preparing *not* to submit to his [Lincoln's] Administration, unless the South has a full guarantee of her rights in the Union," he wrote. "The Governor has convened the Legislature to meet on Monday. . . . I fear we are going to have light times in money matters, but I am decidedly in favor of having this whole matter settled now, in the Union, if we can, and out of it if we must." Howell enclosed a copy of the *Jackson News* with his letter in the hope that Eudora would catch up on local issues, which were now dominated by incessant talk of war. While Hobbs acknowledged his daughter's interest was "more for local news than politics," the sectional turmoil prompted him to gently remind her that "a little of all is well enough—in its place."[2]

Two months later, Hobbs wrote to Eudora about Mississippi's secession from the Union. "We are now an Independent Republic," he informed her on January 15, 1861. "We are all now in a stalemate of uncertainty. We have rumors of wars and are in daily expectation of some declaration . . . but we are determined not to submit to Lincoln's Administration on any terms." Now something more than distance separated father and daughter. "You and I are now in separate Governments," Howell wrote. "I hope however that North Carolina will soon be with us."[3]

North Carolina's reluctance to secede from the Union did not deter Howell from canceling the family's Northern magazine subscriptions, including the *Godey's Lady's Book*. "I have *not* subscribed for the '*Lady's Book*' this year, as we have seceded," he explained to his disappointed daughter. "I would not subscribe to any of their *Papers* or *Books*." Instead, Howell sent Eudora a regular supply of secessionist newspapers and a likeness of Confederate president Jefferson Davis. In 1861, feminine accomplishments were no longer enough for a belle. Now Confederate patriotism loomed large in Hobbs's vision of the quintessential young lady.[4]

OUT OF THE UNION

Mississippi and Louisiana left the Union in a triumphant blaze of color, fanfare, and excitement more reminiscent of a Mardi Gras parade than a prelude to war. In January 1861, secession was celebrated in the streets of New Orleans, Baton Rouge, and Natchez. The church bells rang at Corinth, and crowds of politicians and planters gathered at the state capitol in Jackson, Mississippi. Annie Harper was in New Orleans at the time Louisiana seceded and witnessed the "exultation and demonstrations of joy which filled the city." "For both sexes an open expression of dissent was hardly tolerated, so intense had the feeling become," she commented. "We had burned our boats behind us, and there was no return to the shore. No mutiny was allowed in the crew. In every house the stirring strains of the Bonnie Blue Flag and Dixie were all that the ladies could be induced to sing." The New Orleans Bee declared that the city, "once the most conservative part of the state," had been transformed into "the hot bed of secession."[5]

Cities and towns throughout both states responded with the same patriotic fervor. In Columbus, Mississippi, Northern schoolteacher Caroline Seabury recorded secession celebrations in her diary. "Bells were rung—shouting and tumult proclaimed everywhere that the people were trying to make it a joyful event," she commented. Regina Lee, the daughter of a Confederate congressman from Mississippi, was an active participant in the celebrations. "I heard the cannon fire, the bells ring, the tumultuous enthusiasm, 'South Carolina has gone out of the Union!'" she recalled. "Eleven days afterward, Mississippi wheeled into line, and the bells rang, and the cannon fired, and the mob shouted, and Mississippi had gone out of the Union!"[6]

The excitement and fanfare, however, was but a thin veneer of public unity, only temporarily masking the irreconcilable tensions upon which Confederate nationalism was built. As members of the planter class, young ladies like Annie Harper and Regina Lee were unquestioning in their belief that secession furthered the interests, and generated the wholehearted support, of all Southerners. Not accustomed to socializing with yeoman farmers or poor white families, they failed to see how the impending conflict could be construed as "a rich man's war and a poor man's fight." Nor did they question the loyalty of their slaves, who, they naïvely believed, worked in the interests of the household and therefore accepted the elite ideology that governed relations between masters and slaves. Instead, young women perceived the celebrations they attended as evidence that Southern nationalism was as ironclad as the antebellum social hierarchy it rested upon.

Even as they brushed up on their renditions of "The Bonnie Blue Flag," however, young ladies faced an internal struggle to muster a connection and a sense of loyalty to the cause. Despite the patriotic propaganda that espoused unity and resolve, Southerners soon discovered that nationalist feeling was "not a substance available to people in a certain premeasured amount." Rather, the complex frameworks that tied an individual to the state were founded on one's identity, socialization, and life experiences. Race, class, gender, age, religion, geographical location, and political socialization were just some of the factors that influenced a Southerner's identification with, and relationship to, the Confederacy. While race, class, gender, and age shaped a social group's general nationalist outlook, the other mitigating factors produced a multitude of variations within each group. Some young women, for example, identified more strongly with the cause, or particular parts of it, than others.

Nationalist feeling also differed considerably between groups. Some Southerners reluctantly left the Union, while others ardently embraced secession. Even those who supported secession could not agree on the importance of slavery or its place in the new nation.[7] Like other Confederates, young women contributed to this lack of nationalist consensus by constructing their own understanding of cause based on their life experiences, which were grounded in family and family honor. Their nationalist perspective differed in some ways from that of their parents. The nature of their education and socialization meant that young women possessed little of the political knowledge that formed the cornerstone of an elite white adult's identification with the Confederacy. While young ladies in Mississippi and Louisiana were the daughters and sisters of the men whose interests the South went to war to defend, the rhetoric of secession was couched within complex political, economic, and military frameworks. This rhetoric was understood by elite white men and many politically astute matrons, but it remained unintelligible to the majority of young women whose interest in politics had been sidelined for the cultivation of more feminine accomplishments. In the antebellum South, an active interest in political affairs was nurtured most fully among female members of political families, where kin and politics were explicitly linked.

Annie Rosalie Quitman and her sister Louisa were members of one such family. Their father, John Anthony Quitman, was a prominent politician from Mississippi, serving as governor of that state in the early 1850s. Reared in a household dominated by the ups and downs of political life, the Quitman daughters developed a keen interest in the subject. With her mother's consent, Louisa accompanied John Quitman on official visits and frequently presided over dinner proceedings at the governor's mansion. Her role in her father's career, however, extended far beyond her ability to act the accomplished hostess. Louisa's vast political knowledge furnished her with the ability to advise her father on his campaign to become the Democratic presidential candidate in 1856.[8]

Young ladies like Louisa Quitman were the exception, not the rule. Many elite Southerners regarded politics as a "public," "masculine" pursuit, and women were often socialized, as one father put it, to "attend to studies more important to them and to their happiness." Political science was offered at many academies, but preference was given to learning skills in disciplines such as music and drawing. "We hear more of the sound of the piano here, than the rush of progress, and of the business of mathematics than the 'whirlwind of politics,'" remarked one Mississippian schoolgirl to her sister.[9]

The coming of the Civil War relaxed the link between politics and elite masculinity in an effort to unite all men and women in nationalist thought. Matrons—whose interest in Deep South politics had been nurtured by their antebellum involvement in campaigns, rallies, and committee meetings—embraced the opportunity to celebrate their political savvy.[10] This enthusiasm, however, was not shared by all elite women and was far stronger among Southern mothers than it was among young ladies. Even in 1861, when every Confederate household was captivated by the rhetoric of secession and war, some belles were more absorbed in adolescent concerns, and their political understanding of the cause remained weak and ambiguous at best. Writing to her cousin from her home in Jackson, Mississippi, a young Mollie Whitley remained apathetic about the politics of disunion. "I scarcely know of what to write that would be of interest to you," she commented, "as we hear nothing . . . but Secession or Revolution and I do not suppose you feel at all interested in this."[11]

Other young ladies noted the gulf between antebellum conceptions of womanhood and wartime reality and declared that women should have no interest in political affairs. For Sarah Morgan, this irreconcilable contradiction evoked emotional tension that was expressed by heaping scorn upon the growing number of women who chose to conduct political discussions in public. "I hate to hear women on political subjects," she declared, "they invariably make fools of themselves, and it sickens me to see half a dozen talking at once of what *they* would do, and what ought to be done." Resolved that she had "too much respect for [her] father's memory to adopt so pitiful a warfare," Sarah used her diary as a medium for expressing her thoughts.[12]

Some young ladies embraced the excitement and drama that surrounded secessionist events and enthusiastically attended speeches and rallies with their male kin. Annie Jacobs accompanied her father to a secession convention in Baltimore. "Politics was now the absorbing theme," recalled Eliza Lucy Irion. "Secession was all the talk. General Jefferson Davis came to Columbus and made the most eloquent speeches. This was the first time I had ever heard of him. . . . Great political meetings were now held every night, and the whole country was in a blaze of excitement." Eliza, however, was more engaged with the society present than with the political content of the meeting and failed to refine her thoughts on secession in the pages of her diary. Instead, she recalled the days spent feverishly knitting and sewing for the soldiers with patriotic thoughts of "our cause." Other young women also drew upon vague political jargon to express their opinions. At Wayside plantation, nestled on the banks of Lake Washington, Mississippi, Amanda Worthington was an ardent—although somewhat inarticulate—Confederate. "The South *must* be victorious," she declared, "her cause is the right, and 'right not might should rule the day.'" Amanda, along with fellow Mississippian Ella Pegues, often wrote about the importance of "protecting our rights." Sarah Lois Wadley agreed, stating, "We fight for honor, liberty, life itself." [13]

Kate Stone's brothers fought and died for the Confederacy, but she too was vague about what constituted "the cause." When a neighbor, Mr. Newman, visited Brokenburn in May 1861, he excited "a warm discussion" when he remarked "that if the states had been patient there would have been no war for years and that it would have been better to submit to Lincoln's rule no matter how unjust than to have provoked a war." While Kate "bitterly oppose[d] this view of the subject," she related Mr. Newman's argument in far more detail than her own rather general response. "A nation fighting for its own homes and liberty cannot be overwhelmed," she retorted angrily. "Our Cause is just and must prevail." [14]

While political sentiment initially provided young ladies with a weak foundation upon which to build their connection to the cause, religion fostered more powerful ties and linked God with Confederate justice. In the secession winter of 1860-1861, ministers across Mississippi and Louisiana used their pulpits to defend slavery, justify secession, and rouse nationalist thought. In "A Prayer for Our Armies," Bishop William Green of Mississippi espoused sentiments common to the sermons of the time. "Enable them [Confederate forces] successfully to perform their duty to Thee and to their country," he declared, "and do Thou, in Thine infinite wisdom and power, so overrule events . . . that it may soon end in peace and brotherly love and lead not only to the safety, honor and welfare of our *Confederate States*, but to the good of Thy people, and the glory of their great name." [15]

For pious young women, patriotic ideals were legitimized by their connection to the Lord. Recognizing the powerful role that religion could play in uniting all Southerners under the Confederate banner, Jefferson Davis instituted days of fasting and prayer for the cause. On June 13, 1861, Kate Stone attended a "heartfelt service" to commemorate "the day of national humiliation, fasting and prayer." "Mr. Holbury preached an excellent sermon and made an earnest prayer," she wrote in her diary. "The day was generally observed. Oh! may the prayers of so many ascending, laden with the same petition, bring God's blessing on our Nation." Fellow Louisianian Mary Wright failed to see the point of fasting when the Confederate war machine had already been put in motion. "I am not good enough to understand all about fasting," she wrote. "Prayer will avail, I know. I couldn't help thinking it all a farce to fast when it was too late." Unconvinced by the wartime ritual, Mary refused to attend a service to commemorate the day, preferring instead to stay at home with her prayer book and have a potato for supper.[16]

Sustained by an unswerving faith, young women like Kate Stone believed that God was the most powerful Southern defender and had provided the Confederacy with "wise rulers, brave and successful generals, valiant and patriotic men, and a united people, self-sacrificing and with their trust in God." "God will aid us in our righteous cause," she added. Sarah Lois Wadley agreed. While she conceded that "my heart shrinks and all my bravery seems to fly when I think of what may come upon us," she too summoned enough faith to put her trust in God. "We are in the right," she continued, "and he who ruleth the Earth and who is King however much the people rage together, he will protect us." Kate Foster's beliefs differed slightly from Sarah's. Like many Southerners, she believed the Confederacy had to earn the Lord's approval, and that in time, God would reward their devotion by granting them military success and ultimate independence. During the dark months of mid-1863, Kate clung to the belief that a growing list of Rebel defeats was merely God's way of testing the Confederacy's faith and resolve. "Can any one for a moment think that God will allow so many of His people to fail in what they thought and think a good cause and then for their deaths to be as naught in the balance of peace," she declared. "Because God has it seems to us withdrawn his all-protecting hand are we to lose faith in his power? No, we need chastizement and God is not satisfied with what we consider as bad as can be. If we put our trust in Him he will guide us through darkness into light." Lemuella Brickell agreed. "We will conquer," she wrote. "God is always on the right side." "With God's help we will conquer yet!" added Sarah Morgan. Unlike politics, which was often discouraged in the socialization of the Southern belle, "religious nationalism" drew upon concepts that were both familiar and fundamental to young ladies' understanding of themselves and the world around them. Amid a sea of legal and political justifications for secession, religion cultivated an emotional bond that helped bridge the gap between young women and the Confederate cause.[17]

THE LAST GOODBYE

Young women's political and religious identification with the cause remained weak, however, without a powerful connection to family and family honor. In the heady days of 1861, it was not Jefferson Davis's skillful oratory that fostered young ladies' identification with the cause; rather, the sight of their fathers and brothers leaving for war provided young women with the emotional foundation upon which to build their patriotic contribution to the Confederacy. During the initial months of the war, women bade farewell to loved ones in highly ritualistic community celebrations during which bands played, crowds cheered, battle flags were presented, and speeches made. For many, these events brought the reality of the conflict into sharp focus, pitting the contradictory roles of wife, mother, sister, and daughter against that of the sacrificial patriot.

In Natchez, Annie Harper vividly recalled the Sunday afternoon in 1861 when the Adams Light Guards left for war. "The scene . . . was heart rending," she commented. "Carriages filled with grief stricken women, mothers sweethearts and wives pressed closely as possible to the ranks returning the last fond look of love which left them so despairing. At last the word was given. Forward March! and they filed on board with colors flying, drums beating, bands playing—and canon firing, hurrahing and waving until in the distance faded away."[18]

This scene was repeated hundreds of times across the South. Kate Stone also watched her brothers depart for the battlefield in the spring of 1861. Immediately after they left, Kate sought solace and comfort in her diary. "Our two loved ones left us this morning, but we cannot think it a last farewell," she wrote. "My heart tells me they will come again. They go to bear all hardships, to brave all dangers, and to face death in every form, while we whom they go to protect are lapped safe in luxurious ease. But oh! the weary days of watching and waiting that stretch before us. We who stay behind may find it harder than they who go."[19]

In Yazoo County, Lemuella Brickell watched the Hamer Rifles leave. "It was a *sad, sad* sight," she wrote, perhaps recalling the day when her brother had said goodbye in his uniform of gray. "I saw Sally Dougherty and Pat take leave of each other: he put his arm around her, gave her one long lingering kiss, drew her close up to him, in another moment, the waters of the Yazoo dashed between them! She did not cry, but paled suddenly. I felt *so* sorry for her, a bride of two weeks." Lemuella's nagging anxieties about the outcome of the war effort rendered these "heartrending" farewells even more poignant. While she was proud of the bravery and gallantry of the soldiers, she, like many young ladies, harbored strong doubts about the ultimate success of the military campaign. "Suppose our armies should not be successful?" Lemuella confided in her diary only months after her brother's departure to war.[20]

By grounding their understanding of nationalism so thoroughly on notions of family and family honor, young women connected these ideologies directly to the war effort. As the conflict wore on, a growing list of Southern defeats would force many Confederate belles to separate their understanding of family and nationalism from the war effort in a desperate attempt to preserve the ideals upon which their lives rested. In 1861, however, this connection between family, nationalism, and the war nurtured young women's identification with the Confederacy while also developing their understanding of the cause in a religious and political sense. Politics and military maneuvers assumed new significance when kin were defending the nation on the battlefront. Similarly, prayer and religion helped to sustain women's faith in the cause, gave them a powerful tool to interpret both victories and defeats, and provided them with comfort in anxious, grief-stricken moments.[21]

The act of giving their men over to the Confederacy turned politically inarticulate young ladies into patriotic women. In accordance with the antebellum feminine ideal, patriotic Confederate womanhood emphasized women's self-sacrifice, which was expanded to encompass the war effort. Women's patriotic duty compelled them to urge their men to fight. It also required them to assume the role of custodians of Confederate morale. Through domestic endeavors such as knitting socks, sewing uniforms, and preparing supplies, and especially through their letters to soldiers away at war, women became responsible for equipping the army and maintaining morale.[22] Patriotic womanhood demanded that women make public representations of their commitment to the war effort. These acts were also connected to the exhibition of family honor.

Elite young ladies drew upon this ideal to shape their understanding of and contribution to the Confederacy. They also developed it. For young women, soldiering and patriotism became more than just a wartime duty; such activities also provided Southerners with the opportunity to affirm honor. As in antebellum times, Southern men and women had different yet equally important contributions to make, and each looked to the other to fulfill the obligations of their designated role. For elite Confederate men, defense in combat was analogous to the defense of honor in a duel, and young women looked to their fathers and brothers to display family honor by securing a prestigious promotion or receiving formal recognition for their gallantry in battle.[23]

Sarah Lois Wadley was understandably thrilled when her father, William Morrill Wadley, was appointed Confederate superintendent of railroads. A key player in the Central Georgia Railroad and a planter in Monroe, Louisiana, William's new and important contribution to the cause enhanced his family's reputation and honor both within their immediate community and throughout the Confederacy. A thinly veiled attempt at Christian modesty was overshadowed by Sarah's feelings of patriotic and familial pride. "[Father] has really accepted the position offered him as chief of all the railroads in our Confederacy," she wrote in her diary. "I feel no selfish pride in his elevation to such a conspicuous and important position, though I feel a worthy pride in my Father when I reflect on the change which his own intellect, industry and energy have produced since he set foot on Georgia soil, a youth of twenty, with no fortune but his trade, a half dollar and a few changes of clothes, and—his own genius and will; now he can protect and aid the country which has been his foster mother." Acknowledging that it "will be hard to be separated from him," Sarah tried to fulfill her role as a patriotic woman and suppressed what she regarded as selfish concerns. "I know he can do a great deal of good for the Country," she wrote, "and I feel we ought not to think of ourselves."[24]

Kate Stone and Cordelia Lewis Scales were also proud of their courageous brothers, who chose to defend the cause. Kate brimmed with sisterly pride upon hearing the news that the other young ladies of Monroe found her brother, William, "most captivating in his new uniform." After William enlisted in the Jeff Davis Guards in May 1861, Kate spent hours scanning the papers for some mention of his bravery. In the summer of 1862, she was rewarded. "I am very happy for my darling Brother has been mentioned for distinguished gallantry in the late battles," she wrote excitedly. "We are not surprised for we know him, but it is grateful to have others appreciate him."[25]

Like Kate, Cordelia Lewis Scales was elated when her brothers received recognition for their bravery. "I must tell you the joyful news," she wrote her school friend, Lulie Irby. "Bro. Joe has returned home, and not without laurels, I assure you. Gens. Cox, and Longstreet wrote us word of many interesting accounts of his valorous adventures and daring exploits in the Science of 'Knight Errantry,' all of which we heard before his arrival. He has taken two Yankee officers prisoners and killed unnumberable ones. He has a splendid sword, brace of pistols and spurs that belonged to the officers." Cordelia was also thrilled when two newspapers commended Henry and Dabney for their gallantry in battle. "We heard through Hernando [Mississippi] Press that brother Henry behaved with great bravery at Pensacola in the fight," she wrote. "And in one of the New Orleans Papers we saw two or three days ago a very flattering notice of Dabney's bravery."[26]

Gallantry in battle often led to promotion. This assessment of a soldier's worth was vital to the maintenance of family honor, not to mention its importance to the success of the war effort. The absence of such recognition often caused considerable anxiety among young ladies, who loved to brag to friends and neighbors about the daring exploits of their soldier kin. For Kate Stone, the acknowledgment of William's bravery in a local newspaper seemed inconsequential without a prestigious promotion. In June 1862, Kate admitted her desire to see her brother rise in the ranks in the name of family honor. "He is not ambitious for himself, but I am ambitious for him," she wrote, keenly aware that William's actions reflected on the reputation of the family as a whole. "All my dreams of future glory for our name center in My Brother."

In 1863, her dreams had not been realized. "My dear Brother came home this morning and in perfect health," Kate recorded on New Year's Day. "How overjoyed we are to have him with us, but oh the disappointment that he is still only a captain." "I fear now he will never be promoted," she added in despair. "He has no ambition and a low opinion of his capabilities." In the following months, Kate's anxiety about William's military status grew with each passing battle. "Col. Manlove praises My Brother for great gallantry in the last battle," she commented. "That is something we hear after every fight that he has passed through, and still he is not promoted, which we think so strange for such a gallant young officer. I fear now it will never come." According to Kate, William's bravery meant little if his honor was not publicly affirmed or rewarded. "As the Psalmist says, 'Promotion cometh neither from the East nor from the West,'" she wrote in October 1863, "but I wish it would come from the powers that be. I can write and think myself into a fever about My Brother."[27]

"Died of Shame"

Like Kate Stone, Sarah Lois Wadley's understanding of war was linked to notions of family honor. In 1861, Sarah's excitement over the appointment of her father to the position of superintendent of railroads was coupled with the assumption that her beloved brother, Willie, would also offer his services to the Confederacy. When her father expressed his desire for Willie to manage plantation business in his absence, Sarah wrote with mixed feelings. "I don't know what to wish," she concluded. "I can't bear the thought of Willie's going away, and yet I am anxious for him to serve his country."[28]

In October 1863, Sarah's anxiety turned to despair when Willie decided to hire a substitute, a legal option that was open to all Southerners but only attainable by members of the elite who possessed the money and resources to evade military service. "I could scarcely believe I heard correctly," she confided in her diary, describing the news as "the saddest sorrow I ever have known." Praying that her feelings were not "cruel and unsisterly," Sarah expressed her desire for Willie to do what duty and honor accorded him. "I sometimes fear I am wrong in my feelings about this matter but honor, right, patriotism, all seem to me to point Willie to the army," she wrote. "I would be so unwilling for him to remain at home."[29]

Sarah's protestations on the basis of family honor went unheeded by her father and brother, and on a chilly November evening in 1863, Willie's substitute arrived to confirm the final arrangements. "Michael Fry is his name, from one of the border states of Germany, a strong, stout man, accustomed to exposure and hardship," she commented, "his price is ten thousand dollars in money, a horse, saddle and bridle, and to provide a house and bread stuff for his family during his absence. It is a high price to pay but a little one to receive when one is going to a life of peril and hardships only *for the price*." Unable or unwilling to share her feelings with her family, Sarah wrote in her diary of the shame she felt for her brother and his act. "[I] cannot think of it without pain," she wrote, "which is so much worse that it has none of the softness of sadness, but rather a little mingling of self reproach that I should ever seem to lack affection for a brother who has always been to me the kindest and dearest that a brother can be." While she had always thought of Willie as a dear and honorable brother, Sarah now regarded him and his substitute as "a stain, a cause for blushing" while other men gave their lives to the Confederacy. "I ought to be resigned," she commented, "and yet I cannot be."[30]

When her brother finally relinquished his plans and offered his services to the army, Sarah was quick to question the honor of his assigned duty. "Oh if it were a different service, an honorable service he is going to enter upon," she sighed, adding that it was far from "useful" to be left "inactive in camp." Like Kate Stone, Sarah was neither pleased nor proud when Willie became a clerk, a position she feared "would not be an elevating one." Still, she felt a degree of pride and, more important, a sense of relief that she no longer had reason to feel shame at his manhood. "I cannot help being very much gratified that he is now in a position which I conceive to be the only noble, honorable one a young man can now be engaged in, that is in active service for his country," Sarah wrote. "I do not love Willie any more, my tenderness for him could scarcely have admitted increase, but this feeling is now joined with a sort of proud satisfaction that he is now doing his clear and manifest duty." When military service became a possibility in 1865, Sarah admitted that his final departure made her feel that "he was really a soldier and going to danger." No longer full of reproach, she felt "truly thankful that he is strong and well, and cheerfully inclined to fulfil his duty."[31] For Sarah, and for other young ladies, the Confederate cause embodied more than just a military defense of the South. More than ever before, the war provided men and women with unprecedented opportunities to express their honor. Those soldiers who achieved recognition in the war reinforced their position within their families and their community. Those who did not threatened to blight family honor.

SEWING FOR THE SOLDIERS

Young ladies looked not only to their men to uphold honor, they also looked to themselves. Yet unlike men, whose defense in combat reflected the code duello writ large, young women were forced to cast their gaze from society to the sewing machine in an effort to meet the practical demands of war. Belles who had grown accustomed to exhibiting honor and gentility in the ballroom were now required to assert their commitment to nation (and therefore family honor) through "domestic patriotism," which urged ladies to expand their antebellum role in the household to encompass the war effort. Sewing for the soldiers became a daily staple in every patriotic woman's life, and ladies cheerfully put aside their embroidery to manufacture shirts, pants, socks, jackets, comforters, knapsacks, pillows, and gloves. Lacking the capacity to fit and supply its entire army with clothing, the Confederate government relied on its women to ready their men for war. Southern ladies responded by organizing sewing societies that coordinated the production of soldiers' uniforms and provisions. "A perpetual sock was ever on hand," remarked Annie Harper. "Women knit riding in their carriages and at all visits, ever were the busy needles flying, and some even discussed the propriety of knitting during prayer meeting."[32]

Confederate belles encountered a unique set of challenges as they attempted to fulfill the practical requirements of the domestic patriot. Unlike Southern matrons, whose role as mistress had trained them in the production of clothing, most young women possessed only limited skills in darning, mending, and embroidery. Still, a prerequisite of Confederate patriotism was the willingness to learn. In wartime Mississippi and Louisiana, young women regarded knitting socks, stitching uniforms, and preparing supplies as expressions of female patriotism that also affirmed family honor. They may have struggled initially with these unfamiliar domestic tasks, but with time and effort, knitting and sewing for the troops generated a sense of achievement among young ladies and connected them to the cause in a practical yet conventional way.

While Southern men defended honor on the battlefield, young women used their diaries to document their commitment, which for most involved learning a repertoire of previously unfamiliar domestic skills. Ellen Louise Power was preparing to marry when she began her diary in January 1862. Her moral obligation to the soldiers compelled Ellen to put aside her trousseau in favor of more patriotic tasks. "Ma and I went in town this morning to get some work to do for the soldiers," she wrote in December 1862. A month later, Ellen was knitting socks at a fast pace. "I finished a pair of socks to-day, which is 9 pair I've knit," she recorded with pride. In the following months, she expanded her contribution to include sewing uniforms, stitching comforters, and making pillows. Carefully recording the completion of all these items, Ellen's journal became a physical reminder of her undertakings for the cause. It reaffirmed her patriotic contribution and her commitment to family honor, which had expanded, but not challenged, her role as a young Southern lady.[33]

Other young women vied for important positions on their local sewing committees to demonstrate their commitment to the cause. Like the recognition of a soldier's gallantry in battle, these appointments gave young ladies another opportunity to affirm family honor, which was now bound up in the overt expression of patriotism.[34] On July 14, 1861, seventeen-year-old Sarah Lois Wadley proudly recorded her appointment to the position of secretary of the Monroe Aid Society. A month later, Wadley discussed her first efforts at knitting socks. "Mother has begun her second pair, but I have not finished my first *one* yet," she commented. "It is the second sock I ever knit." Sarah persisted, and during the summer of 1861, her days were transformed from leisurely afternoons of reading and embroidery into hours hunched over the sewing machine, a piece of knitting, or a box of lint. "I have been very busy this week," Sarah wrote in September 1861, "have knit a pair of socks. How many more will I knit before this war closes?" While she complained, "my hand is now quite lame from knitting," Sarah continued to produce socks and gloves, propelled along by her love for the soldiers and the cause. She was not alone. "Everybody seems desirous to do their part of the soldier's work," she remarked with proud satisfaction.[35]

Ellen Louise Power and Sarah Lois Wadley were just two of thousands of young ladies who chose to expand their domestic skills to assist "their soldiers." In August 1861, Kate Stone reluctantly assumed a position on the soliciting committee of her local sewing society, fearful that she would "make a wretched solicitor." Unfortunately, her sewing capabilities were no more developed. While Kate bragged that "Mamma is a famous knitter of socks and can knit one a day," she admitted, "so far I am only capable of knitting comforters of crewel, but I shall advance to socks and gloves." When she took the bold step and "commenced knitting a sock" in September 1861, Kate found the procedure "too complicated for my head." "Shall confine myself to gloves and comforters," she resolved, "I am all right there." Still, a year of perseverance and commitment transformed Kate from a novice into a skilled sewer and knitter. "I am knitting gloves as I can do it well and rapidly now," she exclaimed in September 1862. "Nothing like sticking to a thing to learn it."[36]

In May 1861, Mary Wright volunteered her services to the Cheneyville Sewing Society. "The tailor could not cut out fast enough, so we had to wait a long time for work," she commented. "Seven sewing machines and about that many ladies. We sewed all day until late in the evening." From her home near Natchez, Elizabeth Christie Brown made floral bouquets and biscuits for Confederate soldiers. Her contributions to the local sewing society, however, came to an abrupt end when she made a "wee bit" of a mistake when cutting out a pile of shirts. Confining herself to smaller and more manageable tasks, Elizabeth devoted an entire day to knitting gloves, commenting that she was "tired enough of it, but could not put it by because it was soldier work." "Although I never knew them before, I feel that we cannot do too much for, nor take too great an interest in, anyone that gives up their very life blood, for our dear country," she added. "What a comfort it would be to know that our army was well clothed and did not lack for any necessaries." Sidney Harding and her family were refugees living in a log cabin in Keatchie, Louisiana. Although they struggled to provide food and clothing for themselves, they continued to work for the soldiers. "Oh how I wish now sometimes that I had six pairs of hands," Sidney exclaimed after a long day of sewing and knitting. In New Orleans, Florence Cooney Tompkins recalled the "busy" women and girls who "scraped old linen into lint to be made into packages, and sent to the hospitals." They "accomplished almost incredible results," she commented.[37]

Sarah Morgan also sewed for the soldiers and spent hours picking lint. "What fingers could do in knitting and sewing for them, I have done with the most intense delight," she declared with patriotic pride. Mary Wright was "so busy . . . dying wool to knit gloves etc" that she had no time to write in her journal. Mathilda Todd DeVan of New Orleans aided "in every noble, patriotic undertaking by her means." Her mother described her "patriotic assertions" as manifold: "by knitting scarves, capes, socks and urging others to labor for their [soldiers] comfort," she exemplified young women's commitment to the cause. Helen Johnstone used her family's wealth and resources to generate a massive—and highly honorable—contribution to the cause. With her mother's assistance and a band of women and slaves, Helen equipped a local company for war. To express their appreciation, the troops of Madison County, Mississippi, named themselves the Helen Johnstone Guards.[38]

Young ladies like Helen Johnstone derived great satisfaction and accomplishment from their patriotic domestic role, which required them to become wives of the Southern cause. Knitting socks and sewing shirts for their Confederate family furnished young women with a sense that they too had a place, and a stake, in the success of the new nation. By taking on "wifely duties" that expanded yet reinforced their role as women, young ladies incorporated themselves into their own understanding of nationalism, an understanding founded upon the principles of family and honor.

"For the Benefit of the Soldiers"

Many young ladies did not limit their patriotic contribution to knitting socks, sewing uniforms, or preparing supplies. Beginning in 1861, young women joined with Southern matrons to raise money for the cause. They organized recitations, concerts, tableaux, and charades, drawing upon patriotic themes in an effort to inspire loyal Confederate citizens to donate money. Fundraising galas were often held at schools, where students became patriotic advertisements for the institutions to which they belonged. In other community events, wives and mothers were usually well represented on organizing committees, while young women with polished voices and musical skills were most frequently cast as performers.

While knitting socks had not challenged young women's position in society, these more visible activities did. Performing in public, even if to sing "The Bonnie Blue Flag," was regarded by many Southerners as undignified and unladylike. When Clara Solomon heard the news that a benefit for the soldiers was to be held at the Normal School in New Orleans, she grew indignant at the thought of her school friends performing for money. "Mary Ames is going to sing at the concert," she wrote in disapproval. "She is bold enough to do it. I do not approve of such publicity being given to a young girl. They can contribute their aid for our 'absent soldiers' in some more appropriate manner."[39]

In the following weeks, preparations for the event dominated school proceedings, and by the day of the concert, patriotic fervor won out over previously rigid standards of decorum. After "obtaining seats very far back" in the "packed" hall, Clara and her sister, Alice, were entranced by the performance. "I was very much pleased, and they all acquitted themselves creditably," she wrote. "The 'Bonnie Blue Flag' was the feature of the evening. It was encored, and at the conclusion called for. . . . We were all exceedingly entertained." Although she was initially shocked by the impropriety of young ladies performing in public, Clara and many other elite ladies soon realized that far from challenging women's place in the public arena, such activities reinforced—and celebrated—a belle's role as the guardian of Southern gentility.[40]

Without balls and parties to occupy their attention, it was not long before young ladies embraced concerts and tableaux as a form of entertainment that bolstered morale, raised badly needed funds, and filled in the long, weary hours waiting for news. Women fashioned costumes out of antique relics discovered in attics, props and sets were decorously arranged, and flowers were picked to adorn the halls and the heads of the lead performers. Organizing committees spent hours, sometimes weeks, devising programs and conducting rehearsals to ensure the ultimate success of the performance, which gave young women the opportunity to reconstitute the gentility they had exhibited in the ballroom and transfer it to the stage. In Confederate Mississippi and Louisiana, both patriotism and refinement could be affirmed by singing a Southern song, reciting a poem, or acting out a tableau of war. By adapting genteel honor to the patriotic demands of war, belles were able to affirm their commitment to the new nation while flaunting their accomplishments, expanding their social network, and strengthening elite ties. War may have curtailed the expression of genteel honor, but it had not banished it completely as a mechanism for assessing social worth.

Planter society relished these rare and enjoyable occasions, and an upcoming concert was not to be missed. In January 1862, Amanda Worthington's sister attended a concert in Greenville, Mississippi, for the benefit of the soldiers of Washington County. "The music was very good and the house crowded," Amanda commented. "She [sister] says she reckons they made about $400. I hope they did. Bettie Miller sang the 'Marseilles Hymn' and 'Robert,' and Mrs. Lonsdale played a piece from the Opera 'Trovatore.'" Annie Harper attended a benefit concert in Vicksburg, where she "saw a young lady recalled twice to the footlights to repeat the 'Bonnie Blue Flag,'" while Lemuella Brickell was present at a benefit in Benton, Mississippi, where Aggie Cheatham and Mary Bowman both performed patriotic arrangements.[41]

Kate Stone attended a similar event at Milliken's Bend in September 1861, where she socialized with "a number of the girls before the concert for the benefit of the soldiers." "It went off splendidly," she remarked, "most of the girls we know being performers. Mary Gustine looked beautiful. She is the handsomest girl in the parish and has an excellent voice, which she has just recently discovered, and is now taking singing lessons." The benefit gave accomplished young ladies like Mary an alternative way to play out their bellehoods—on stages instead of in ballrooms. As Kate noted, the event also established or renewed social ties among the guests. After the concert, the Stone women were pleased to "make the acquaintances of Mrs. Maher, Miss Carrie Lowry, Mr. Campbell, Mrs. Coney Morancy, Mrs. Bence, Miss Orr, [and] Mrs. Reading's sister."[42]

Cordelia Lewis Scales was the star performer of a gala benefit in Holly Springs, Mississippi. "We had a great deal of fun and every one seemed to enjoy it so much," she related in a letter to her friend. "I opened the exercises by singing 'The Volunteer' on the guitar. A Volunteer was standing by me dressed in his regimentals." "The first scene was Faith, Hope, and Charity," she continued. "Faith was represented by a girl dressed in white with a little child kneeling at her feet with its hands together. . . . I was Hope—I had on a white dress, my sleeves looped up with white rose buds and green leaves. . . . Charity was a girl dressed in white with a little baby in her arms." Admitting that it would not "be interesting to you to read all about the tableaux," Cordelia urged her friend to come and see for herself. "We are going to have a grand exhibition Christmas for the benefit of the soldiers," she wrote excitedly. "I wish so much you would come and spend Christmas with me, and join in our sport."[43]

For Cordelia, concerts and tableaux filled a void that had once been taken up with antebellum frivolities. Her contribution to these events, however, reflected something much more. Up on a tiny stage, surrounded by the admiring glances of family and friends, Cordelia's participation in the performance highlighted her personal refinement, as well as her family's honor and patriotic commitment. While she may have been deprived of the opportunity to impress elite families and beaux with her graceful waltzing style or her elegant appearance, Cordelia maintained her role as the lead actor in the theater of gentility—she was still being watched and judged by her peers and affirming her membership to their select group. Cordelia's participation in the "Faith, Hope, and Charity" tableau meant that she also represented and embodied the ideals that Southern men went to war to defend, expressing her patriotism through socially acceptable channels that stopped far short of any overt engagement with the male-dominated world of politics. The powerful concepts of family and honor were inextricably tied to the new Confederate nation and profoundly shaped young ladies' identification with and commitment to the cause. In 1861, it prompted them to seize their knitting needles and learn new skills with patriotic vigor. Yet as the war stretched on, family and honor would provide young women with the blueprint to negotiate their way through a ravaged, unrecognizable world.

CHAPTER THREE

Keeping House

The Southern Belle in the Confederate Household

> Mamma went to Vicksburg today and I am left at home as commander-in-chief with Little Sister and the two boys, Johnny and Jimmy. We are getting on bravely today, pickle making, weaving etc. etc.
>
> *Kate Stone, November 10, 1862*

On a fine spring morning in May 1861, Kate Stone opened a blank notebook and began her Civil War diary. Perhaps when sitting at her writing desk or on Brokenburn's long gallery, Kate was often carried away by visions of gallant soldiers risking all in defense of their families and their beloved Confederacy. "Throughout the length and breadth of the land the trumpet of war is sounding," she wrote with patriotic fervor, "and from every hamlet and village, from city and country, men are hurrying by thousands, eager to be led to battle against Lincoln's hordes. Bravely, cheerily they go, willing to meet death in defense of the South, the land we love so well." In her patriotic visions, Kate perceived the war as something that transpired on a distant battlefield while "much indulged" young ladies like herself kept the home fires burning, knit socks, and worried anxiously over the fate of soldier kin.[1]

In 1861, Kate's innocent portrayal of the heroic conflict was yet to be tainted by the bloody reality of war. While friends, neighbors and newspapers in Monroe talked relentlessly about the Confederate cause, the daily rhythm of plantation life remained the same. At sunrise, while Kate slumbered in her bed, most of Brokenburn's 150 slaves trudged out to the fields to work the cotton crop. After Kate woke, dressed, and consumed a wholesome breakfast prepared by "Annie" the cook, she often retired to her room or the parlor while her mother, Amanda, and

"Aunt Lucy" ensured that "all household affairs moved smoothly." A nap, reading, embroidery, or visiting often took up the rest of Kate's day while her family's slaves toiled in the fields, prepared her supper, washed her clothes, and cleaned her home.[2]

Not accustomed to domestic work of any kind, Kate dreaded the occasional times when a bout of sickness prevented her mother from managing the household. "Mamma is sick again today," she wrote anxiously in June 1861. "I hope she will be relieved by tomorrow. It upsets everything for her to be sick." Terrified by the prospect of having to assume her mother's domestic role, Kate buried herself under three large volumes of Motley's *Dutch Republic* while leaving the servants to do the "best they could."[3]

As Kate Stone escaped the drudgeries of housekeeping in mid-1861, the effects of the Confederate war edged ever closer to her homelife at Brokenburn. Looking to the battlefield as the place of war, Kate did not foresee the consequences that her brothers' soldiering, the blockade, and Federal invasion would have on her life and her role within the Big House. In the antebellum South, the structure of the household, the delegation of power, and the duties allotted to each individual had always been distributed according to race, class, gender, and age. The exodus of white men to the battlefield left a gaping void at the very apex of this hierarchy, leaving old men, young boys, and women to struggle in households where clearly defined roles and responsibilities no longer existed.

The Southern mistress loomed large in this wartime landscape, and her responsibilities grew to encompass every facet of domestic and plantation affairs. As matrons struggled to oversee crops, slaves, households, and finances, young women found themselves in a different, but equally daunting, role.[4] Armed with only the most basic training, belles were suddenly thrown into the domestic regime, both as participants and as managers. The ability of the mistress and her daughters to rise to the challenge was essential to the survival of the Confederate household.

WAR CONFRONTS THE CONFEDERATE HOUSEHOLD

The war began to encroach on every Confederate household the day that husbands, sons, fathers, and brothers left for the battlefield. When Kate Stone and her mother bade farewell to their soldier kin, they immediately confronted the reality of changed households and changed lives. While thirty-six-year-old Amanda Stone had proven herself to be a capable and resourceful manager after her husband's death in 1855, she, like many planter widows, relied heavily on the assistance of her brothers, Bohanan and Ashburn Ragan, and her sons, William, Coleman, and Walter, to run Brokenburn. The management of the plantation was no small task. Spanning 1,260 acres—"eight hundred cleared and deadened"—Brokenburn's success was founded upon a lucrative cotton crop, which provided Amanda with the finances to purchase slaves and construct a sawmill, slave quarters, and a Big House. On the eve of war, Amanda admired her bountiful crop, which, she anticipated, would allow her to pay off all her outstanding debts, take her children on a delightful Northern tour, and commence building an elegant mansion in "the large grove of native water oak, sweet gum and sycamore": "a house," Kate remarked, "that would be a pride and pleasure to us all."[5]

Growing sectional tensions profoundly altered Amanda's vision—along with Kate's daily existence. When "the trumpet of war sounded" in 1861, William Stone was among the first to enlist. On the eve of his departure, Kate began to contemplate the ramifications of her brother's absence to her family and the household of which he was a part. "The parting will be dreadful for Mamma," she acknowledged. "She so depends on My Brother, her oldest and best beloved." In the following months, Bohanan, Coleman, and Walter also departed for war, leaving Amanda Stone to occupy the roles of master and mistress. Aside from her duties in the Big House, which had been further complicated by wartime shortages, Amanda assumed responsibility for crop production, consulting with the overseer, managing slaves, and transacting business. Her already onerous duties were compounded by the Confederate government's wartime strategy, which called upon all Southerners to sow vegetables in preference to the more lucrative staples of cotton and sugar. It was hoped that this shift in production would establish a subsistence economy with enough surplus to feed the army.[6]

The day after her beloved son's departure, Amanda set her slaves to the task of agricultural adjustment. "Mamma is having quantities of peas, potatoes, and all things eatable planted, as our only chance for anything from this time until the close of the war will be to raise it ourselves," Kate wrote. "It is probable that meat will be very high, and by advice of Mr. Fellowes, Mamma will try to raise enough to do the place. She has put Jeffery to devoting his whole time to the hogs and cattle. We have not a great quantity of either just now, but they will soon grow."[7]

Grappling with new crops and increased responsibilities, Amanda

Stone also encountered growing problems with her slaves. Rumors that the North was fighting to abolish the South's "peculiar institution" prompted many slaves to challenge the boundaries of white authority, which had already been slackened by the departure of men to the battlefront. In June 1861, Kate remarked that "the house servants have been giving a lot of trouble lately—lazy and disobedient." "I suppose the excitement in the air has infected them," she added. As these acts of "disobedience" grew in frequency, Kate viewed the servant problem with concern. "Still trouble with the house servants," she wrote days later. "Aunt Lucy, the head of them all, ran away this morning but was back by dinner. Mamma did not have her punished. All of them are demoralized from Charles up."[8]

Amanda Stone must have worried anxiously about the tumultuous state of affairs, yet she was not alone. During the war, mistresses throughout Mississippi and Louisiana encountered a set of domestic problems unlike anything they had experienced before. Planter women like Amanda confronted a set of problems different from those of their urban counterparts, but shortages, inflation, and "impudent" slaves also took their toll on elite women living in towns or cities. In New Orleans, Emma Solomon was also left to manage domestic affairs when her husband relocated to Virginia to work as a sutler. As the cost of bread and meat skyrocketed, Emma was no longer able to rely on Solomon Solomon's irregular pay packets to make ends meet. "Ma's finances are in no better a state, and she has an attack of the 'blues,'" Clara remarked only months after her father's departure. By 1862, Emma was forced to take in sewing in a desperate attempt to feed and clothe herself, her six daughters, and the family's increasingly "disobedient" slave. While Clara acknowledged that most women took work from Mr. Weilman out of necessity and were "glad of the small pittance," she was indignant at the exploitation of her mother's labor. "It is a perfect imposition to give only a dollar!" she cried. Yet as Emma Solomon knew, twelve pairs of drawers furnished her family with a pleasant supper of shrimp, and the "imposition" was far preferable to heavy hearts and empty stomachs.[9]

In Natchez, Kate Foster's "Aunt Jenny" faced a similar predicament. She struggled to maintain authority over her slaves while also worrying about the fate of her husband, who had been taken prisoner by Federal troops. Unable to confront the crisis that had befallen her household, Jenny took to her bed with "a head-ache brought on by excitement." When a Federal lieutenant informed Jenny that Ralston was to be transferred to Camp Chase, she gave up in despair. "I felt more for Aunt J. than

I did for Uncle R.," Kate admitted. "My heart ached and I was powerless for I could do nothing as she was so much disturbed and would not be comforted." In the meantime, Kate tried to maintain some order within a household now bereft of slaves or a master's patriarchal command.[10]

While their gender had always limited their authority over slaves, mistresses like Amanda Stone, Emma Solomon, and "Aunt Jenny" were now given the insurmountable task of maintaining the master's authority from their position on the second rung of the social hierarchy.[11] They were required to uphold the image of the "paternal provider" at a time when money was scarce, goods were high, and reciprocal obligations to slaves (such as the provision of food and clothing) could not be adequately met. Most important, they were charged with the task of maintaining control over their slaves through a hierarchy that had always invested complete authority in the head of household. In wartime, mistresses found themselves caught between their training in submission and benevolence and the need to embrace the masculine concept of dominance, which drew upon violence as an underlying mechanism of slave control. Elite men may have returned home after the war to realize they had lost their authority as masters of slaves. Planter women and their elite urban counterparts saw this authority weaken firsthand and disintegrate in daily acts of black resistance.[12]

THE YANKEE PROBLEM

Young women's participation in the wartime household was necessitated by a number of factors besides the absence of men. In an effort to starve the Confederacy into economic submission, the United States instituted a naval blockade of all Southern ports from Virginia to Texas and a partial blockade of the Mississippi River. In theory, no goods could be shipped into or out of the Confederacy. While enterprising blockade runners smuggled goods into the South for sale at exorbitant prices, this strategy had profound repercussions on a region whose manufacturing and industrial capabilities remained underdeveloped at the outbreak of war.[13]

The effects of the blockade began to disrupt Confederate households as early as 1861. In New Orleans, Clara Solomon was astounded by wartime inflation. "Things are daily increasing in price. Soap which formerly was 20 cts. a bar, is now $1.00!" she wrote in disgust. "Coffee $1. per pound, and Ma has notified us that we must soon say 'good bye' to it. . . . Meat, which in former times we would consign to the Mississippi, now sells for 40 and 50 cts. per lb." Clara and her sister, Alice, were particularly concerned about their inability to purchase good quality cocaine, which they believed was a most effective treatment for headaches. After visiting a number of drugstores, Clara and Alice were forced to accept a "similar" but inferior "preparation." "I am so sorry that we are deprived of this excellent article," Clara lamented. "Oh thou art the cause of this sorrow Abe Lincoln." In the coming weeks, Clara's anguish intensified as more and more of her favorite consumer goods disappeared from the shelves of the most popular stores in New Orleans. "What are we coming to?" she cried. "The Blockade must be raised."[14]

Goods that had previously formed the staple of domestic life in Mississippi and Louisiana disappeared or were sold at highly inflated prices. Flour, meat, fruit, vegetables, coffee, soap, and medicines were all conspicuously absent from the pantries and smokehouses of many wartime households. As early as 1862, young women and their mothers spent days traveling the countryside in search of the most basic commodities. On a shopping trip to Clinton, Louisiana, Ellen Louise Power was shocked by the high prices and lack of available stock. "I never heard of goods being as high as they are, and rising every day," she exclaimed. Sarah Morgan recorded her exasperation at her inability to purchase either basic foodstuffs or nonessential items, both of which she considered necessary to her elite existence. "Next time I go shopping, I mean to ask some clerk, out of curiosity, what they *do* sell in Clinton," she commented sarcastically. "The following is a list of a few of the articles that shop keepers actually laugh at you, if you ask for. Glasses, flour, soap, starch, coffee, candles, matches, shoes, combs, guitar strings, bird seed—in short, everything that I have heretofore considered as necessary to existence." Sarah soon discovered that any homemade or inferior substitutes were suitably referred to as "Confederate." "In present phraseology, 'Confederate' means anything that is rough, unfinished, unfashionable or poor," she remarked. "You hear of Confederate dresses, which means last year's. Confederate bridle, means a rope halter. Confederate silver, a tin cup or spoon. Confederate flour, is corn meal, etc." In Rapides Parish, Louisiana, Mary Wright braved "bad weather"—a combination of rain and sleet—to make her much anticipated trip to town. Unfortunately, her shopping expedition was not worth the effort. "Monday morning we went all over town shopping, but found very little, and that little selling very high," she wrote in her diary. "We bought the only tooth brushes we could find and gave $2 for them."[15]

For young women, wartime shortages represented far more than an inconvenience. Unable to procure items such as lace, combs, or even guitar strings, they began to feel the effects of the war chipping away at their elite identities. While patriotic womanhood called for the sacrifice of all such things for the good of the cause, young ladies struggled to relinquish what they had heretofore considered the most basic prerequisites of Southern gentility. Without these physical expressions of their status, Confederate belles were well aware that there would be little to distinguish them from other patriotic women of lower social orders.

After more than one fruitless shopping trip to town, many young women became increasingly angry and frustrated by their inability to purchase fashionable items that had once been considered essential to the attainment of the belle ideal. In Natchez, Annie Harper remarked that "the scarcity of toilet soap was . . . a greater deprivation to our women than the loss of fine clothes." "An abundance of the common article was made and [while] many attempted to produce something more refined, the last cake of perfumed soap was treasured for fete occasions." Fine material—a prized article among belles—also became a sought-after commodity. Appalled by the thought of having to submit to wearing homespun, Kate Stone proclaimed that "the ladies are raising a cry for calicos and silks that echoes from the Potomac to the Gulf." Clara Solomon was more concerned about the scarcity of fashionable gloves. "What will we do for Kids (kid gloves, that is!)" she remarked. "They are now $1.50. There will not be many in the city. Abe Lincoln! Abe Lincoln!"[16]

Imported boots, once a staple in every young lady's wardrobe, also disappeared early in the war. After a long afternoon searching the stores in New Orleans, Clara Solomon's mother, Emma, finally met with some success. "Ma came in very much fatigued," Clara remarked. "She had been walking to obtain some things, and had made some small purchases of shoes, crockery, etc. She startled us with the high prices of every thing. . . . And shoes! They are almost impossible to be got. What will we do? They are *now* exorbitantly high. All dry goods will be scarce this winter, and there will not be much dressing." Young ladies like Sarah Morgan were often forced to settle for less genteel alternatives. "I have had such a search for shoes this week, that I am disgusted with shopping," she exclaimed. "I am triumphant now, for after traversing the town in every direction and finding nothing, I finally discovered a pair of *boots* just made for a little negro to go fishing with, and only an inch and a half too long for me, besides being unbendable." "Behold my tender feet cased in crocodile skin, patent leather tipped, low quarter Boy's shoes, No. 2!" she remarked, "from my pretty English glove kid to sabots made of some animal closely connected with the hippopotamus!"[17]

Sitting down to dinner in her crocodile-skin boots, Sarah and other young ladies were often forced to submit to a basic diet they would have once considered more appropriate for slaves. "How many articles we considered as absolutely necessary, before, have we now been obliged to dispense with!" Sarah commented in September 1862. "Ice cream, lemonade and sponge cake was my chief diet; it was a year last July since I tasted the two first, and one since I have seen the latter. Bread I believed necessary to life; vegetables, useless. The former I never see, and I have been forced into cultivating at least a toleration of the latter."[18]

Kate Stone agreed. "A year ago we would have considered it impossible to get on for a day without the things that we have been doing without for months," she wrote. Amanda Stone's commitment to agricultural adjustment, however, meant that Kate enjoyed a plain yet bountiful table well into 1862. "It is not such hard living," she admitted. "Common cornbread admits of many variations in the hands of a good cook—egg bread (we have lots of eggs), muffins, cakes, and so on. Fat meat will be unmitigated fat meat, but one need not eat it. And there are chickens, occasional partridges, and other birds, and often venison, vegetables of all kinds minus potatoes; and last but not least, knowing there is no help for it makes one content. There is hardly a family in the parish using flour constantly. All kept some for awhile for company and for the sick, but it is about exhausted now."[19]

While Annie Harper was thankful that "the hens did not refuse to lay or the cows to give milk," many young ladies quickly grew tired of common Confederate fare and longed for the foods more indicative of their class and gentility. Culinary delicacies that had formerly been taken for granted were now transformed into symbols of lost elite culture to be longed after. "We have just repaired from the dining room, where we have been indulging in bread and molasses," sighed Clara Solomon, "and wishing for one of those nice fish suppers, of which nothing but the memory of them, now remains." Clara also longed for the simple pleasures that had once been a part of the Solomons' diet. "You cannot imagine how we miss our butter, as though a friend had departed," she commented. Even if she had been lucky enough to purchase some butter, Clara and most Confederates in New Orleans had no bread with which to enjoy it. "It is an utter impossibility to obtain *bread*," Clara related in April 1862. "The bakers have suspended baking, and flour is selling at enormous rates. Our 'motzoes' are so miserably sour that I don't think I have eaten a whole one. A little bit of corn-bread suffices me." "I expect before long we shall all starve," she added.[20]

Fellow Louisianian Sarah Morgan shared Clara's anguish. "If any one had told me I could have lived off of corn bread, a few months ago, I would have been incredulous; now I believe it, and return an inward grace for the blessing, at every mouthful. I have not tasted a piece of wheat bread since I left home, and shall hardly taste it again until the war is over." On a "rainy and dismal" Sunday afternoon, Sarah and her family whiled away the time recalling other "wonderful delicacies of old." "Lydia, lying by me, sighed for a single oyster," she remarked. "Miriam thought some fruit would complete her happiness; Anna talked most pathetically of the delights of roast chicken, while I thought that a piece of bread, and a cup of coffee would be the greatest treat in the world."[21] Sarah, and many other young ladies, struggled to define their place in a world where food, clothing, and possessions no longer marked out the boundaries between masters and slaves, rich and poor. Clinging to their elite identities through fond remembrances of oysters and ice cream, they were forced into the realization that patriotism and the antebellum tenets of the belle ideal did not sit comfortably together in the wartime landscape of the Deep South.

Not every young woman had the luxury of dreaming about delicacies while partaking in a plain yet wholesome supper. In Mississippi and Louisiana, regional location and the extent of military activity often transformed the inconvenient absence of favorite foodstuffs into a daily struggle for survival. By mid-1862, the Federal presence in the Mississippi region extended far beyond the shortages produced by the blockade. As the Union army sought to gain control of the Mississippi River, New Orleans, Baton Rouge, and Natchez were captured and the surrounding regions invaded. In an effort to disable the Southern war machine, Confederate households were pillaged for food, medicines, livestock, and other provisions. At Tennessee Landing, Mississippi, Mattie Jarnagin described her family's loss in the aftermath of a Union raid. "They broke open all the doors that were locked, went into the smokehouse, took the meat, and threw what they could not use to the dogs, taking everything else with them, such as sugar, coffee, and a few jars of preserves," she recalled. "None of these things could be replaced so it was a great loss to us."[22]

Oakland, the Scales family's three-story mansion near Holly Springs, Mississippi, became an obvious target for Federal raiders. Nineteen-year-old Cordelia related her family's sudden destitution in a series of letters to her school friend, Lulie Irby. "I must tell you about the Yankees as you are so anxious to know how they behaved," she wrote. "You may congratulate yourself, my dear friend, on being slighted by them. They came and stayed in our yard . . . and they use[d] to order the milk to be churned any time and they took corn, fodder, ruined the garden and took every thing in the poultry line." Three months later another body of cavalry robbed the Scales household of all its provisions. "When the waggon trains were passing thirty and forty of the Yankees would rush in at a time, take every thing to eat they could lay their hands on, and break, destroy, and steal every thing they wanted to—all of our mules, horses and waggons were taken, 42 waggons were loaded with corn at our cribs, and a good many more after," Cordelia wrote. "I'll tell you what I thought we would certainly starve."[23]

After a Union raid on her family's smokehouse, Letitia Dabney Miller was forced to consume "game, partridges and squirrels" caught by her brother, John. The plight of Confederate refugees was even more desperate. After fleeing their homes and abandoning every physical symbol of their gentility, refugees possessed neither the resources nor the capital to raise vegetables or buy stock. Their hardships were not alleviated by the Confederate government, which failed to provide a decisive course of action to deal with shortages. Instead, they found themselves at the mercy of a wartime economy of scarcity.[24]

After growing accustomed to the abundance of vegetables available at Brokenburn, refugee life brought Kate Stone down to the realities of wartime existence. "So little to eat," she commented from her accommodations in Tyler, Texas; "*biscuit*, for we can get plenty of flour; syrup made of sugar, for we have a hogshead of sugar; and rusty, rancid bacon, absolutely all the meat we have been able to buy, no eggs, chickens, milk, butter, or fresh meat, and not a vegetable. Nothing more to be bought." Unlike her mother, Kate found it increasingly difficult to be thankful for the coarse fare that now graced the supper table. Unable to relinquish the last vestiges of her socialization in culinary elitism, Kate preferred to partake in plain "bread and milk three times a day" as a preferable alternative to the other "delicacies" offered. "The others have come down to the stern realities of life and really seem to enjoy sassafras tea, coarse cornbread, and fat bacon," she admitted. "I am nearly starved."[25]

Sarah Morgan grew desperate at the plight of her sister, Lilly, and her small children, who had also been forced to flee their home. "Letter from Lilly to day has distressed me beyond measure," Sarah wrote in her diary. "Starvation which threatened them seems actually at their door. With more money than they could use in ordinary times, they can find nothing to purchase. Not a scrap of meat in the house for a week, no pork, no potatoes, fresh meat obtained *once* as a favor, and poultry and flour, articles unheard of." By the end of the month, her situation had worsened. "Lilly has been obliged to put her children to bed to make them forget they were supperless, and when she followed their example, could not sleep herself, for very hunger," Sarah commented anxiously. "So with money enough to purchase a comfortable home among respectable people, they . . . live on from day to day with empty stomachs and full pockets. Can anything more aggravating be imagined?"[26]

Sidney Harding's refugee life was similar to that of Lilly Morgan's. Living in a log cabin in Keatchie, Louisiana, Sidney grieved the loss of her beloved home and community. "O how homesick I am lately," she cried. "Think of dear old St Mary [Parish] more than ever." Sidney's depression was heightened by her family's destitution. Once wealthy planters, the Harding family members were now forced to live day to day, not knowing when their next meal would come. "Poor Ma is always worried about provisions," she wrote. "Everything so scarce and high. She does not know how to provide. Eggs five dollars a doz., chicken five, no beef to be had—no sugar, butter, or flour." While kind neighbors such as Mrs. Edwards and "Miss Mattie" assisted the family by sending over fresh ham, vegetables, and butter when they could, Mrs. Harding and her daughters were often forced to go hungry. "Poor Ma she sat down in despair and cried," Sidney wrote in anguish. "Nothing in the house to eat."[27]

For young ladies like Sidney Harding and Cordelia Lewis Scales, war was no longer something that transpired on a distant battlefield. By 1862, it came to dominate the Confederate households of Mississippi and Louisiana. The structure of domesticity collapsed, and with it, the leisure filled days of the Southern belle. In peace, young women had been the guardians of gentility. In war, they became responsible for preserving the vestiges of domestic life that had always defined family honor and elite culture. No longer able to languish on their daybeds or potter in the garden, they moved from the fringes of the household to the center. Young women were often overwhelmed by their new and daunting responsibilities. A complex mix of honor and necessity led them to embrace the challenges of their wartime domestic role.

"Fixing and Patching"

The repercussions of war overturned the antebellum domestic land-scape that had governed relationships between masters, mistresses, and slaves. The blockade, the absence of men, the Federal presence, and the loss of slave labor created a crazy-quilt pattern across the landscape of the Mississippi region, rendering the wartime predicaments of each household unique. Some families lost all their slaves, while others lost only one or two. Some women were able to draw on the assistance of male kin or overseers. Others were left to sort out the challenges of man-aging a wartime household or plantation on their own. Some households possessed good supplies of food and clothing. Others scratched out a poor existence by catching game or relying on the kindness of neigh-bors. The size of the family unit, the number of slaves, and the presence of male kin all influenced both the strategies the mistress employed to survive in this wartime world of necessity and, ultimately, the amount of domestic work her daughters were required to undertake.

The overarching effects of the blockade, however, meant that all Confederate households were forced to revert to a system of home man-ufacturing, a system that had long been abandoned with the increasing availability of consumer goods. "Necessity and *war*," Clara Solomon remarked, became the "mother of invention," and young ladies, who had often done little more than assist in making preserves, now assumed a pivotal role in the production of an array of household items. In a cli-mate of scarcity, mothers and daughters devised ingenious recipes for making common household items such as coffee and bread, and they either instructed their slaves or tried the new Confederate methods themselves. In the process, young women acquired a wide range of culi-nary skills and, more important, an education in improvisation.[28]

Without coffee or tea, Southern mistresses and young ladies con-ducted endless experiments in the search for a more pleasing alterna-tive. "For tea, we dried blackberry leaves," recalled Letitia Dabney Miller. "Coffee was made of parched corn, and we cut sweet potatoes into little squares, dried them, then roasted them. The drink, if flavored with just two or three grains of real coffee, was good enough." Annie Harper and Kate Stone preferred okra coffee. "After experimenting with parched potatoes, parched pindars, burned meal, roasted acorns, all our coffee drinkers decided on okra seed as the best substitute," declared Kate, who was an avid coffee drinker herself. The scarcity of sugar in parts of Mississippi and Louisiana did not deter Ellen Louise Power, Kate Stone, or Elizabeth Christie Brown from baking "Confederate cakes," which were made from a concoction of cornmeal and molasses. In Washington County, Mississippi, Amanda Worthington was so impressed by her recipe that Confederate cakes were included as part of the family's Christmas dinner in 1862.[29]

Nowhere was the reversion to a home economy more evident than in the production of clothing. While Mississippi had produced more than 20 percent of the world's supply of cotton in 1860, the South had overwhelmingly concentrated its efforts on exporting the staple crop for production in the North and in Britain. As a result, the Confederacy's manufacturing sector remained woefully underdeveloped at the out-break of war. By 1862, the blockade had stemmed the flow of goods into the Confederacy, and the Union army's ability to destroy the few South-ern textile mills that were established sent the prices of even the most basic materials soaring.[30] For the first time in their lives, fashion-con-scious belles were unable to purchase fabric, lace, ribbons, trim, petti-coats, or stockings. With even the most basic items suddenly out of their reach, young ladies were forced to assume an increasingly active role in maintaining their wardrobes, a role that extended far beyond selecting patterns, material, or trim.

Accustomed only to light sewing or decorative needlework, young ladies worked tirelessly to acquire the broad range of skills that would enable them to cling to the vestiges of the stylish, but now elusive, belle ideal. Sarah Lois Wadley's desire to maintain her elite appearance fueled her enthusiasm to learn the art of dressmaking. "This past week has been a very busy one, with us," she wrote. "Mother has been making two or three winter dresses and altering some old ones, I made a dress for myself this week, it is only the second one I ever made." "I have been very busy sewing every day and this morning I worked too," she added, filled with pride at her accomplishment.[31]

Kate Stone also extended her domestic skills in a desperate attempt to remodel old clothes. "There is so much to be done now . . . I hard-ly know where to commence—three pairs of gloves and a necktie to be knit, three dresses to make, and all my clothes to be mended. Things are certainly mended as long as possible now. As Mr. Stenckrath used to say, 'Be kind to my old shirts, Emma'—they just *had* to *last*." Unlike Sarah, Kate often hinted at the frustration of mending and remodeling. "We have all been busy this week trying to make 'auld claes look arnaist as weil as new,' a tiresome and hopeless job," she wrote in exasperation. In New Orleans, Clara Solomon cried "a flounce, a flounce a kingdom for a flounce" as she spent days sewing on the family's clothing. "Renovating, altering and making Flannels for the children," fixing a cantankerous sewing machine in need of repair, sewing on men's drawers for extra money, attaching a flounce to her sister Alice's dress, and "'ending' some hdkfs. after Ma had hemmed them on the machine" occupied most of Clara's sewing time. Household chores and wartime shortages, however, did not deter Miss Solomon in her quest for elegance and gentility. While she admired her sister's beautiful barege, Clara was compelled to make do with her existing yet somewhat limited wardrobe. "I have been employed in ripping a flounce off of last summer's dress," she commented, "and I intend to convert it into two diminutive ones." It was not long before Clara remodeled her own tired yet beloved barege. "In these times," she added, "people must devise all sorts of means." Also "without fashion plates," Helen Gardner and her friends "fashioned [their] dresses according to individual taste." "They were more than once ripped, sponged and remodeled," she remarked.[32]

The daughter of a highly successful and esteemed sawmill owner in Natchez, Elizabeth Christie Brown had spent her antebellum days learning how to embroider—not sew. Like most other young ladies, she was less than acquainted with the heavy-duty sewing and mending often undertaken by the mistress and a band of slaves. Yet necessities born of the blockade also forced Elizabeth to extend her capabilities in an effort to keep her wardrobe in a respectable, if not fashionable, condition. "In the afternoon, I embroidered a stocking, that had rather more holes in it than were necessary for its beauty," she wrote in January 1863. "Spent the evening in knitting but did not get along very rapidly." Mending a dress, "put[ting] buttons on another," and darning stockings became regular activities in Elizabeth's wartime day.[33]

Other young ladies like Kate Foster expanded their skills to encompass the art of "plaiting palmetto hats." "[They] are quite the fashion as we cannot get them any other way," she explained. Sarah Lois Wadley became so skilled in the manufacture of palmetto hats that her friends and neighbors relied on her handiwork. While she did not regard the hats as "very pretty for girls," Sarah admitted they were "quite serviceable, and *are all we have.*" After altering a hat for Margaret Craig and making others for her father and friends, she remarked, "I am getting to be quite a milliner." "If misfortunes should reduce me thus far," she added, "might set up a shop after a short apprenticeship." Despite all her efforts to learn the craft, Elizabeth Christie Brown possessed neither the talent nor the dexterity required to model a fine hat. "I sewed Pa's

Palmeto hat, and thought I was getting on nicely with it," she remarked, "when Ma said she thought it too large, and so it was, I had all my morning's work to undo, and almost had a cry over it, but such is life, we toil and struggle on, and when we think we have reached the goal, some slight thing sets us back and frustrates all our hopes." Elizabeth's failed attempt marked the end of her contribution to Confederate millinery.[34]

Often unable to purchase shoes of any description, other young women became experts in fixing and patching last year's fashionable footwear. In Aberdeen, Mississippi, Jennie Pendleton grew tired of searching for shoes and made her own. Kate Stone and her family also became "quite expert" at making shoes. "We cut up an old pair of gaiters and slippers for a pattern," she explained. "We make the uppers of broadcloth, velvet, or any strong black goods we can get, and the shoemaker for the Negroes puts on the soles. They are not to say elegant looking but we are delighted to be able to make them, and they are far better than bare feet." Despite her distinct lack of respectable footwear, Sarah Morgan dismissed any thought of making her own shoes. Instead, she waited patiently for a local man to fashion her a pair. "I have been with Mrs Badger to a Mr Powell who has started quite an extensive shoe making establishment, in the vain attempt to get something to cover my naked feet," she commented in October 1862. "This was my second visit there, and I have no greater satisfaction than I had at first. He got my measure, I got his promise, and that is the end of it, thus far." That was, indeed, "the end of it," and Sarah was unable to purchase any other shoes until her exodus to occupied New Orleans in April 1863.[35]

In the later years of conflict, the exorbitant cost and scarcity of material forced many young women in Mississippi and Louisiana to learn the art of spinning, an art long before performed by their ancestors and, up until the Civil War, a task often performed by slaves. Textile production of all kinds was most fully revived in rural communities, where physical space and the equipment used for spinning or weaving were both readily available. Confederate politicians such as Governor Charles Clark of Mississippi urged women to dust off their spinning wheels to fulfill the ideal of patriotic womanhood. In his inaugural address to the Mississippi legislature on November 16, 1863, Clark proclaimed, "The spinning wheel is preferred to the harp, and the loom makes music of loftier patriotism and inspiration than the keys of the piano." According to Clark, textile production captured the essence of the patriotic feminine ideal. Spinning and weaving became an extension of women's commitment to the new nation and to their kin who chose to defend it.[36]

In an attempt to elevate the status of this complex and laborious task, Kate Stone recalled images of Revolutionary matrons busily working at their spinning wheels in the name of their cause. "It is like going back to the days of the Revolution," she wrote excitedly, "to see the planters all setting up their looms and the ladies discussing the making of homespun dresses, the best dyes, and 'cuts' of thread." For many young women, it was still a harrowing, tiresome, and complex task. Sarah Lois Wadley became increasingly frustrated after many failed attempts to learn the craft. "I am so very, *very* tired, I have commenced to learn to card and spin, and I never tried anything so difficult to me, or so very tiring," she wrote. "I never remember having learned anything which was at the same time difficult and discouraging." "I forgot one exception," she added, "music." Wartime necessity, however, compelled Sarah to persevere. She was not alone. Sarah commented that her neighbor, Mrs. Craig, "spin[s] and weave[s] all the cloth the family wear." "This is but one of many such families in the south, once so rich and prosperous," she added.[37]

Near Jackson, Louisiana, Ellen Louise Power also documented many days spent at the spinning wheel, while Sallie McRae of Mudville, Mississippi, became skilled in spinning, weaving, and warping thread. Lucy Paxton Scarborough recalled hearing, as a child, the "swift whir of the reels twirling the thread into hanks" as women prepared the fibers to be spun into cloth. While she "dreaded the roughness and 'smelliness' of the new cloth and greatly hated the prickly feel of the 'linsey-woolsey' which the children were condemned to wear during the winter," Lucy commented on the superior cloth—"spun finer by carding into the rolls raveling of old silks"—which was made and worn by the ladies. In Louisiana, Sophie Collins admitted that "I can't learn to spin, but like to weave very much." "Kate and I have both learned," she wrote her mother. "We know how to warp it and put it in the loom, we think we are very smart." In an ironic twist of fate, belles sacrificed their leisurely, genteel lifestyle in a desperate attempt to keep up appearances. With hands tired and worn from stitching and weaving, they knew all too well that the loss of some spare time at home was a far preferable alternative to the loss of status abroad. In their patched and remodeled creations, Confederate belles were still judged by others.[38]

Without "Help"

While Kate Stone had associated spinning and weaving with the patriotism of Revolutionary matrons, the widespread loss of slaves in wartime households in Mississippi and Louisiana compelled young ladies to become acquainted with the less genteel aspects of slave work. By 1863, the pervasive Federal presence prompted a massive slave exodus from Vicksburg to New Orleans. For the first time in their lives, members of many elite families confronted households without cooks, washerwomen, nursemaids, and house servants.[39]

Without the knowledge or the skills required to maintain a household, young women were thrown into the domestic regime in a desperate effort to fill the void created by the loss of slaves. Young ladies in urban households frequently worked under the direction of the mistress. Young planter women, however, were often compelled to assume a larger portion of the domestic burden while their mothers attended to other matters such as finances or crop production. Armed with brooms and dustpans, many young ladies struggled to reconcile the widening gulf between their antebellum lives filled with reading, embroidery, and visiting, and the wartime reality, which necessitated their participation in the most menial of household chores.

While they regarded their work for the soldiers with a sense of patriotic pride, many belles struggled to view their new domestic role in the same light. In April 1863, Amanda Worthington was shocked to learn that her friend Sallie had been forced to take up housekeeping after her family's slaves left their plantation in search of freedom. In a well-meaning attempt to help her friend, Amanda invited Sallie to Wayside so that she could learn a few domestic tips off her family's "loyal" servants. "Sallie came over to learn off Aunt Charity how to make coffee," she commented. "All of their house servants left them and nearly all their others too, and Sallie and Mary have had to cook for the last day or two!! I think that's coming down to the stern realities of war sure enough." As she indulged in a leisurely afternoon playing the piano, Amanda did not anticipate that her friend's unfortunate predicament would soon become her own. Only weeks later, when the majority of the Worthington family's slaves left for Yankee lines, Amanda and her mother also faced the prospect of how to manage their auspicious home without a bevy of servants. Their only option was to complete the work themselves, and in June, Amanda settled into a rigorous and "tiresome" domestic regime. "Yesterday morning I got up and set the table and brought in breakfast, helped wash the dishes, cleaned Bert's room, the linen room and the lumber room, swept two long porches and one short one—set the dinner table and brought dinner in—polished five pairs of andirons and rubbed two brass candle sticks—skimmed the milk for the churn," she wrote. "—In short, I acted the part of a perfect chambermaid."

Besieged by a host of unfamiliar household chores, Amanda associated her new responsibilities with servitude, not patriotic sacrifice. Tired of churning butter ("the most tiresome work I ever did, without a doubt"), washing dishes, sweeping, dusting, and preparing rooms, Amanda had no time, or energy, to complete an elegant toilette in anticipation of the arrival of evening guests. After a long day of housework, a disheveled Miss Worthington greeted her Aunt Anne in a "soiled dress" and was happy to meet strangers looking like a "chambermaid" instead of an elite young lady. "Sallie was over this evening and she, Sister and I walked down to the Lake," she wrote. "We were all somewhat *soiled* in appearance so we had the luck of meeting two soldiers." A little embarrassed by her appearance, Amanda took comfort in the fact that the men "couldn't boast of being much cleaner than we."[40]

Kate Stone was even less embracing of her duty to her family and her nation. While she had managed domestic affairs at Brokenburn, the loss of her home and possessions quashed Kate's desire to acquaint herself with the peculiar domestic duties of the refugee. During her stay at a house in Trenton, Louisiana, she commented that the furniture was "dirty and dusty," but made no attempts to clean it herself. "Should Jimmy [her brother] get any of the house servants, we will certainly have it all overhauled," she declared, "and such a washing of bedclothes there will be." Later, Kate commented on "the comfort" of having one slave to complete what she regarded as tiresome chores. Annie "keeps our room in such nice order and washes our few clothes beautifully," she wrote with satisfaction, confirming that the most ingrained assumptions about gentility could survive even the war's worst moments.[41]

Other young ladies regarded their new responsibilities as an opportunity to embrace the Southern patriotic ideal. Natchez belle Kate Foster resigned herself to the prospect that the family's slaves would soon depart for Union lines. "We think all [slaves] will go," she commented. "We have been obliged to do a greater part of the house work. It is not hard to do." "Taking out the slops is the only part that I do not like," she added. It was only when slaves left her friend Mrs. Dunbar that Kate became indignant at the inconvenience. "Mrs. Dunbar's two house servants Nancy and Mary Ann left Thursday morning and the latter took all of her children," she wrote. "Now Mrs. D. has to do the house clean-ing and nearly all the house work. It seems that if the rest who are here if they had any feeling they would feel sorry for Mrs. D. and remain faithful." Kate's sympathy for her friend prompted her to visit often. "I nurse the baby and wonderful to say get along famously," she later remarked with pride. "Who would have thought two years ago that I who hated children would ever nurse one." Kate's enthusiasm, however, did not extend to hard physical tasks such as doing the washing. When "John, Sarah and Rose" left the plantation, Kate was compelled to do all the washing until a replacement could be found. Much to her hor-ror, the chore became a part of her domestic routine for six long weeks. "Came near ruining myself for life," Kate exclaimed in disgust, "as I was too delicately raised for such hard work."[42]

Other young women were also forced to undertake domestic duties that expanded their previously limited knowledge of, and role in, household affairs. When Elizabeth Christie Brown's slaves left in 1863, she was forced to complete much of the work herself. In her diary she recorded days of housekeeping, "preparing dinner," and performing other domestic duties, including "setting hens" and chickens, cleaning rooms, darning, patching, and remodeling the family's clothes. House-hold affairs, however, did not always run smoothly, and Elizabeth was prone to tearful outbursts if her work was not duly acknowledged or appreciated. "Today I thought I was very smart, and was going to have the dining room look so pretty, with the lace curtains up to the windows, and got them all arranged before dinner," she wrote in April 1863. "But alas my work was not appreciated, but instead of praise I caught the most terrible blowing up, and instead of taking it like a woman I cried like a spoiled baby." Conscious of her new role in the household, Elizabeth made a firm resolution to "try and control my feelings better and be a woman, in some things at least." Belles, Elizabeth believed, had the right to indulge in tears; women with responsibilities did not.[43]

After the Federal attack on Baton Rouge, Sarah Morgan and her mother concentrated their efforts on cleaning up the mess that the Yankees had left in their wake. They did so alone. "Here mother and I are alone, not a servant on the lot," she related. "The dirt and confusion was extraordinary in the house. I could not stand it, so I applied myself to making it better. I actually swept two whole rooms! I ruined my hands at gardening, so it made no difference. I replaced piles of books, crockery, china, that Miriam had packed for Greenwell; I discovered I could empty a dirty hearth, dust, move heavy weights, make myself generally useful and dirty, and all this is thanks to the Yankees!"[44]

In New Orleans, Clara Solomon minded children, moved furniture, washed dishes, bottled preserves, "suppered" her young sisters, and often took on the role of "housekeeper." When the Solomon's unreliable Irish servant, Ellen Deegan, failed to arrive for work, Clara was often assigned her rather disagreeable duties, which included the care of baby Josephine. "Josie was bad as usual," Clara remarked angrily after a morning of childcare, "and I accomplished nothing in any other line than minding her, and not much in that, for I would *never, never* do for a nurse." Other days were not so bad. After rising at six o'clock on a mild October morning, Clara "studied until breakfast; and after disposing of the dishes, putting Josie to sleep, . . . made a complete wash of the gas fixtures, which was by no means a task destitute of difficulty." Necessity and war had furnished Clara with the skills to fulfill her new role as a capable participant and superintendent of her household. Like Clara, Sidney Harding remarked that "one day has been pretty much as another. Work, eat, and sleep." In Mudville, Mississippi, Sallie McRae's days were busy indeed. With no time for introspection or reflection, Sallie merely used her diary to jot down the array of chores she had completed during the day:

January 27, 1862	I rose quite early. Went to spooling thread. . . .
January 29, 1862	Making my dress. Warped the thread. . . .
February 1, 1862	Ironing and drying clothes. . . .
February 11, 1862	Spinning again. Scoured the parlor. . . .
February 27, 1862	Bet and myself washing. Kate weaving. . . .
March 21, 1862.	Ironed in the morning and spun in the evening.[45]

As they struggled with additional tasks of their own, elite women in urban and rural locations also began to rely heavily on their inexperienced daughters to assist in the management of household affairs. For the first time in their lives, young ladies were trained to become mistresses and assumed their new role under the most difficult wartime conditions. In 1861, Kate Stone had retreated to her room at the mere prospect that she may be asked to assist her mother in taking up the carpets. By 1862, the war had transformed her existence. When the blockade made it exceedingly difficult for her mother to manage Brokenburn, Kate was often left as "commander-in-chief" while Amanda Stone attended to business matters in Vicksburg. Caring for her younger siblings and managing household affairs, Kate found the responsibility tiring and arduous. "I think I should like keeping house if I were forty years old and had no one to interfere, but now it is horrid work, vanity and vexation of spirits," she complained. Practice, however, furnished Kate with the skills to manage the household without slaves or her mother's guidance. During Amanda's absence in May 1863, Kate ensured that domestic affairs ran smoothly while also taking care of Aunt Laura, who remained "quite ill" in bed.[46]

Sarah Lois Wadley, fatigued by the completion of light housework in 1860, also became the mistress of her household many times in the following years. Often, these duties kept her mind off the state of the war effort. "There is nothing like work for me," she remarked, "idle and aimless days make me melancholy and miserable." Although she threw herself into her work, Sarah's transformation from a Southern belle into a capable Confederate mistress was fraught with challenges and setbacks. "I never before realized half the care of housekeeping, nor half the trial it is to the patience," she wrote, tired and overwhelmed on a hot summer's day. "I have not borne it very well, have several times been very much fretted, our house is so large, and there is so much sweeping and dusting to do about it. It has not been quite a week since Mother left, but it seems to me like months."[47]

While Sarah struggled to come to terms with her wartime responsibilities, Clara Solomon and Cordelia Lewis Scales were extremely competent in their role as "acting mistress" and Lise Mitchell managed the household, meals, and poultry yard at Fleetwood as "a sort of general superintendent." Proud of her newly acquired accomplishments in the domestic realm, Lise was more than a little disgruntled when her brother returned home on a furlough and complained about the "simple fare" and "poor housekeeping." "[He] soon began to see I performed my part as well as possible under the circumstances," she wrote later, feeling somewhat vindicated. "It is certainly hard for housekeepers to supply their tables now, and especially for one with as little experience as myself, and it seems a pity for me to have undertaken my task for the first time when things are so difficult." By 1865, Sarah Morgan reflected on her changed circumstances. "My life changes, changes," she sighed. "I am nominally housekeeper; that is to say I keep the keys in my pocket, and my eyes on the children, and sit at the head of the table."[48]

For young ladies like Sarah, the war transformed their understanding of and relationship to the household. In the wartime chain of events, masters became soldiers and mistresses became acting masters. Young ladies, whose lives had been filled with education, visiting, and prospects of marriage, frequently moved from the margins of the household to the center. Domestic work provided them with practical training in a host of previously unfamiliar chores while also furnishing them with the skills to manage a large household without, in many cases, the assistance of slaves.[49] These advantages, however, came at a price. The effects of war on the Confederate home front had forced young women to confront the growing tension that existed between Southern gentility and patriotic sacrifice. When working to aid the soldiers, they had been able to incorporate their sense of gentility into their patriotic endeavors. The increasing demands of the conflict, however, soon left young ladies in a desperate struggle to bridge the gap between the belle ideal and wartime reality.

CHAPTER FOUR

The Confederate Belle

> Your family are very well, cheerful, in excellent spirits and getting along very well, do not be anxious on their account.
>
> *Emma Walton to her father, James B. Walton, August 6, 1862*

> Tom tells me you are down in the mouth all the time. I do not like to hear this. This is the time when we must keep a bold front and it is rather a sign of weakness to despond.
>
> *William Bisland to Caroline Pride, August 11, 1862*

The emotional cost of the Confederate War bore an indelible mark on the lives of young ladies in Mississippi and Louisiana. In Terrebonne Parish, Caroline Pride grew anxious and withdrawn waiting for news from her fiancé, William A. Bisland. A member of the 26th Regiment, Louisiana Volunteers, Bisland was stationed at Vicksburg during the battle for control of the Mississippi River. At home, Caroline's knowledge of the campaign spawned fears for William and for ultimate Confederate victory. While she continued to sew for the soldiers, Caroline struggled to appear outwardly cheerful and optimistic about the war effort. Instead, the melancholy that pervaded her days spilled over into her letters to her beloved.

In Vicksburg, William grew increasingly concerned about his fiancée's devotion to the cause. Unsettled by her gloomy correspondence, William regarded Caroline's emotional outbursts as unwomanly at a time when ladies were expected to support their soldiers in the field. "What are you so low spirited about?" he wrote tersely in August 1862. "Is it at the success of our arms? or what? Tom tells me you are down in the mouth all the time. I do not like to hear this. This is the time when we must keep a bold front and it is rather a sign of weakness to despond. If we cannot bear some of the ills and trials of life, we are not deserving of our independence—and at the same time it shows a distrust of the good providence who can overrule all these things to our good." "Cheer up," he instructed Caroline, "and be more of a woman, more deserving of the esteem and affection of a soldier."[1]

William's attempts to rouse his fiancée's spirits failed dismally, and months later he was again angered by reports of Caroline's persistent depression. "You say everyone says that you are very much changed. You say yourself that you have lost all your spirit and take no interest in anything," he wrote from his camp. "Now this is not a very lovable picture you draw of yourself. I don't know that I should be satisfied with it." "These are times that try men's souls and women's too and to show what they are made of," he lectured. "Cheer up and know that you are at home. Take an interest in everything about you. Assist your Mother in all her household duties, and be continually employed, and take my word for it, after trying this awhile, you can draw a picture of yourself that I, at least, will admire and love more than the other." William regarded Caroline's fears and anxiety as a weakness, a blight on family honor and the honor of the cause. He insisted that it was her duty to uphold the ideal of patriotic womanhood: to knit socks, to keep the home fires burning, and to sustain morale by writing cheerful, optimistic letters to soldiers away at war.[2]

In New Orleans, Emma Walton also had many reasons to feel discouraged and war weary. In April 1862, her beloved Crescent City had suffered humiliating defeat and subsequent Federal occupation. Union soldiers victoriously patrolled the streets, and in May, a group of "blue devils" raided the Walton home in search of Confederate uniforms and flags. Without her father, Colonel James B. Walton, to protect them, Emma and her mother felt overwhelmed and vulnerable in a Southern city swarming with Yankees.[3]

Yet when Emma sat down to write to her father, she put all her worries and concerns aside. Unlike Caroline, Emma fulfilled the wartime feminine ideal by composing patriotic letters, assuring her father of the safety of his family and the optimistic spirits of the people. "We are all cheerful and *hopeful*," she wrote in July 1862, "looking through the thick clouds by which we are encompassed in New Orleans to the bright future in store for us." During more than a year of Federal occupation and at a time when other young women were despondent about the ultimate success of the cause, Emma Walton wrote to her father about their family's "admirable spirits." "Our faith in God, and our devotion to that which we hold so dear and sacred, will sustain us amid all our trials," she declared. "Everyone feels as I do."[4]

On the fall of Vicksburg and Port Hudson—a time of universal gloom in the Deep South—Emma stated that "we have not yet become depressed." "We of course feel badly," she admitted in July 1863, "but we have just the same confidence in the success of our cause as ever. . . . We know that the capture of Vicksburg and Port Hudson will not open the river, there will never be commerce as long as we have room to plant a battery to fire upon their boats." By 1864, she no longer wrote to her father about the state of the war effort or the sentiments of the people. Instead, she just reassured him, "We all laugh when we can and keep the blues at their distance."[5]

Emma Walton fulfilled the ideal of Confederate womanhood—an ideal that encouraged women to draw upon their "natural" piety to become the "virtuous conscience" of the new nation. Patriotic women expressed their honor by cheering troops, preparing supplies, and lifting Confederate morale. In her letters to her father, Emma Walton achieved this ideal by subsuming her personal fears and anxieties about the war effort to write confident and glowing pronouncements about the cause. For other young ladies, however, the transition from Southern belle to patriotic Confederate woman was fraught with difficulty, and many lost their footing trying to make the giant leap into womanhood without the traditional, and previously essential, rite of passage.[6]

In many ways, Confederate womanhood had developed the ideal of the Southern lady by demanding the extension of women's domestic and familial responsibilities to encompass the war effort. A mistress's sewing and knitting, once completed for family members, was extended to include Confederate soldiers. A woman's role as a spiritual guide to her husband and children was reworked to encompass "Confederate morale." Southern matrons, therefore, were able to expand their existing role to embrace the war effort. In contrast, young ladies were expected to discard their "bellehood" for the patriotic wartime ideal. Suitors, fashions, balls, and parties were replaced with sewing societies, wartime fundraising, and the sacrifice of men. The extension of honor through marriage and the public display of gentility were increasingly suppressed for more patriotic endeavors.

The dominance of the patriotic ideal was also strengthened by the repercussions of war. By 1862, the Federal presence in Mississippi and Louisiana led to a scarcity of provisions and the loss of homes and possessions. A young lady's induction into womanhood was no longer possible for many elite families who had always relied on their wealth to exhibit gentility but were now faced with a wartime struggle to maintain supplies of food and clothing. The absence of eligible Southern men also transformed the nature and purpose of elite society, and the loss of thousands of soldiers to the battlefield altered the fate of many promising young belles.

At a pivotal time in their lives, young Confederate ladies were confronted with the impossibility of attaining the customary belle ideal. Their visions of ball gowns and dashing gentlemen, however, were not given up without a fight. Between spinning, sewing for the soldiers, minding the children, and praying for the cause, young women struggled with their new wartime identities. They worried about their very survival, but they also worried about their appearance, their social graces, and their prospects of marriage. In a world that had always made wives out of its adolescent girls, the young Confederate ladies of Mississippi and Louisiana were forced to reconcile the belle ideal with unfamiliar notions of sacrificial patriotism and wartime realities.

THE HOMESPUN DRESS

As they bade farewell to their soldier kin in the spring of 1861, young ladies would have scoffed at the suggestion that they might be forced to make do with their existing wardrobe through four long years of war. Clothing had always been a central concern for young women, because fashion enhanced female attractiveness and provided a physical representation of status. Necessity and war, however, revolutionized elite Confederate ideas about dress. Genteel frills and furbelows were swapped for homespun dresses that were made from cloth previously worn by poor whites and slaves. The significance of the homespun dress as part of the wartime patriotic ideal was reflected in a popular Confederate song, which urged young ladies to sacrifice their finery in the name of the cause.

> The homespun dress is plain, I know,
>   My hat's palmetto too;
> But then it shows what Southern girls
>   For Southern rights will do.
> We sent the bravest of our land,

> To battle with the foe,
> And we will lend a helping hand—
> We love the South, you know.[7]

Notions of feminine patriotism—and necessity—dictated that belles sacrifice their finery. By 1862, the Union blockade of Southern seaports and the dislocations born of Federal invasions had made the attainment of high fashion impossible in Mississippi and Louisiana. Supplies of hoops, bonnets, lace, and elegant fabrics dried up within months of the onset of hostilities. Available goods were marketed at considerable cost, depending on rarity, demand, and wartime inflation. One woman in Hinds County recorded the prices of some items in 1864: boots cost $200; shoes were $125; coats, $350; and calico could be bought for $10 per yard.[8]

Young ladies who had been raised to value their appearance found this wartime reality difficult to reconcile with their socialization as Southern belles. At the beginning of 1861, Kate Stone was the proud owner of an array of beautiful dresses, including day outfits and evening gowns. Her wardrobe also contained a good supply of fine corsets and hoops, imported stockings, and the most elegant French slippers. By 1862, war and necessity forced Kate to redefine some of her ideas about fashion. "It looks like we may have difficulty in getting summer clothes," she wrote anxiously in January. "We have spent less this year than ever before. Have bought only absolute necessaries—no frills and furbelows for us." In 1863, Kate was happy to trade items for secondhand clothing and marveled at the repercussions of war. "'Times change and men change with them'—trite but true. A year ago would we have thought of receiving, or of a friend offering, clothes as a present?" she wrote. "Now we are as pleased to receive a half-worn garment from a friend as the veriest beggar that goes from door to door. How else shall we cover our nakedness?"[9]

When Amanda Stone purchased a number of secondhand items in a desperate effort to replenish her family's depleted wardrobe, Kate was charged with the unenviable task of remodeling the clothes into respectable and well-fitting garments. "I am busy every day trying to make up the cloth Mamma bought, but it is slow, tiresome work for one person with no sewing machine," she complained. "The only things Mamma could find to buy belonged to the Lowrys, and they sold them at awful prices. . . . Mamma bought some of Olivia's things for Sister. Jimmy is fitted out with a suit belonging to a Mr. Mc-something, and I have two dresses and an embroidered skirt of Carrie Lowry's. It seems funny to be wearing other people's half-worn clothing, but it is all we can get." Kate's younger sister received the most unfashionable purchase of all. "Mamma bought some Turkey-red calico at $3 a yard for a dress for Sister," she remarked, probably relieved that that the fabric had not been assigned to her.[10]

Kate also noted that the Federal blockade had inadvertently plunged fashion-conscious belles into a state of complete ignorance. While young ladies had spent 1862 dying and remodeling their dresses, by 1864 few had any idea of the popular trends in Europe or Britain. Kate was struck by this alarming realization when she tried to assist a friend with her trousseau in May 1864. "Every day or so Julia comes with something to be cut or remodeled, and we have grand consultations on the fashions," she remarked, "which is an exemplification of the blind leading the blind, as we are all in a state of dense ignorance." Natchez belle Annie Harper regarded women's newfound ignorance as a blessing that allowed ladies to nurture their individual style rather than conforming to the seasonal dictates of the fashion world. "Of fashion we knew nothing but were a law unto ourselves," she confessed. "And I must say I never saw our girls look prettier, . . . because each one only studied that which was becoming, and with true feminine instinct unperverted by outside influences generally succeeded in attaining it."[11]

Most young ladies were unable to regard the wartime economy of necessity as anything but a disagreeable inconvenience and grew increasingly frustrated when they compared the high standard of antebellum fashion to their modest Confederate garb. Sarah Morgan declared that she was "not quite equal . . . to the young lady, who when told she must leave New Orleans instantly as it was to be shelled, said if her trunks could not go too, she would remain and share their fate." Still, she acknowledged that she would mourn the loss of her "blue flounce," her "magenta muslin," and her "pretty barège," which she would be forced to leave behind in the event of an attack on Baton Rouge. When her family became refugees, Sarah made do with a couple of older dresses, and she dreaded the winter months when her entire wardrobe would consist of "a handsome blue silk I bought two years ago last spring, and one heavy blue merino that does not fit me." "What an out-fit for winter!" she cried in despair. Instead of her bonnet made of "black velvet, purple silk and ostrich feathers," Sarah was forced to wear a "black straw walking hat with its curled brim, trimmed in black ribbon with golden sheaves of wheat." "Two years ago this fall, father threw me a banknote

at table," she remarked, "—and I purchased this with it. Now it is my
only headgear, except a sunbonnet."[12]

Clara Solomon was also disgusted with her limited wardrobe. "Nothing to wear!" she exclaimed in September 1861. "I finally donned my
pink barêge, and went down stairs not in a *very* amiable mood." As
autumn drew to a close, Clara became irritated and upset by the thought
of what she would be wearing next season. "If it continues warm, I have
nothing to wear, if it gets cold, I am in the same predicament," she
wrote in despair. Unsatisfied with her appearance, she sometimes
regarded staying at home as preferable to going out in "Confederate
attire." In May 1862, Clara and her sister, Alice, refused to attend the
synagogue, "the principal reason being," she wrote, "that we had no
new bonnets." In Monroe, Louisiana, Sarah Lois Wadley's vanity even
triumphed over her sense of patriotic duty. "There is to be a concert and
supper in Monroe tonight, for the benefit of the Ladies Volunteer Aid
Society," she wrote in July 1861. "I have been pressed to go by all my
acquaintances around here, and Aunt Jane invited me to spend the
night of the concert with her, but I thought it would be better for me
not to go, I have no appropriate dress to wear."[13]

While Clara Solomon and Sarah Lois Wadley struggled with their
wartime appearances, some young women were able to redefine their
antebellum understanding of fashion and glorified homespun in patriotic terms. "The ladies here have beautiful homespun," wrote Sophie
Collins to her mother in Louisiana. Annie Harper declared that young
women looked far more becoming "in their palmetto hats and simple
garments" than they had in antebellum times. "The last wool dress often
went to warm our absent soldier boys," she added, "and homespun was
cheerfully worn instead." Annie Jacobs was pleased with her successful
attempt to remake two old dresses into one fine garment. "In all my life
I have never had a dress that gave me more satisfaction," she declared.
Sarah Morgan was often frustrated by her deplorable wardrobe, yet she
too wrote with pride about the dignity of Confederate ladies. "Blessed
abode of maidens who scorn not to worship in church with bonnets that
had passed their prime three years ago, and in sunbonnets of unbecom-
ing hue," she remarked.[14]

Other young ladies continued to define their gentility by their clothing. While Clara Solomon patched and remodeled her own attire,
Elizabeth Christie Brown of Natchez wrote of the "unpleasant" duty of
getting fitted for a new dress. "I went this morning to have done what I
dislike *very much* and that is to have a dress fitted," she commented,

"but I like to have my clothes look well when I have them on so I must put up with some of the disagreeables for the sake of the pleasures." The occasion, however "disagreeable," provided Elizabeth with a rare opportunity to affirm her status in a world where most representations of gentility had become casualties of war. In Columbus, Mississippi, Eliza Lucy Irion was also furnished with an array of "nearly new" dresses after her sisters went into mourning. "I had a nice supply of clothes although 'twas war times," she recalled. "People were not so proud about wearing their sister's old clothes, and as two of my sisters were in mourning, I had a nice supply and then Sis Hattie had exchanged two dresses with a lady for two splendid silks—more antique. These completed my wardrobe." Extremely proud of her appearance, Eliza was one of the few young women to enter society during the war.[15]

Without fine attire of her own, Kate Stone clung to the idea that gentility and elegance were the intrinsic qualities of an elite Southern lady—even if a wartime economy of scarcity compelled her to dress in remodeled, patched, or secondhand clothing. She may have been clad in homespun, but Kate declared that she knew how to wear it with style: something, she added, that the women of Lamar County, Texas, did not possess. "We saw several nice-looking families, but all were in the fashions of three years ago," she scoffed in disgust. "If they would only leave off their tremendous hoops, but hoops seem in the very zenith of their popularity. Mamma and I were the only women folks without the awkward, ungraceful cages. No doubt the people thought us hopelessly out of date. We have not worn them for a long time. Nothing looks funnier than a woman walking around with an immense hoop—bare-footed." While lamenting the loss of her elegant wardrobe, Kate drew comfort from the fact that even though her clothing was similar to that worn by women of lower social orders, her comprehensive education in gentility somehow set her apart—and above—them. "I must still cling to my calfskin *chaussures*, homeknit stockings, and brogans," she confessed in July 1863, "something different from the lace-like clock stockings and French slippers of the olden times. I miss nice things for my feet now more than anything. I feel so slovenly with these horrors on exhibition. But a truce to complaints. I might be dight out in a large hoop and bare feet."[16] While they patched their skirts and fashioned palmetto hats to replace pretty bonnets, young ladies like Kate continued to judge themselves and others by the antebellum feminine ideal. The blockade, wartime necessity, and the dictates of patriotic womanhood had forced them to sacrifice their finery for homespun. Their complaints, however, reveal the tensions they confronted as they tried to reconcile their antebellum socialization in genteel honor with patriotic ideals and wartime reality.

BALLS OR SEWING PARTIES?

Without fashionable dresses, elegant bonnets, imported boots, or lace stockings, young ladies were probably relieved that their change in appearance corresponded with massive changes in the nature and purpose of society. The blockade and the presence of Federal troops limited the types of social occasions held in Confederate Mississippi and Louisiana. So too did the absence of men. In antebellum times, parties and balls had been the meeting grounds for belles and gentlemen. With the coming of war, women organized tableaux and sewing parties, and functions were held to raise money for the Confederacy. Most young women participated in these events. Kate Stone, Sarah Lois Wadley, and Mary Wright attended sewing societies. Annie Jeter Carmouche organized groups of neighbors for afternoons of sewing and knitting. Southern women also turned hospitality into a patriotic gesture as they opened their homes to entertain or nurse honorable Southern soldiers.[17]

Busily sewing and knitting, many young ladies looked upon balls and parties in an entirely different light. While Sarah Morgan was happy to attend a party in 1863, sobering thoughts of war prompted other young women (and some soldiers) to reflect upon the propriety of dancing while thousands of men gave their lives to the cause. Confederate soldier William Bisland was relieved to hear that his fiancée did not partake in such lighthearted affairs. "I was glad to see how little inclination you have to attend parties and balls in such times as these," he wrote her in February 1863. "I truly think it is no time for such things. The whole country should be in mourning, instead of dancing."[18]

In Natchez, Elizabeth Christie Brown noted the absence of the "May-day frolics" in 1863. "What has caused the omission of the usual festive scene at the Hall today?" she wrote. "Listen to that noise like distant thunder, and look on the blood stained turf, and your question is answered. The women and children of the South have hearts, and how could they enter into the May-day frolic, when all they hold dear, may be bleeding on the *Battle* field, with no one to give assistance, or hear their last wishes, and messages to the loved ones at home." With three brothers in the Confederate army, Cordelia Lewis Scales refused to indulge in a day of shopping and visiting in nearby Holly Springs. "We were all going to the Springs, but since the battle of Manassas I don't feel inclined to take any pleasure when I don't know that my brother is alive or not," she admitted. Instead, she preferred to wait at home, praying for the welfare and safety of her brothers Joe, Henry, and Dabney.[19]

Sophie Collins had been a self-confessed "belle of the ball" in antebellum Mississippi, but the war also subdued her love for such occasions. In November 1862, she wrote to her mother stating her relief that there were no dances in Canton, Mississippi. "[It] would seem as if [we] were dancing over the graves of our dead soldiers," she wrote. That was exactly how nineteen-year-old Eliza Lucy Irion felt after she attended a dance in 1862. "I felt that I had been so remiss in my love and anxiety for my dear beloved brother," she cried. "Such vanity and folly had been in my mind and had filled the place which should have been devoted to his welfare! Oh! how awful to feel remorseful on account of neglect to our loved ones! I was glad when the gentlemen left and when I laid my head upon the pillow, I was very regretful."[20]

At wartime gatherings, young women often found it difficult to perform their patriotic duty and appear cheerful and optimistic. Anxiety, grief, war weariness, and frustration often undermined their youthful vivacity, and many young ladies reflected on the life they had eagerly anticipated and their wartime world. With her father and brother away at war, Sarah Lois Wadley experienced frequent bouts of depression and struggled to overcome "the melancholy that takes hold upon me." "I suffer much from debility and low spirits the last few weeks, sometimes I am so overpowered by melancholy and find myself in such fits of abstraction that I fear I am losing my mind," she wrote tearfully. "I must struggle more against it, sometimes my body feels so weary and weak and my mind and heart so sad that I can scarcely sit up, and feel cross and pettish whenever I am spoken to." At these times of great sadness, Sarah grew despondent and entertained the possibility that she was losing her youth before it had even begun. "Lately in my moments of bodily weakness the sad thought comes over me that I am losing my youth," she confessed. "I have never had any beauty, I have always known and sadly known that I was *ugly*, but I have lost my color, my eyes are often surrounded by a purple band of coloring, my hair used to be the only beautiful thing about me, and now it has fallen out till it is not more than half as thick as formerly." Unable to break free from her depression, Sarah shut herself up in her room, away from the cares and sorrows of a wartime world.[21]

Sarah Morgan felt "a thousand years old" and shed the "bitterest tears" in the confines of her room. "I can't stand it much longer; I'll give way presently, and I know my heart will break." Reflecting on happier times only made Sarah more miserable. "It is the Past that is killing me now," she cried, "contrasting what Ought to be with what Is. It is wearing me out, drinking the very life from my heart." In a log cabin in Keatchie, Louisiana, refugee Sidney Harding felt "bowed down with low spirits" and "perfectly miserable at times." Lemuella Brickell also suffered from depression when she came to the realization that her intended life as a belle was not to be. "Many hopes and fears have been crushed, and I await my 21st birthday to find *my life* almost a blank," she wrote somberly. "What times to live for—what is the use of living."[22]

Young ladies who had once found pleasure in parties and visiting now shunned all social gatherings. After the death of her beloved brother and the loss of her home and possessions, refugee Kate Stone lost all interest in the pleasures of society. "There is no dearth of company," she wrote from Monroe, Louisiana, "but I cannot enjoy it. I feel out of place with a party of gay young people. Their mirth jars my heart. Life seems too sad a thing to spend in talking nonsense. I feel fifty years old." Sarah Lois Wadley also struggled to maintain a cheerful image. After tea with Eliza Baker, she recorded the evening had passed "heavily to me." "I have been so little in society for so long a time that the light conversation which generally forms the *staple* between young ladies and gentlemen is quite strange and distasteful to me," she wrote, adding that she was "utterly unable to carry it on with any spirit." Fellow Louisianian Mary Wright felt so "low-spirited" and "tired of living" that she too spent her days "moping" and "pray[ing] for patience to see the end." "My health is very poor now," she conceded. "I stay at home constantly —scarcely see any one visiting at the house." When her sister, Esther, insisted that the pair attend Ellen Sneade's wedding in December 1864, Mary admitted that it had been a "merry" occasion. "I cannot enjoy myself for long at a time," she added hastily, suddenly overcome with guilt at the thought of partaking in any pleasure when family and friends were fighting and dying on distant battlefields. Weeks later, Mary came to the realization that her "ceaseless repining" and "selfish mode of living" had "accomplished nothing." "It is alienating me from my friends," she wrote, "who look upon me as a stranger, and even my own family think me willfully selfish to withdraw so much within myself. Ettie understands me more than the others, but she cannot feel at all times as I do. . . . I stay upstairs and feel more like crying."[23]

As the war dragged on, young women revealed the tensions that existed between their patriotic role as the upholders of morale and the reality of their lives in Confederate Mississippi and Louisiana. In her letters to her father, Emma Walton fulfilled her wartime duty by sounding confident and hopeful. Others, like Lemuella Brickell, struggled to reconcile the widening gulf between patriotic optimism and wartime grief. "Everyone looks at me and thinks how happy—envys me perhaps my gay spirit," she commented. "—O God and if they only knew the misery I feel, they would sink down on their knees and say 'God protect me from such happiness.'" Confederate patriotism demanded that Lemuella and other young ladies sacrifice their men, homes, possessions, clothing, and society for the wartime good. For many young women, the immensity of this sacrifice became almost too much to bear, producing cracks in the patriotic façade of Confederate femininity.[24]

To Become an Old Maid

Perhaps this tension reached its climax when young women assessed their possibilities of marriage. Marriage was the goal of all Southern belles, and a young lady's social and educational pursuits were directed toward the attainment of this ideal. Yet the Civil War and patriotic womanhood demanded that women assume the duty of encouraging men to enlist, and shaming those who did not. As self-sacrificing patriots, Southern women where also asked to give their own men to the cause, and to do so became an expression of their commitment to the new nation.

These sacrifices, however, came at a price. Many young ladies lost their fiancés, sweethearts, or potential suitors to the bloody battlefield. In Mississippi, Annie Jacobs was visiting her godmother, Louise Yerger, when she received the tragic news that her "soldier lover . . . was killed fighting in one of the great battles in Virginia." In the days that followed, Annie could only watch helplessly as Louise spent many grief-stricken hours in "her darkened room, where she was lying in bed with his picture on her breast." Mary Wright was inconsolable after her cousin (and suitor) Dave died in a battle at Fisher's Creek in December 1864. After repulsing his advances on the eve of his departure to war, Mary was now overcome by grief, and guilt. "I cannot help my eyes filling with tears at strange and unwelcome moments," she cried. "I think of poor Dave so often, never with indifference, I can never do that again.

If he could only come back—I would let him love me as much as he wanted—just to make him happy. I know I made him feel miserable very often—What would I not give to replace those unhappy days with happy anticipations for the Future!"[25]

As men like Dave gave their lives to the Confederacy, young ladies were still subjected to the same pressures to marry. In antebellum times, the most accomplished belles had the luxury of choosing a husband from an array of eligible gentlemen. The repercussions of wartime, however, curtailed a young lady's options. Thousands of soldiers died, and those who returned from the battlefront were often maimed in body and spirit. The ability to meet potential suitors was also governed by military maneuvers and patterns of wartime invasion. Southern women living in occupied areas encountered Federal soldiers, not their "boys in gray." While Kate Foster had heard reports of young women "receiving attention from the Yankees" in occupied Natchez, she believed that "it shows so little character not to resist love of admiration more." Flirtations with the enemy, she argued, were nothing less than treason. "We ought to remember that we all have relatives, friends or lovers in our army and if they hear these things it might weaken a strong arm in time of battle and sicken a stout and loving heart." When Kate Stone heard reports that "Miss W. Richardson" "had caught a Yankee beau," she used the incident to affirm her self-worth. "Imagine any girl falling so low," she exclaimed in disgust, reassuring herself that a single life was far preferable to this desperate and unpatriotic alternative. As Kate knew, family honor may not withstand such a scandal.[26]

Romantic liaisons with honorable Southern soldiers were far less problematic, and in areas under Confederate control, young women still met and entertained Rebel soldiers who bivouacked nearby or were passing through on their way to another destination. These brief encounters often led to romance and even marriage. During a stay with her sister-in-law's family near Port Hudson, Louisiana, Sarah Morgan enjoyed the frequent company of a select group of elite Confederate soldiers stationed in the area. Sarah soon captured the attentions of John Halsey, a Pointe Coupee Parish lawyer who served as a private in Captain James L. Bradford's battery, 1st Mississippi Light Artillery. After a deluge of gifts—including novels, a bird, and a pet flying squirrel—Sarah was forced to acknowledge her conquest. "Think I can do pretty much as I please with 'John,'" she commented smugly, "though of course it would never do to let him, or anyone else know it. . . . He is not a stupid man by any means; yet he says some dreadfully foolish things to me sometimes; *so* foolish that I dont like to tell on him because I know he has better sense and feels ashamed of it afterwards." John's removal to the battlefield and the Morgan women's relocation to New Orleans put an end to Sarah's flirtations. "If he is really killed, I will doubtless persuade myself that I always did like him," she confessed.[27]

At Wayside plantation, Amanda Worthington also relished the company, and the attentions, of a steady stream of gallant Southern soldiers. When five Confederate scouts stayed for supper, Amanda "was delighted to think we once more had some 'rebels' under our roof." When a "Mr. Bailie" arrived for a meal, Amanda could not resist the opportunity to bask in his attention. "Mr. Bailie staid till nearly five o'clock and every body left him for me to entertain from dinner time till then. I liked him very much better than any of the other soldiers who have been here," she remarked, "but he's the only one I've talked to much." Later, Amanda noted that it was commonplace for her father to invite up to eighteen soldiers to have supper with the family each night. "Father . . . never will let one pass without either taking a meal or staying all night," she wrote, delighted by the prospect of more soldier beaux.[28]

Elizabeth Christie Brown also collected a number of admirers in wartime Natchez. "Lt. Duncan McDonald . . . came, and stayed until sundown. We chatted on various subjects, he tried to make me tell him whether I was engaged or not, but I did not gratify his curiosity," she commented. "He said he wanted to know for Capt. B's benefit." "I think that gent is too susceptible," she declared, "if he has taken such a fancy to me when he has only seen me twice." In Columbus, Mississippi, Eliza Lucy Irion enjoyed an eventful summer with "the 36th Mississippi Regiment encamped in one of our fields right in front of the gate." "Long be remembered the summer of '62!" she exclaimed. "Our house was crowded with company. Girls were very fond of visiting me, and the evenings were pleasantly spent with parlor, hall and gallery filled with 'nice beaux.'" Much to Eliza's delight, the strict courtship rituals that had governed antebellum society were largely abandoned with the coming of war. Without male chaperons, young couples encountered less parental influence and acquired more freedom of choice. Courtship procedures were also shortened to accommodate the demands of war, in particular, the movement of troops to the battlefield. In Confederate Louisiana and Mississippi, belles could be courted and engaged within weeks, sometimes days, of meeting a suitable gentleman.[29]

Still, the absence of a traditional courtship procedure through society and the loss of thousands of men to the battlefield made many young women reflect on the possibility of never realizing their intended role. Kate Stone dreamed of suitors "but to no purpose." "Nobody coming to marry me, nobody coming to woo." When an acquaintance told her about the "scores" of beaux she had "all waiting in trembling apprehension of yes or no," Kate felt a pang of jealousy. "What a garment of comfort self-satisfaction is," she sighed enviously. "Oh, for a nice cloak of self-appreciation."[30]

In her log cabin in Keatchie, Louisiana, refugee Sidney Harding also dreamed that "a handsome soldier" would find her. "I wonder why it is that I have not had more offers[?]" she questioned. "I know I am not ugly." Lemuella Brickell also hoped and prayed that she would not become an "old maid." "I don't want to be an old maid and won't if I can help it," she declared. Without any romance in her life, Clara Solomon had to be content to watch a pair of lovers courting on a gallery opposite her home in New Orleans. "If ever I felt envious it was when I looked at them," she wrote in her diary. "How devotedly he regarded her, and how affectionate were his caresses. Oh! how my lonely heart craved for love, some one to love. Will its cravings ever be satisfied?"[31]

Young women's anguish was understandable. As Southern belles, their primary goal was to marry. Wartime necessity had refashioned an ideal of womanhood into one that supported the war effort while contradicting the underpinnings of their antebellum role. Often such frustration vented itself in discussions of the lives of single women, a solitary existence that many would be forced to "endure" because of the war. In a rare frank moment in her letter writing, Emma Walton addressed the possibility that she, like many others, might become an "old maid." "The writer is no longer as young as she 'used to be' and that she can see the shadows of an *old maid* flitting before her not yet impaired vision," she wrote her father, reminding him that this was the common sacrifice of a wartime belle. "You know it's no fault of hers but of the war," she added, "therefore we will not murmur but *endure* like true patriots for the good of our country." Unlike other diarists, Emma slotted her matrimonial sacrifice into the larger framework of Confederate sacrifice. By so doing, she fulfilled her patriotic role while reconciling it with her inability to fulfill the belle ideal.[32]

Other young women failed to make this connection in their diaries, and struggled with antebellum ideals and wartime reality. Sarah Morgan saw spinsterhood as the only alternative; and so, vowing to "take hard crusts and bitter words; take poverty, and hardships" before dependence, she planned a single life with a close friend. "Marie and I say to each other almost daily with an emphasis that makes it almost ludicrous, 'We will never, never marry,'" she remarked. "Every one laughs at us, and prophesies that before another year has elapsed we will recant our vow at the altar. Never! We speak knowing what we say, and firmly resolved (at present) to carry out our resolution." Clara Solomon also contemplated sharing her "old maidenhood" with her sister, Alice. After learning their school lessons, the pair "remained some time *enjoying* ourselves *alone* in the little cozy room, and picturing ourselves in the days, when as old maids we would occupy a like apartment." "We would surely be *happy*," she added, "for it would be impossible, while in each other's society, to be otherwise." In Monroe, Sarah Lois Wadley intended to prove "false the sentence, 'if matrimony have many trials, celibacy has no pleasures,'" while Kate Stone and her friend, "Missie Morris," proposed that they would wait two more years before laying "down the flower-wreathed scepter of girlhood and don[ning] the badge of spinsterhood."[33]

Some young ladies looked with revulsion to the schoolroom and the dreaded life of the governess as the only way to survive in a world stripped of wealth and destroyed by Federal occupation. Amanda Worthington had always been a reluctant scholar and wrote in her diary of her inability to apply herself to her work. Yet after witnessing the many horrors of war, not in the least her family's loss of wealth, she perceived her academic pursuits in an entirely different light. "I came to the conclusion yesterday that I would commence studying some today as I may have to be a school teacher some of these days in order to make a living," she commented. Lemuella Brickell had similar thoughts. "I am reading French and cyphering every day," she wrote. "Perhaps I may have use for it very soon." "I don't know what else I can go at," she added. "I had rather teach than wash and cook." Like Lemuella, Eliza Lucy Irion recognized that the days of leisure she had experienced in 1862 were probably gone forever. "I must indeed try to be more useful," she wrote on her birthday. "—If I can't be a fashionable lady—perhaps I can be a useful one."[34]

After passing her examinations at New Orleans' Normal School, Clara Solomon tried her hand at substitute teaching. "Imagine me at the head of 60 children," she remarked. "I was almost inadequate to the task. As I expected, the children were quite unruly in the absence of their teacher, and it resisted my efforts to reduce them to a state of quietude. . . . The continual buzz in which I was surrounded had a powerful effect upon me for at the dismissal of school I was worn out." The harrowing experience did not deter Clara in her quest to obtain an academic position, nor did it quash her "dream of happiness . . . for A. [Alice] and I to be teachers in the same school." Instead, Clara made plans to look for a permanent teaching post in the nearby Garden District.[35]

Jennie Pendleton dismissed the idea of ever teaching because she would "lose all [her] dignity" among her former schoolmates, but Florence Cooney Tompkins maintained a different perspective, describing the foresight of her mother, who believed that economic necessity would shape life in the postwar South. After enrolling Florence in a "Yankee school," her mother defended her actions among a group of patriotic Confederate women. "I foresee great disaster for our Southern people," Florence recalled her mother saying. "With no money, slaves freed, homes confiscated, what is left but education? No, although it may break my heart and the children's, I see no alternative: 'tis the only inheritance left for Southern women, and my girls must and shall be educated." While only a small minority felt that women needed to be furnished with employable skills in order to survive in the postbellum South, war and necessity prompted some young ladies to consider a lifestyle outside the traditional boundaries of elite womanhood. These feelings were heightened by the staggering loss of Confederate military personnel and women's emerging realization that marriage could no longer guarantee them financial stability. Most young elite women nevertheless saw teaching or the life of a governess as desperate final options. Sarah Morgan commented that she would undertake such a life only from necessity and would probably die as a result.[36]

Although few young ladies were shipped off to teaching academies, elite Southerners demonstrated an ongoing commitment to educate their young women, in part to reinforce the class boundaries that had blurred considerably with the loss of homes, possessions, and slaves. As in antebellum times, educational standards varied greatly across wartime Mississippi and Louisiana. Some young ladies were tutored at home, others attended day or boarding schools. Some young women taught their siblings, while others were sent to academies along the Confederacy's eastern coast. By 1862, Federal raids and occupation constantly threatened to disrupt or terminate this educational process as families responded to the changing circumstances of war.[37]

After a period of anxiety when Sarah Lois Wadley conceded that she was "fast approaching ladyhood" and was "very ignorant," her family finally employed a tutor who taught her French, ancient geography, astronomy, rhetoric, and mythology at her home near Monroe, Louisiana. "I am to take philosophy, physiology and arithmetic when the books come," she added. Emma Walton, Martha Josephine Moore, and Clara Solomon learned arts and languages at various ladies academies in occupied New Orleans, while another young Crescent City lady described her musical training to her brother, a lieutenant in the Confederate army.[38]

As they honed their painting skills or spent time practicing on the piano, these young women were preparing for a genteel world that had been destroyed by the ravages of war. With the terrifying realization that life may never be the same, young women in Mississippi and Louisiana looked to the battlefield and to Confederate victory for a sign that better days were coming. What they saw provided them with no comfort or assurance of Southern triumph. Clinging to education as a means to assert their elite identities, young women struggled to navigate their way through a world that pitted patriotic sacrifice against marriage, and wartime practicality against gentility. Struggling to fulfill their role as belles or as patriotic women, young ladies were left in a limbo, somewhere between an irrelevant standard and a reality, a place where the region's elite women would remain long after the Civil War's conclusion.

Photograph of slaves in front of library on Joseph E. Davis's Hurricane plantation, south of Vicksburg. Lise Mitchell was Joseph's granddaughter and was born at Hurricane in 1842. *Courtesy Old Courthouse Museum, Vicksburg, Mississippi.*

Elite life in the cities and towns of the Deep South. A photograph of Church Street, Baton Rouge, taken in 1863. Sarah Morgan's home is in the middle of the photograph, partly hidden by the tree. *Courtesy Charles East.*

Carte de visite of Ellen and Mary Wright, ca. 1854, Wright-Boyd Family Papers. *Courtesy Louisiana and Lower Mississippi Valley Collections, Louisiana State University, Baton Rouge, Louisiana.*

"Southern Women Hounding Their Men to Rebellion," engraving, *Frank Leslie's Illustrated Newspaper*, May 23, 1863.

Sarah Lois Wadley. Raoul Family Papers. *Courtesy Special Collections and Archives, Robert W. Woodruff Library, Emory University.*

Kate Stone. John Q.
Anderson Papers, Mss. 2162.
*Courtesy Louisiana and Lower
Mississippi Valley Collections,
Louisiana State University,
Baton Rouge, Louisiana.*

Carte de visite of Amanda
Worthington. Amanda
Dougherty Worthington
Papers. *Courtesy Mississippi
Department of Archives and
History, Jackson, Mississippi.*

Carte de visite of Sarah Morgan, taken in New Orleans in 1863. On the back of the photograph Sarah wrote: "Hold me upside down if you want [to] improve the picture—It is really better looking—don't hold it near as it looks coarse." *Courtesy Morgan Potts Goldbarth.*

Clara Solomon. *Courtesy Alice Dale Cohan.*

Ruins of Baton Rouge, 1862. Andrew D. Lytle Collection, Mss. 893, 1254.
Courtesy Louisiana and Lower Mississippi Valley Collections, Louisiana State University, Baton Rouge, Louisiana.

The Ladies of New Orleans before General Butler's Proclamation.

After GENERAL BUTLER's Proclamation.

"The Ladies of New Orleans Before and After General Butler's Proclamation,"
Harper's Weekly Illustrated, July 12, 1862.

"Cemetery in New Orleans—Widow and Daughters in Full Mourning," engraving, *Frank Leslie's Illustrated Newspaper*, April 25, 1863.

"Searching for Arms," *Harper's Weekly Illustrated*, November 16, 1861.

"ACCOMPANIED BY ONE OF THESE SMILING 'INDISPENSABLES.'"—*Page 4.*

Southern belle with an "indispensable" servant at her feet. Drawing by W. A. McCullough, reproduced from a plate in Letitia M. Burwell, *A Girl's Life in Virginia Before the War* (New York: 1895). *Courtesy Rare Book, Manuscript, and Special Collections Library, Duke University, Durham, North Carolina.*

Entry for September 20, 1863, Kate D. Foster Diary, 1863-1872. *Courtesy Rare Book, Manuscript, and Special Collections Library, Duke University, Durham, North Carolina.*

108

Eliza Lucy Irion-Neilson. Irion-
Neilson Family Papers. *Courtesy
Mississippi Department of Archives
and History, Jackson, Mississippi.*

Sarah Morgan Dawson, 1886.
Francis Warrington Dawson I
& II Papers. *Courtesy Rare
Book, Manuscript, and Special
Collections Library, Duke
University, Durham, North
Carolina.*

CHAPTER FIVE

"How Has the Mighty Fallen"

Defeat in Mississippi and Louisiana

Death is nothing in comparison to dishonor.

Sarah Morgan, March 1864

In April 1862, Sarah Morgan peered anxiously from a window of her home on Church Street in Baton Rouge. For three days, rumors had been circulating that the Union army was preparing to shell the city. While "nothing [could] be heard positively," reports indicated that the Confederate gunboat on its way to defend Baton Rouge had been sunk by the enemy, who were organizing en masse in an attempt to "take possession" of the city. "There is no word in the English language which can express the state in which we are all now [in], and have been for the last three days," Sarah wrote excitedly. "I believe that I am one of the most self possessed in my small circle of acquaintance, and yet, I feel such a craving for news . . . that I believe I am as crazy as the rest, and it is all humbug when they tell me I am cool."[1]

Realizing that they "had best be prepared for anything," twenty-year-old Sarah gathered together a "running bag" filled with a host of essential items as well as many sentimental keepsakes. "My treasure bag being tied around my waist as a bustle, a sack on my arm with a few necessary trifles and a few *unnecessary* ones—I had not the heart to leave the prayer books father gave us—carving knife and pistol safe, I stood ready for instant flight," she wrote. "My papers I piled on the bed, ready to burn, with matches lying on them."[2]

On this occasion, the Yankees did not arrive. Sarah's reprieve, however, was short lived, and in the following days she came to the realization that her childhood home would have to be abandoned for safer quarters. As Sarah reflected on the likely fate of her rosewood furniture, the elegant parlor, and the pleasant balcony where she had often sat strumming her guitar, precious memories came flooding back. It was in this home that she had received the news of her brother's death in a duel. In her bedroom, she had spent many nights crying over his loss. Months later, in the parlor, Sarah had kissed her father, Judge Thomas Gibbes Morgan, as he lay on his deathbed. She had also bade farewell to her soldier brothers, Gibbes, George, and James, as they set out to defend the Confederate cause. "O my dear Home!" she sighed as she watched for the Yankees. "How can I help but cry at leaving you forever? For if this fight occurs, never again shall I pass the threshold of this house where we have been so happy and sad, the scene of joyous meeting and mournful partings, the place where we greeted each other with glad shouts after ever so short a parting, the place where Harry and Father kissed us good bye and never came back again!"[3]

For Sarah Morgan, notions of family and family honor were linked to memories that had been played out in the parlor, the kitchen, and the bedrooms of her Church Street home. Yet with the coming of war, the powerful ties of family and honor were also linked to the Confederate cause. Gibbes, George, and James Morgan defended home, family, and nation on the battlefield, and Sarah upheld her duty by knitting and sewing for the soldiers. All prayed earnestly for the success of the cause. In the Deep South, their prayers were not answered. As the list of Confederate defeats continued to grow, young women were compelled to reassess their familial understanding of nationalism that had tied family honor and the ideals of the cause to the war effort.

"The Future Looks Threatening"

The Civil War came early to the civilians of Mississippi and Louisiana. "1862 dawned upon us gloomily," remarked Eliza Lucy Irion. "The very weather seemed prophetic of the misfortunes which were to come too quickly to our cause."[4]

The year began ominously. The Mississippi and adjacent rivers were soon targeted by Federal forces, which recognized the strategic importance of these Southern waterways as transportation routes for armies and supplies. "Whatever nation gets the control of the Ohio, Mississippi and Missouri rivers will control the continent," declared Union general William T. Sherman. In their quest to conquer the mighty Mississippi, Northern troops moved the scene of battle from the river to the shore, attacking—and occupying—the most strategically valuable towns in the region. By early 1862, Forts Henry and Donelson in Tennessee had fallen to General Grant, and over the next year or so the Confederate army experienced defeats at Island No. 10, Corinth, Port Gibson, Natchez, and Jackson in Mississippi, and New Orleans, Baton Rouge, and Port Hudson in Louisiana.[5]

The fighting and subversion of their homeland profoundly affected young women like Kate Stone, who watched with alarm at the steady advance of the enemy. "The whole Northern Army is now on the move preparing to attack us at all points," she wrote anxiously in January 1862. "The manner in which the North is moving her forces, now that she thinks us surrounded and can give us the annihilating blow, reminds me of a party of hunters crouched around the covert of the deer, and when the lines are drawn and there is no escape, they close in and kill."[6]

In Washington County, Mississippi, Amanda Worthington also voiced her concern over the strength and capability of the Confederate army. "Today has been the very sort of a day to give any one the blues and I have had them considerably," she wrote on a gloomy February afternoon in 1862. "I got to thinking about this dreadful war and how many advantages the North has over us, and then about Willie and Bert being at Columbus which is such a dangerous post, and how long it will be before I see them again, and it made me miserable, and no wonder for such a combination of sad things, is enough to make any body miserable." A string of defeats confirmed Amanda's worst fears about the war effort. "Our people are having a dreadful time now, we have been defeated in six successive battles. Everybody has the blues and feels out of heart." "I almost begin to despair," she added, "they have *so* many more men than we have I am afraid we can't possibly whip them." After hearing that President Jefferson Davis had declared a day of fasting and prayer, Amanda resolved "not to eat a bite all day." "I think our country is in such a condition that she needs fasting and praying for," she concluded. Ellen Louise Power shared similar feelings in her journal. "We are continually hearing bad news about the war," she conceded, "every one seems very much distressed on account of it."[7]

While Amanda Worthington regarded Northern superiority as "enough to make anybody miserable," Lemuella Brickell began to contemplate the ramifications of defeat at Columbus, Mississippi. "O I can't bear to think about it," she wrote in late 1861. "What if they should take it all would be lost." Worrying about the war effort, and her brother's safety, soon wore down Lemuella's already fragile health.

"I am having chills yet some every day," she admitted. She was not alone. In September 1861, Clara Solomon described the solemn atmosphere in New Orleans. "Winter is at the threshold, but its approach is not heralded with bright hopes and joyous anticipations," she wrote. Instead "the dreaded war" with all its "incalculable horrors" stared New Orleans in the face. "And with these gloomy forebodings, can thoughts of pleasure and enjoyment intrude themselves," she questioned. "On previous occasions how many hearts have bound with joy at the idea of participating in the enjoyments presented by our 'gay city.' But now, how different!"[8]

Sarah Lois Wadley also struggled to remain optimistic about the war effort. "These times make me feel sad, sometimes my spirits fall dreadfully, but I try to battle against the ideas that creep unawares into my mind and I endeavor to free myself from the melancholy that takes hold upon me." When William Wadley warned his daughter that the conflict might develop into a long and bloody affair, Sarah grew disconsolate at the news. "I pray that God in his mercy may avert this trial," she wrote feverishly. "I have never contemplated a long war, I have steeled myself to bear great and bloody battles and many privations and even sufferings for a little while, but four long years of war, of suspense which is worse than defeat almost; my heart sinks, my courage utterly fails; *can* I bear it?" The link between family, honor, and the cause added another set of worries to Sarah's wartime burden as she contemplated the ramifications of defeat on the structures of family, household, and community. "This is one of my dark days, one in which I feel the burden of humanity pressing too heavily to be borne," she wrote tearfully. "The future looks threatening, the present is clouded with doubt, and uncertainty; our country is in turmoil and danger, and our family seems like a ship floating upon a troubled sea, with no particular destination." By placing her understanding of nationalism within a framework that incorporated family members and honor into the war effort, Sarah feared the physical and ideological survival of the family unit. Her sense of patriotism had not faltered, but she had begun to question whether Southern troops could indeed triumph over Northern military might.[9]

Part of the answer came on April 25, 1862, when David Glasgow Farragut and his Union fleet captured New Orleans, "the Queen City of the South." "Oh! *never* shall I forget the 25th Apr. 1862," wrote Clara Solomon. "Such expressions of woe as were on the faces of every one, and such sadness as reigned in every heart. Oh! that that day should ever come." The humiliation of defeat was compounded by the realization that one of the Confederacy's largest and most prosperous cities had been unable to fend off its first Northern attack.[10]

As the "Federal flag" flew triumphantly over the Customs House, Clara Solomon was filled with a sense of hopelessness and despair. "A gloom has settled o'er my spirit, a gloom envelopes our dearly-beloved city," she wrote in her journal. "When I am in the street I do not seem to breathe a free atmosphere. It is not free. Laden with the breath of those invaders." "I am sick at heart," she added. "What a victory. The taking of New Orleans." While Clara remained adamant that "our *cause* is not *dead*, it is only *sick*," she conceded in her diary that the Union army now had "the valley of the Mississippi at their command."[11]

The Federal occupation of New Orleans shook the Deep South to its very core, and even those young women who lived some distance from the city suddenly began to question their fate. "It is reported the Federals have possession of our city [New Orleans]," Ellen Louise Power wrote from her home in East Feliciana Parish, Louisiana. "Oh what dreadful news it is, what is to become of our once happy country and its inhabitants?" Like Clara, Kate Stone and Amanda Worthington were well aware of the consequences of this Union victory. "They have free passage of the dear old Miss. river and our Valley is completely in their power," cried Amanda, as thoughts of "blue devils" and Yankee depredations edged closer to home. "Fair Louisiana with her fertile fields of cane and cotton, her many bayous and dark old forests, lies powerless at the feet of the enemy," added Kate Stone. Not only had the Confederate people experienced a terrible defeat, the land itself—as perceived by these diarists—also had suffered the humiliation of Northern conquest.[12]

While Kate Stone was furious that "the proclamation on taking possession of New Orleans . . . [had] the cool impudence to say 'the State of Louisiana,'" it was only a matter of months before Federal forces dominated the river from Natchez to New Orleans. In early May, Sarah Morgan clutched her running bag, pistol, and carving knife and prepared to flee Baton Rouge. Unable to leave without one more precious book or another treasured keepsake, mayhem gripped the Morgan household minutes before their departure. "Miriam flew around everywhere; mother always had one more article to find, and the noise was dreadful," she wrote later. "Besides the inevitable running bag tied to my waist (which invariably throws me in a violent perspiration), . . . I had my sunbonnet, veil, comb, tooth brush, cabas filled with dozens of small articles, and dagger to carry; and then my heart failed me when I thought of my guitar; so I caught it up in the case, and remembering father's heavy inkstand, I seized that too, with two fans."[13]

Armed with as many items as she could possibly carry, Sarah staggered along the road with dozens of other terrified women and children. In her diary, she later described the exodus from Baton Rouge as "a heart-rending scene." She recorded seeing "women searching for their babies along the road, where they had been lost, others sitting in the dust crying and wringing their hands, for by this time, we had not an idea but what Baton Rouge was either in ashes, or being plundered, and we had saved nothing." In her account, Eliza McHatton Ripley captured the state of confusion that ensued after the attack. "These are not sheep but human beings, running pell-mell," she wrote, "panting, rushing tumultuously down the hot dusty road, hatless, bonnetless, some with slippers and no stockings, some with wrappers hastily thrown over nightgowns."[14]

Baton Rouge fell on May 12, 1862, and Federal forces continued their advance up the Mississippi River. Alone and unprotected, elite women braced themselves for a visit from the Yankees. With her brothers away defending the honor of the cause, Kate Stone and her mother were left to protect Brokenburn plantation. They were among the few who chose to stay. "There has been no attempt at resistance," Kate stated in July 1862. "Some of the plantations have been deserted by the owners, some of them burned by the Yankee bands, and some of them not molested. It depends on the temper of the officer in charge. If he feels malicious, he burns the premises. If a good-natured enemy, he takes what he wants and leaves the buildings standing." "Most of them are malicious," she added fearfully.[15] For Kate, the constant anticipation of attack culminated in feelings of despair and a loss of hope. "For the last two days we have been in a quiver of anxiety looking for the Yankees every minute," she wrote, "sitting on the front gallery with our eyes strained in the direction they will come, going to bed late and getting up early so they will not find us asleep." Kate described this wartime existence as a "miserable, frightened one—living in constant dread of great danger, not knowing what form it may take, and utterly helpless to protect ourselves." "It is a painful present and a dark future," she added. An unexpected bout of inclement weather provided Kate and Amanda with their only respite from anxious, suspense-filled days. "Today as it is raining, they [Yankees] are apt to remain in camp," Kate wrote happily, "and so we have had a little relief."[16]

Unreliable reports and a lack of regular news inevitably heightened feelings of anxiety and desperation among women. Without newspapers, or supplied only with censored coverage of the war, many young ladies experienced "near panic." In early 1861, Kate Stone read "*Harper's Weekly* and *Monthly*, the *New York Tribune*, *Journal of Commerce*, *Littell's Living Age*, the *Whig* and *Picayune* of New Orleans." By 1862, Kate commented that the "papers had dropped off one by one," and she rarely received mail from her brothers and uncle. "We long for news from the outside world, and yet we shudder to think what evil tidings it may bring us," she admitted. "Could we hear that all our soldiers are well, the troubles here at home would seem but light ones."[17]

In Monroe, Sarah Lois Wadley heard "nothing but vague rumors," while in occupied New Orleans, Clara Solomon was exasperated by the "extravagant and absurd" stories that circulated the city. "By these reports a person is plunged into a continual state of excitement and for nothing," she wrote angrily. "Some one will tell you that a certain place has been seized. You will relate it to another party only to receive from them a decided contradiction." The newspapers, now controlled by the occupying forces, were of little help. Clara later reported that her beloved *Delta* had become nothing more than a "Yankee paper": Its front page carried the slogan "The Union—it *must* and *shall* be preserved." "It was curiosity which prompted me to read it," she admitted, "but no honorable person should contaminate themselves by a contact with it."[18]

Sarah Morgan encountered similar difficulties in Baton Rouge. "If we could keep all the dispatches that have passed between us . . . what a collection of absurdity and contradiction it would be! 'Forts have been taken.' 'Their ships have passed; forts safe; Yankees at our mercy' . . . and so on, sometimes three times a day, each dispatch contradicting the other, and all equally ridiculous." News was no easier to come by in the countryside, where mail deliveries were rare and households were increasingly forced to rely on information from passing soldiers. At Wayside plantation in the Mississippi Delta, Amanda Worthington grew increasingly anxious as her hopes were raised by one report—only to be dashed by another. "We hear so many contradictory reports we don't know what to believe," she wrote in frustration. Elizabeth Christie Brown simply dismissed the most positive reports, describing them as "improbable" tales that were "too good to be true."[19]

Anxious, alone, and afraid, young ladies worried about the precarious state of the war effort and the safety of soldier kin. Doubtful of ultimate victory, women like Sarah Lois Wadley grew increasingly concerned about the preservation of family honor. While they had drawn upon this powerful concept as a way to build a connection to the cause, defeat and Federal occupation rendered the link between family, honor, and patriotism quite tenuous. If family honor was connected to the war effort, what did military defeat by an "inferior" adversary say about Southern men or the Confederate cause? To preserve the ideals that Southerners went to war to defend, young ladies were forced to redefine their understanding of the Confederacy. Wartime reality collided with patriotic ideals. Pervasive military defeat in 1862-1863 debilitated civilian morale in the war effort. It also compelled young women to separate (as far as possible) the concepts of family honor and nationalism from the war and defeat. By separating these two seemingly intrinsic notions, young ladies were able to sustain their belief in the cause while allowing their morale in the war effort to falter. Indeed, their feelings about Confederate nationalism (or the cause) remained strong, even when the reality of military defeat made them doubtful of ultimate victory.

Separating family honor and the lofty ideals of the cause from the war effort was a difficult thing to do, especially for young ladies who had brothers and fathers in the army. Amanda Worthington's brothers, Bert and William, fought in many minor battles that were later described as Confederate defeats. So did the brothers of Kate Stone and Sarah Morgan. Yet all these young ladies chose to separate their kin from the military defeat by focusing on individual acts of bravery and connecting these to the exhibition of family honor, rather than on the outcome of the military campaign.

In doing so, their response was also in keeping with antebellum conceptions of Southern honor that utilized the duel as a public expression of familial worth. While this dangerous exchange often resulted in death, Sarah Morgan's diary indicates that men who died in duels were not regarded as "failures" in the antebellum South. Sarah's brother Henry had died in a duel in 1861. In the pages of her journal, Sarah praised her brother as a hero who had defended family honor. "Courage is what women admire above all things and that he possessed in the most eminent degree," she wrote. "It was stamped in every line of his face, and all might see that he was a man who did not know fear. . . . No! there never was a braver man than Harry." "New Orleans rung with the story of his death," she added. "Men talked of his coolness, and applauded his bravery, while his broken hearted mother and sisters wept over him at home." Henry lost a duel to another man, but Sarah did not question his masculinity or honor. He had affirmed his self-worth and his courage, regardless of the outcome. Like duelists, Confederate soldiers were acting on the traditions of Southern manhood and, by doing so, brought honor to both themselves and their families. "In defeat or victory, were they not still fighting for us?" Sarah wrote. "Had they not done their best? . . . Were we the less grateful when they met with reverse?"[20]

Just as Sarah Morgan had separated her brother's courage from the ultimate outcome of the duel, Confederate belles separated individual acts of bravery from the outcome of the military campaign. Amanda Worthington brimmed with pride when passing soldiers described her brother as an "invaluable guide." "They seemed to think there never was such a woodsman as Bert," she wrote, "—he had guided them through the woods and helped burn the cotton when the first yanks were here." In 1865, Amanda was again buoyed by news of William's valor in battle. "Sergt. Wolf . . . spoke in very high terms of Willie, said he was ever where the balls fell thick." "Every one, though, speaks of how gallant and brave Willie is," she added, "and it pleases me so much." Kate Stone's hours of watching and waiting were made bearable by news of her brother's gallantry in battle. In Holly Springs, Cordelia Lewis Scales was proud to relate news of her brothers' soldiering exploits to her friend Lulie Irby. "I know that three braver and nobler boys never lived," she declared. Like other young ladies, Amanda, Kate, and Cordelia reflected on the individual acts of bravery performed by male kin and connected these to family honor and individual character, not to the final outcome of the military campaign. This mode of valuing enabled women to theoretically separate their kin from the failure of the war effort in a way that was consistent with the antebellum code of honor.[21]

Similarly, the most trying of circumstances did not culminate in a lack of faith in Confederate ideology. As the Yankees advanced and life became harder to bear, young ladies clung to their belief in the cause. It would take much more than lowered standards of living to subdue Sarah Morgan's patriotic fervor. One afternoon, while remembering the culinary delicacies of old, she cried, "If it was put to the vote, 'Corn bread in the Confederacy, or wheat in the Union,' I think I'd cry 'Sawdust and Independence for ever!'" Clara Solomon agreed. "We are willing to make sacrifices," she stated. "With corn meal we can never starve." Sarah Lois Wadley also reaffirmed her commitment to the cause. "I should be willing to endure poverty, willing to labor for my bread all the rest of my life if I could see my country in peace," she commented, "[and] see the South take her place among nations and be able to say with grateful pride, I am a southerner."[22]

"This Is War with All Its Horrors"

The young women of Mississippi and Louisiana may have used their diaries to separate individual bravery from the war effort, but they could not separate their soldiers from the realities of military service. Campaign after bloody campaign produced immense casualties, and few Southern families were left untouched by the dreaded lists of "killed and wounded." For women whose lives were so inextricably tied to the family unit, the long absence of male kin and the possibility of death shook the foundations upon which they had built their identities and their lives. Yet by separating their understanding of the cause from the war, young ladies were able to express their anguish over the untimely death of Confederate soldiers without compromising their loyalty to the cause.[23]

In this way, their expression of pain and distress became a reaction against the war but not a rejection of the cause. While Sarah Lois Wadley declared that she would endure almost anything for Southern independence, she could scarcely comprehend the bloody sacrifice that would have to be made to achieve this end. "My heart sickens when I think that under this beautiful blue sky . . . thousands of men are mingling in mortal combat, and groans and shrieks sounding amid the roar of artillery and the trampling of cavalry," she wrote. "The picture is too dreadful; how many Mothers and sisters and wives and children sit in despair or suspense this day." After a battle near Keatchie, Louisiana, Sidney Harding accompanied her mother to the local hospital. The sights, sounds, and smells of the dead and wounded gave her a new and terrifying understanding of war. "Oh the sickening sights," Sidney recorded with horror, "some shot in face, both eyes out, head bent arms, legs, everywhere."[24]

By 1862, many young ladies mourned the loss of relatives and friends. Ellen Louise Power recorded the death of John Griffith: "Another one of our young men *gone*." Sarah Lois Wadley also heard of deaths "either from disease or the sword nearly every day." Two months later, Sarah recorded the tragic story of a young woman who had traveled with her baby to be with her wounded husband, only to find him buried on her arrival. "Oh! how many, many such widows this war will make," she wrote tearfully as she listened to the woman sobbing in the adjoining room, "nay, has already made; scarcely a family but has lost one member." In Natchez, Kate Foster commented that the "church is gradually filling up with black dresses and mourning veils." "Almost every time we hear from the army one or two more we have to add to our list of those who have at last found peace and quiet in a Saviour's bosom," she added. "Our Troop has been spared 'till lately and one after another dies gloriously for his country. Dunbar Shields, Tommie Medcalf, Major Conner, Mr. Bob Dunbar and some of our noble men in other companies have fallen to save our loved South. Dunbar died like a hero, so glad, he said, to give up his life for his cause."[25]

Kate soon received news that her brother had been wounded. "The surgeons said at first it was mortal," she wrote. "When he was told this he said 'Oh! my sisters.' He had lived twenty-three days when we last heard from him and my constant prayer is that he may be spared to us in future years as a monument of God's exceeding mercy for which we have had to thank Him *so* often before. Brother is my pride, ambition and love. Pa has gone on and by his not returning Brother is alive." Kate's hopes were soon dashed. Writing two months after his death, she added her own loved one to the list of "noble men" who had sacrificed their lives for the cause. "Just as the sun was setting one Friday afternoon the last in Sept. passed our precious Brother's soul into heaven," she wrote tearfully. "He was willing to go if God willed it so but did not want to die as he was too young to wish to leave this world whilst it seemed to him so fraught with hopes unrealized. It seems as though when he my pride left us my heart became flint."[26]

Kate Stone endured seven weeks of heartache and uncertainty before she received confirmation that her brother Walter had died of pneumonia at Cotton Gin, Mississippi. "We cannot realize that he is gone forevermore," she wrote in disbelief. "Even as I write, I feel his tears on my cheek and see him as I saw him last when I bade him good-bye in Vicksburg, reining his horse on the summit of the hill and turning with flushed cheeks and tearful eyes to wave me a last farewell." Yet even in the midst of her own grief, Kate acknowledged that her family was just one of many to experience "trouble and sorrow." "Nearly every household mourns some loved one lost," she commented. "A letter from Amelia Scott yesterday tells of the death of her brother Charley on the bloody field of Chickamauga. Allen Bridges, a bright little boy not more than sixteen, Robert Norris, and Mr. Claud Briscoe all fell in the same engagement. Of that band of boys who used to assemble at our house to hunt, play, and amuse themselves, only Joe Carson and Ben Clarkson remain."[27]

Like Kate, Amanda Worthington experienced this anguish firsthand when her brother Bert was killed by a band of Union soldiers only hours after his return home on a furlough. Almost a year after his death, she summoned the courage to write of "the bitter waters of sorrow" she had drunk since receiving the terrible news. "God only knows the agony I have suffered and the many many times I have prayed for death since I saw my darling lie dead before me," she cried. "Oh! how willingly would I have given my life for his! It is my first sorrow and as it rushes over me I feel as if I cannot bear it, I dont see how I have lived these long ten months since he ceased to breathe."[28]

The death of relatives and friends made young ladies increasingly anxious for the safety of those kin still in military service. Cordelia Lewis Scales prayed nightly that "holy angels, those 'white winged messengers' of love and mercy might ever hover o'er and protect" her brothers from "all harm and danger." "I could stand almost anything except the death of one of my dear brave brothers," she concluded. "Oh! my God, that would kill me." Lemuella Brickell also worried about her brother, James. "What should I do if mine were taken?" she wrote. "God, father in Heaven, spare me that bitter, *bitter* sorrow—let us keep him, he is my *all*."[29]

In Epnon, Mississippi, Mattie Burkett wrote letters to her brother expressing her concern for his safety, while in New Orleans, Clara Solomon recorded the scenes she witnessed as women waited anxiously for news of another battle. "My heart ached as I looked around and saw the many occupied seats," she wrote. "Many awaiting either to hear the confirmation of the fears respecting dear relatives and friends, while to others the suspense was ended, the sad tidings had been communicated." "Every face bore as sorrowful an expression and then did I realize this slaughter of human lives," Clara added, "—this, this is war; war, with all its horrors." In their diaries, young women took comfort in the fact that their kin upheld family honor through valorous acts of courage. Yet they could not separate their soldiers from the possibility of death in battle. By reworking their understanding of the war and the cause, young women were, however, able to express their grief and hatred of war without undermining their loyalty to the cause.[30]

Separating Confederate ideals from the wartime reality also made it easier for young ladies to express their despondency over military defeats, which had increased considerably since the fall of New Orleans and the Federal advance up the Mississippi River. "I get nervous and unhappy in thinking of the sad condition of the country and of the misery all prophesy [h]as in store for us," Sarah Morgan conceded in June 1862. Months later she tried to convince herself that all was right in the Confederacy. "Better days are coming," she wrote. "—I am getting skeptical, I fear me." In New Orleans, schoolgirl Martha Josephine Moore admitted that she had "but a weak foundation on which to build" her ideas that the Confederacy would prevail. Clara Solomon agreed. "My feelings accord with the state of my beloved country," she remarked. "A cloud dark as that which hovers over her is above me. In these terrible times who can feel otherwise?"[31]

Many young ladies began to long for peace. "Oh! how I do long for peace to be declared!" sighed Amanda Worthington as she watched anxiously for the appearance of Yankee raiders. "I never thought in times of peace what an awful thing war was, but now I have . . . brothers and . . . cousins in the army I can realize it." "If the war was only over," wrote Elizabeth Christie Brown, "and peace once more reigned through our land, we could not be too thankful." "O for Peace!" cried Sarah Morgan. "Think of meeting your brothers and friends again—such as are spared! Think of the blessing of lying down in quiet at night, and waking in safety in the morning, with no thought of bomb shells breaking the silence of the night, or of thieving lawless soldiers searching for plunder. Think of settling quietly into the life Heaven has appointed for you, whether in comfort or poverty, content because He sends it, and because either will be rest, and quiet at last! O Peace! how it will be appreciated by those who have suffered in this struggle!" In the following months, Sarah often mentioned her desire for peace. "O War how I wish you were over!" she wrote in September 1862. "How thankful I will be when all this fuss and trouble is done away with, and the boys come home!" Six months later, Sarah voiced her commitment to "sawdust and independence forever," indicating that she too had separated her understanding of the war from her loyalty to the cause.[32]

HOPING AGAINST HOPE

Those young ladies who still prayed for Confederate victory looked to Vicksburg as the last bastion of hope. Nestled on the banks of the Mississippi, this bustling river town held enormous strategic and psychological value to both sides. "Vicksburg," said Jefferson Davis, "is the nail that holds the South's two halves together."[33]

During 1862, Confederate forces had successfully defended Vicksburg against attack, and citizens throughout the Deep South looked to this Mississippi town as an example of Southern patriotism triumphing over Northern military might. By May 1863, however, Confederate forces had lost their stronghold, plunging Vicksburg into a forty-eight-day siege. As Union artillery shelled the city, women and children sought refuge in caves dug out of the hillside. As supplies of fruit and vegetables dwindled, soldiers and citizens were forced to subsist on a diet of rice and mule meat. Death from shelling or disease became an everyday occurrence, and by July, the Confederate army could hold out no longer. On Independence Day 1863, Vicksburg surrendered to jubilant Northern troops.[34]

For the young ladies of Mississippi and Louisiana, this defeat extinguished what little hope they had in military success. Down the river at Natchez, Elizabeth Christie Brown refused to believe all the initial reports of the surrender. "We were almost crazed at the news of the capitulation of Vicksburg (which came today)," she wrote on July 7. "We could scarcely credit it, yet felt it was possible." Convinced that unreliable and contradictory reports were a positive sign that the city had not yet surrendered, Elizabeth and her mother "came to the conclusion that it was all a Yankee fourth of July story, and talked it over so much that we nearly believed it was." When the "terrible news" was finally confirmed—together with the "correct news of the surrender of dear, brave, little Port Hudson"—Elizabeth was overcome with feelings of sadness and foreboding. "We now felt at the mercy of our merciless foe," she conceded. "What a neglected, deserted feeling came over me, I do not know if any one else felt as I did, but really I felt as if our own Country had cast us off."[35]

Fellow Mississippian Amanda Worthington was also heartbroken. "Vicksburg fell! Oh! that I should have to write it! I was perfectly stunned when I heard it and utterly refused to believe it for several days—but at last I was compelled to yield to the stern reality of it," she cried, lamenting the "humiliating" defeat and shuddering at the thought of all those victorious Yankees. "I felt so humiliated to think that Vicksburg my pride and boast had fallen and to think how the hated yankees would exalt over it." Kate Stone agreed. "How has the mighty fallen," she wrote from her refugee outpost in Lamar County, Texas, "and to give up on the Fourth of July to make it even worse. We wish they could have held on at least one day longer, but we know nothing of the hardships our soldiers have endured there in the last eight months." "The loss of Vicksburg has stunned the whole country," she added. "It is a grievous blow, and there is great discouragement at least on this side of the Mississippi River. But the reaction will come. The people will rally to strike a more deadly blow, to fight till the last armed foe expires, to conquer or die."[36]

Far closer to the scene of battle, Natchez belle Annie Harper was unconvinced of the South's ultimate success and the resolve of its war-ravaged people. She noted that "with the fall of Vicksburg the first notes of the Confederacy's death knell rung with clanging harshness on our ears." While Kate Foster remained optimistic that the loss of Vicksburg was a sign from God "to show us our cause does not rest upon the mere fall or holding of any one city," Lise Mitchell believed that the siege had been nothing more than a futile endeavor. "What anguish to think that all those months of brave defense, or superhuman endurance, had been brought to nothing," she concluded. Sarah Morgan made a half-hearted attempt to convince herself that although the "skies *are* dark, . . . there is a bright side somewhere." Initially, she refused to believe the news. When her brother confirmed the report, Sarah spent the day in tears. "How the mighty are fallen!" she sobbed. "I cry hourly. . . . Up to Vicksburg our prospects were glorious; now they are the reverse." Sarah Lois Wadley was devastated. "Vicksburg has fallen, Vicksburg, our hope and pride," she wrote in despair. "Oh god, have mercy upon us, all is dark, all hearts are sad, this is the worst blow we have had." "I cannot look ahead," Sarah conceded. "I shudder to think of the future. Should the Confederacy fall I feel I can never know joy again."[37]

While the Confederate belles of Mississippi and Louisiana lamented the crushing defeat of Vicksburg and Port Hudson, they nevertheless revered the gallantry of the honorable Southern men who had held on to the last. In occupied New Orleans, Emma Walton exalted the efforts of the soldiers who had valiantly fought—and lost—the siege. "I cannot describe to you my feelings upon learning the particulars," she wrote her father, who was defending the cause in faraway Virginia. "The grief for our misfortune, gave way to the pride which swelled our breasts at the noble endurance of our brave boys who during this siege, have so heroically and cheerfully borne all the hardships." Sarah Morgan agreed. "O dear, noble men! " she cried. "I am afraid to meet them; I should do something foolish; best take my cry out in private now. . . . Port Hudson does not matter so much; but those brave, noble creatures! The *Era* says they had devoured their last mule before they surrendered."[38]

When the Confederate troops captured at Port Hudson were transferred to the New Orleans Customs House, Sarah and her sister, Miriam, boasted of their friendships and associations with a number of the prisoners. Clearly, the men's inability to hold "dear little Port Hudson" had done little to diminish their bravery or heroism in the eyes of multitudes of young patriotic women. "Miriam and I are looked on with envy by other young ladies because some twenty or thirty of our acquaintance have already arrived," Sarah wrote with delight. "To know a Port Hudson defender is considered as the greatest distinction one need desire." While Sarah and other young ladies were prohibited from visiting their heroes, they expressed their appreciation by sending baskets of food and "a number of cravats and some handkerchiefs" to the jail.[39]

Such expressions of gratitude toward the soldiers did not cloud young women's realism about the war effort. While women in other Southern states still hoped and prayed for victory, the young ladies of Mississippi and Louisiana accepted ultimate defeat. "I cannot now look forward," cried Sarah Lois Wadley, "a mist shuts in my mind which has hung over the hills for several days, only the past is ever present with me." Months later, she commented on the failure of the people to embrace the war effort. "We have so many disloyal persons amongst us now," she conceded. "The public sentiment in Louisiana is very much demoralized. . . . The universal sentiment is that this side of the river at least, is lost to us, and there is even now and then a low murmur that we will soon be altogether subjugated."[40]

With broken hearts, women in Mississippi and Louisiana sought only to care for their loved ones, to knit for their soldiers, and to bear with resignation to God the trials and hardships that had befallen them. For most, regional Confederate defeat signaled the beginnings of a new struggle as "hateful Yankees" occupied their homes and communities. Yet by separating Southern honor from the humiliation of defeat, young ladies were able to preserve their understanding of family and honor. They would meet their captors, not as defeated women, but as dignified and patriotic young ladies who would do anything to preserve Confederate ideology and family honor.[41]

CHAPTER SIX

"The Yankees Are Coming"

We will miss himself [father] and his protection, for I think it quite unsafe to leave a parcel of females in a house without, in these times, a male. We know no one whom we can get to remain with us, and if we did, we have no accommodations.

Clara Solomon, June 24, 1861

If Confederate defeat had tested young women's faith in the war effort, the arrival of Yankee soldiers threatened to obliterate what little hope they had left. Ladies who had been raised to depend on male protection were now confronted with a daunting and unfamiliar social landscape that left Confederate soldiers out of the equation. In New Orleans, Clara Solomon's devastation over the fall of her beloved city was heightened by her family's precarious situation as a group of seven women living alone in an occupied territory. With her father, Solomon Solomon, working as a sutler in Virginia, Clara, her mother, and her five sisters "did not know what to do," and waited anxiously for a telegraph from "Pa" as terrified friends and neighbors fled the city.

"Mrs. Miller, I deeply regret to say, has left the city and gone up to her relatives in Mississippi and in a short time I presume that she will join her husband. May we meet again. The Smiths have also evacuated this place, and I suppose upon inquiries for many of our friends, we shall find that they have acted likewise." Clara, however, preferred the "loathsome" sight of victorious Yankees to an uncertain existence as a refugee, and vowed to meet her fate in fair Louisiana. "I would not like to desert my native city in this, her hour of trial," she declared, "but feel it the duty of every native to stand or fall with the fortunes of their own Louisiana." Still, Clara remained uncertain as to how this goal might be achieved without her father's protection. Two weeks after the surrender, she and her mother were still waiting for definite news from Solomon. "I ask myself the question 'what are we going to do?'" she cried in despair. "Is not Pa coming home, or he is going to send for us[?] Can we live in this isolated condition, cut of from all communication with him[?]" Unaccustomed to protecting herself or making decisions without Solomon's counsel and consent, Clara and her mother were now compelled to look for new ways to safeguard their family's reputation and honor.[1]

Confederate defeat and Federal occupation had dismantled the Southern code of reciprocity: an arrangement where men granted women protection and respectability in return for their deference and submission. While elite white men defended family and nation on the battlefield, they struggled to fulfill their obligations at home. Unable to protect their kin or the sanctity of their households from Union soldiers, Southern men temporarily charged their women with the task of upholding family honor. Young Confederate women, who had already negotiated their role in the household to accommodate the absence of men, were now compelled to abandon their gendered socialization in honor and reciprocity. Alone and afraid, they assumed responsibility for defending their households, their reputations, their bodies, their sense of family honor, and the patriotic ideals of the cause against the powerful Northern army. At the same time, young Southern ladies were also expected to maintain an unwavering belief in the men who had failed to protect them.

THE YANKEES ARRIVE

By mid-1863, Mississippi and Louisiana had succumbed to the enemy. Northern troops occupied the major river towns from Vicksburg to New Orleans, and massive areas on either side of the river were subjected to regular visits from raiding soldiers as the army attempted to break the supply link between the Confederate household and the battlefront. After the surrender of Vicksburg, Ida Barlow Trotter recalled that "the entire section from Jackson toward Vicksburg was one vast field of smoking ruins, standing chimneys and devastated fields."[2]

The Federal presence in Mississippi and Louisiana generated a different set of wartime challenges for every woman, regardless of her age. The location of a household, its proximity to other communities or battlefronts, the age and mobility of family members, the climate, the surrounding terrain, and a commander's style of occupation all influenced women's contact and interaction with the enemy. In occupied cities such as New Orleans, Baton Rouge, or Natchez, civilians like Clara Solomon, Elizabeth Christie Brown, and Kate Foster encountered Union troops on a daily basis. While the pervasive Federal presence minimized the pillaging or destruction of homes, churches, schools, and commercial buildings, clothing and provisions were often scarce and patriotic behavior was strictly policed. Women living in households located just outside occupied areas were frequently subjected to regular visitations from parties of Northern soldiers looking for additional food or provisions. Uncertain of when the next group of raiding soldiers would arrive, these citizens eked out an uncertain existence and faced the daily prospect of losing all their livestock, meat, vegetables, and other provisions. Other women, such as Eliza Lucy Irion, knew little of this desperate wartime experience and lived comfortably in the pockets of countryside seldom visited by soldiers or subjected to the ravages of war.[3]

Despite these variations, the Federal presence in the Deep South was successful in systematically unraveling the code of reciprocity. In wartime, soldiering conflicted with a Confederate man's familial responsibilities. Separated from their loved ones by distance and for long periods of time, soldiers found themselves caught between their duty to defend the Confederacy and their obligation to protect their families. In June 1862, Kate Stone's brother Walter acknowledged the tension between familial and patriotic duty. After hearing reports about Yankee soldiers in Louisiana, he wrote home in distress. "He says that it will kill him to remain idle in Virginia when we are in such danger and that he must come back to see about us and fight with the Mississippi Army," Kate wrote. "He seems so desperate. We fear he will do something rash and get into trouble."[4]

Even if he had been present, Walter Stone and other Confederate men could have done little to protect their female kin. Instead, those who remained at home relied on their women to defend the hearth while they ran from the clutches of the enemy. In 1862, Clara Solomon was well aware that the men of New Orleans would be of little assistance in an impending attack. "Every man would be sent away in preference to being taken prisoners," she noted. "And the women—they will have to protect themselves." Southern men who were caught by the Union army often faced imprisonment or death. At Wayside plantation in the lush Mississippi Delta, Amanda Worthington grew accustomed to the "commotion" associated with a visit from the Yankees.

One autumn day in late 1863, Amanda was skimming milk for supper when "a cry of 'yankees' [was] raised." "I hurried out and saw they were yanks," she related. "By that time the whole house was in commotion—Ben, Mr. Bill Peak, Mr. Hutchinson, Mr. Cobb and Mr. Kelly had all saddled up and when I went out on Mother's balcony I could see them galloping furiously in one direction and the yanks riding up in another about two or three hundred yards apart from them." As Amanda watched her chivalrous Confederate soldiers make their escape, she was more concerned for their welfare than her own. "Oh! I was so scared, for I expected to hear shots exchanged, but happily the yanks didn't give chase."[5]

Amanda's brother Bert was not so lucky. When he returned home for a brief furlough, the joyful family reunion was short lived. Minutes after his arrival, a group of Federal soldiers from the 4th Illinois Cavalry rode up to Wayside in search of food and provisions. As Bert fled to the safety of the back pasture, his excited hounds followed him in quick pursuit. One of the soldiers noticed the dogs and, after a spirited chase, caught Bert Worthington and shot him dead. Fearful of subjecting her sister-in-law's father to a similar fate, Sarah Morgan finally convinced General Albert Carter to abandon his post in the face of Union troops at nearby Port Hudson. "The General left this morning, to our unspeakable relief," she commented. "They would hang him, we fear, if they should find him here." Sarah and the Carter women preferred to be "left alone here to meet them [Yankees]" without the added burden of General Carter's life in the balance.[6]

In wartime Mississippi and Louisiana, the antebellum code of protection had been reversed, leaving all women unsure of how to defend family honor or safeguard their reputations without the men whose presence had previously been essential. As young ladies nervously anticipated the arrival of the "blue devils," horrifying rumors of Yankee depredations only served to heighten their feelings of vulnerability. At Brokenburn, Kate Stone felt anxious and overwhelmed without male protection. "It was a time to be scared last night, and I, for one, did feel frightened with Mr. McRae, Brother Walter, and Jimmy all away and Johnny the only man (he is twelve) about the place," she wrote. "We have heard such horrible stories of the outrages of the Yankees and Negroes that it is an anxious time for only women and children." As the months wore on, Kate and her mother often found themselves in the same unsettling predicament. "We are in a helpless situation," she admitted, "three ladies and two little girls and not a white man or even a gun on the place, not even a boy until Johnny gets back. And the scouts may take him. We can find rest only in the thought that we are in God's hands." In Keatchie, Louisiana, Sidney Harding lamented the absence of a soldier to protect them on their travels, while Sarah Morgan regarded her brothers as the only viable form of defense against the Yankees. "Oh my brothers, George, Gibbes and Jimmy, never did we more need protection!" she cried, "where are you?" Later, Sarah concluded that her family was utterly "helpless" without them.[7]

Confederate belles like Sarah, however, had less to fear from the enemy than did their slaves. In the first flush of Federal invasion, most Union soldiers limited their military conquest to the rape and assault of black women, thereby preserving the white feminine ideal that dominated the collective consciousness in the North and the South. While they may have stopped short of physical violence, soldiers found other ways to dishonor patriotic Confederate ladies. By invading their private chambers, taking their underwear, or using obscene language, the Federal army degraded Southern men by symbolically violating their women.[8]

The young ladies of Mississippi and Louisiana recorded many acts of "symbolic rape." "The Yankees committed great depredations about Bastrop," reported Sarah Lois Wadley, "they were very insulting to several ladies, but committed no actual violence upon them." In Holly Springs, Cordelia Lewis Scales was shocked by the behavior of the Union soldiers who camped in Oakland's front yard. "I never heard such profanity in all my life," she declared, "and so impudent, they would walk around the house and look up at the windows and say, 'wonder how many Secesh gals they got up there.'" When Sarah Morgan returned to her home after the Federal attack on Baton Rouge, she "actually sat down to laugh" at the sight of a contorted bonnet that had been "remodeled" by a Northern soldier. "One was mother's velvet, which looked very much like a foot ball in its present condition," she remarked. "Mine was not to be found, as the officers forgot to return it. Wonder who has my imperial? I know they never saw a handsomer one, with its black velvet, purple silk, and ostrich feathers."[9]

Later, Sarah was horrified to hear about the antics of the Yankees who had mocked and vandalized her family's most elegant attire. "In the pillaging of the armoirs, they seized a pink flounced muslin of Miriam's, which one officer placed on the end of a bayonet, and paraded around with, followed by the others who slashed it with their swords crying 'I have stuck the damned Secesh! that's the time I cut her!' and continued their sport until the rags could no longer be pierced. One [soldier] seized my bonnet, with which he decked himself, and ran in the streets. Indeed, all who found such, rushed frantically around town by way of frolicking, with the things on their heads. They say no frenzy could surpass it. . . . Our clothes were used for the vilest purposes, and spread in every corner—at least those few that were not stolen." The Morgan women were not the only young ladies to suffer this injurious fate. Sarah also noted the experience of her neighbor, Miss Jones, who helplessly watched as the Yankees rummaged through "her clothes bag and took out articles which were certainly of no service to them, for mere deviltry."[10]

Confederate soldiers had promised protection for women like Sarah Morgan. In Mississippi and Louisiana they had failed dismally. Victorious Northern troops shattered the idea of the invincible Confederate soldier and left Southern wives and mothers feeling "abandoned and betrayed" by their men. In many cases, the Confederate soldier's inability to fulfill his reciprocal obligations in wartime not only "eroded" these women's confidence in their men but culminated in their placing self interest before self sacrifice. Instead of suffering in silence, women "deserted the ranks."[11]

While these findings may indeed be reflective of the general civilian population, a woman's age influenced her reaction toward, and understanding of, Federal occupation. Young ladies may have longed for male protection, but unlike older generations of Southern women, they felt neither abandoned nor betrayed by their men. Using honor as a compass to guide them through the challenges of war, young ladies had separated the soldier's bravery from the outcome of the military campaign. By doing so, they were able to revere the honorable actions of Confederate men, irrespective of military success or defeat—and even in the face of Union occupation. Living in Federally controlled areas of Mississippi and Louisiana, Elizabeth Christie Brown, Emma Walton, and Sarah Lois Wadley continued to write with pride about the "brave" and "gallant" soldiers of the Confederacy. "I love all Confederate soldiers and am friendly and polite to all," proclaimed Amanda Worthington. "Noble boys!" added Emma Walton. "We could kiss the very ground you walk upon." Kate Stone—who had been forced to flee her home in the face of advancing Federal troops—also wrote with pride about the brave soldiers defending their glorious nation. "Our gallant Southern soldiers," she boasted, "—who can praise them enough? as much as they deserve?"[12] Clinging to this ideal through Southern military success—and defeat—young ladies looked to the image of the "barbarous Yankee soldier" to justify the further negotiation of their roles as young Confederate women.

"Villainous Yankees"

As Yankee forces edged closer to their homes and communities, young ladies focused their anger on the barbarity of the invading enemy—not on the failure of Confederate men to protect their women. Lionizing the brave and honorable Rebel soldier, they embraced a binary image of Union soldiers as men without honor. In New Orleans, Emma Walton described the occupying troops as "blue devils." Sarah Lois Wadley referred to them as "impudent invaders," while Lise Mitchell described them as "tyrants." Clara Solomon and the Shannon sisters of Vicksburg regarded the Northern army as "vandals."[13]

Sarah Morgan felt bitter contempt for the soldiers who had attacked the "defenseless women and children" of Baton Rouge. After the shelling had stopped, Sarah was quick to mock the Union victory. "Does it take thirty thousand men, and millions of dollars to murder defenseless women and children?" she wrote angrily. "O the great nation! Bravo!" Sarah was further enraged when she received news that one woman had been killed in the attack, and described the "valiant" and "industrious" Flag Officer David Farragut as "the Woman Killer." Chiding the Union army for "wreak[ing] . . . vengeance" on women and children, Sarah emasculated Northern men for making war on Southern women.[14]

As slaves fled to Union lines, the image of the disreputable Yankee became an alternative way for belles to mark out their status in a world where Northern soldiers had assisted in obliterating other symbols of Southern gentility. In Natchez, Kate Foster questioned the honor and intelligence of her captors. "What consummate fools and knaves these Federals are," she exclaimed. Martha Josephine Moore was no more impressed by the soldiers who occupied New Orleans. "I should think from their appearances [they] had not been washed or combed in six weeks," she remarked in disgust. In Vicksburg, the Shannon sisters were repulsed by the "common looking men" they encountered, while Kate Stone was not surprised to hear that General Grant had been "very rude" to an elite lady when she "applied for protection." "What else could she have expected from a Yankee general?" she commented.[15]

As they met "blue devils" in the streets and, increasingly, in their homes, Confederate belles used the image of the "barbarous" Yankee soldier to justify their new role as "defenders of the hearth." Fulfilling the requirements of this role, however, proved far more difficult. In wartime Mississippi and Louisiana, young ladies confronted the prospect of negotiating a path between the belle ideal, patriotic womanhood, and wartime reality. Antebellum femininity had sought the protection of men. Patriotic womanhood had extended women's moral and domestic role to encompass the war effort. The realities of life on the Confederate home front extended this role even further, requiring young ladies to defend their homes and persons against the enemy. Many soon recognized the gulf between the women they were and the women they had to become. Young ladies such as Cordelia Lewis Scales were forced to act in assertive ways for which they were ill prepared. Without the presence of her brothers, Kate Stone was compelled to defend her family's honor, undertaking a task that was previously an obligation of her male kin. The transition from Confederate belle to martial defender challenged the boundaries of antebellum femininity, forcing young ladies to temporarily revoke their position within the family hierarchy in order to defend it. Abandoning deference and submission for courage and bravery, young women drew upon male codes of honor to work their way through this unrecognizable wartime world.

"We Are All Men"

For the first time in their lives, young women across Mississippi and Louisiana were charged with the task of protecting themselves. The war had stripped most households of all their men, and those who remained were often too old, too young, or too sick to serve. In this changed social landscape, practicality and wartime necessity demanded that young ladies learn to arm themselves against Northern troops, a task in direct contradiction to the genteel belle ideal and the patriarchal ethos. On an autumn afternoon in 1860, Sarah Lois Wadley and her friend Miss Julia took their "first lessons in shooting." She described the activity in her diary that evening. "Miss Julia, Mr McJunkin and I were up at the spring when Mr McJ. asked us if we would not like to shoot," she related. "Upon our answering in the affirmative . . . he loaded it, put up a mark, and gave it into my hands to shoot. After being instructed how to hold it, and to take sight, I pulled the trigger and when the flash was over he took it from my trembling hands, and almost unable to stand I sat down." Sarah regained her composure to shoot again. "Miss Julia and I both shot twice," she wrote proudly, "but neither of us hit the mark." Kate Stone also enjoyed an afternoon of rifle practice with her brothers in 1861. "Ashburn, Brother Walter, and I ate cantaloupes and practiced rifle shooting," she recorded in her diary.[16]

Some young ladies threatened to employ these skills in their encounters with the enemy. Cordelia Lewis Scales dressed like a "guerilla" and proudly displayed her rifle for all Federal soldiers to see. "I never ride now or walk without my pistol," she remarked to her friend, Lulie Irby. "Quite warlike, you see." On one occasion, she threatened a soldier from the 7th Kansas Jay Hawkers after being warned about her flagrant disrespect for the enemy. "One of them sent me word that they shot ladies as well as men, and if I did not stop talking to them so and displaying my Confederate flag he'd blow my damn brains out," she wrote. "I sent him word by the lady that I did not expect anything better from Yankees, but he must remember two could play at that game." Kate Stone also felt brave "in appearance with a five-shooter in my hand," but found out "afterwards it was only dangerous to look at as it was not loaded." Unlike Cordelia, she acknowledged that "guns are of no use to people in our dilemma. To use one would only be to invite complete destruction from the soldiers."[17]

With her brothers away defending the honor of the cause, Sarah Morgan resorted to carrying about a cabas filled with hairpins, starch, embroidery, and combs, with the whole menagerie "crowned by [her] dagger." In May 1862, she used her diary to record a warning to any Yankee who attempted to "Butlerize—or brutalize" her. "And if you [Yankees] want to know what an excited girl is capable of," she declared, "call around, and I will show you the use of a small seven shooter, and large carving knife which vibrate between my belt, and pocket, always ready for use." Days later, she was shocked by her transformation from a genteel young lady into a bloodthirsty Confederate. "I, who have such a horror of bloodshed, consider even killing in self defense murder, who cannot wish them the slightest evil, whose only prayer is to have them sent back in peace to their own country, *I* talk of killing them!" she cried. "For what else do I wear a pistol and carving knife?" Caught between notions of feminine propriety and the need to defend herself, Sarah Morgan struggled with her feelings of vengeance and her socialization as an elite young lady.[18]

Confused and a little daunted by her new wartime role, Sarah and other Confederate belles often fantasized about dispensing with their "useless" femininity. Glorifying her brothers' honor and highlighting the irrelevance of her upbringing in her current predicament, Sarah described women as "useless trash . . . of no value or importance to ourselves or the rest of the world." "What is the use of all these worthless women, in war times?" she questioned. "I dont know a woman here who does not groan over her misfortune in being clothed in petticoats." Cordelia Lewis Scales agreed. "It seems so hard that we who have the wills of men should be debased from engaging in this great struggle for liberty just because we are ladies." Sarah Lois Wadley and Kate Stone also felt frustrated that it was woman's lot to wait and pray. "My spirit often makes me chafe at the regulations which it is right a woman should submit to," Sarah admitted. "If I were a man—but I am not . . . and I will not encourage it by giving way to vain wishes and vaunting, 'if I were a man.'" [19]

Other young ladies exercised less restraint. "I feel almost like fighting myself," wrote Amanda Worthington. After news of another Confederate defeat, her desire to fight was tempered by frustration. "Oh! If I were only a man, how quickly would I go to the War and try to put some of those vile Yankees out of our way!" she exclaimed. Within the pages of her diary, Sarah Morgan fantasized about "donning breeches" and "slaying" Yankees. After the Federal attack on Baton Rouge, she even made an attempt to "try on" her brother's suit. "I advanced so far as to lay it on the bed, and then carried my bird out—I was ashamed to let even my canary see me," she wrote, "but when I took a second look, my courage deserted me, and there ended my first and last attempt at disguise." Sarah had already reflected on the changed state of wartime femininity. "Pshaw! There are *no* women here!" she scoffed. "We are *all* men!" [20]

By wishing to become men, young ladies 'tried on' masculinity at a time when they questioned the value of womanhood. Frustrated with their contribution to the war effort—which had been curtailed by the arrival of Northern troops—they looked to the battlefield and to their brave men as the most honorable way to serve the Confederacy. They glorified Southern manhood and described themselves as "useless," even when armed with pistols and knives. Still, by commenting that ladies "could set the men an example they would not blush to follow," they looked to themselves, not to their soldiers, for protection. By expressing their desire to fight, young ladies unknowingly challenged Southern masculinity at its very core by exposing the deteriorated state of reciprocity between men and women. [21]

"WOMAN'S TAUNTS": PATRIOTISM AND FEMININITY

The steady advance of enemy troops may have prompted young ladies to fantasize about becoming soldiers, but the actual arrival of the Yankees did not require such dramatic actions. Widespread occupation did, however, transform the ways in which young women were able to express their patriotism. A Confederate belle's newly acquired skills in knitting and sewing were of little use in occupied areas where civilians were barred from any contact with their troops. In regions still under Confederate control, many families were subjected to bouts of Federal raiding, during which supplies of food and clothing were confiscated or destroyed. Civilians soon came to the realization that their efforts to aid Southern soldiers were instead benefiting the powerful Northern enemy, whose military might allowed them to come and go at will.

Deprived of the means of expressing their patriotism and honor in conventional domestic terms, young ladies abandoned their antebellum socialization in deference to engage in small yet symbolic acts of political resistance. Meeting the invaders on their doorsteps and in the streets, young women sang "Dixie," taunted Federal soldiers, and waved Confederate flags. Behavior that would have been regarded as shocking, unladylike, and "political" in the antebellum South was now embraced by belles, who affirmed their patriotism for the cause through flagrant acts of defiance. Shifting the boundaries of public behavior, young women legitimized their actions by pointing to the barbarity and social inferiority of their captors.[22]

The young women of New Orleans led the charge against the Yankees, spurred on by the polices of General Benjamin Butler, whose ironfisted command of the occupied city quickly earned him a reputation as "The Beast." Scorned by Confederates for his unceasing efforts to quash any signs of "disloyalty," Butler's "dehumanization" prompted the young women of New Orleans to push the boundaries of feminine resistance to the limit. Union soldiers "are subjected to every silent insult by the ladies," remarked Clara Solomon with an air of delight. "A car on Camp St. containing a number of the last named articles was hailed by some Fed.[eral] officers and as they walked in the ladies walked out." Clara and her sisters seized upon every opportunity to taunt the "unwelcome" soldiers. After observing "a number of Yankees . . . parading up and down the street," Clara called a friend outside and exclaimed, "don't they look like they've got yellow fever." "Such looks as were cast at me!" she commented with satisfaction. Later, Clara was delighted when her young sister cried "Hurrah! For Depp Dabis and Beauregard," as a Federal soldier passed by her home.[23]

New Orleans schoolgirl Martha Josephine Moore participated in similar acts of resistance. When Federal soldiers entered her school with the purpose of confiscating any Confederate books or flags, Martha and a friend refused to submit to their demands. "They asked for any books that had flags in them," she wrote. "Now I did not have them in any books, but I did have one small one on a composition. Compositions and books being very different things in my opinion, I did not give it up." Martha's school friend was a little more outspoken. "Lizzie Davis sat on her desk hugging a book, as tho' it were her dearest friend, and, declaring she would not give it up, no, indeed, she wouldn't, for it had a flag in it, and she would not resign the emblem of her country." "In years I do not think my passions have been so roused as they were to-day," she added, "and if it were possible I *hate* the Northerners with a deeper, more lasting hatred, than ever before." Living in an occupied city, Martha hated passing houses "stolen by the Federals" on her way to school but resolved to continue walking her regular path, declaring, "I wouldn't want to go even a half square out of my way for any Yankee that ever lived." On another occasion she and the other ladies of her congregation chose to enter church via the back way, as being "preferable to walking under their [Union] banner," which hung victoriously over the front entrance.[24]

In occupied Baton Rouge, Sarah Morgan vowed to "devote all my red, white, and blue silk to the manufacture of Confederate flags." Still, she struggled with her antebellum socialization and her new role as a public defender of the cause. After pinning a Confederate flag to her dress and unexpectedly encountering a group of Federal officers on the street, Sarah "felt a painful conviction that I was unnecessarily attracting attention by an unladylike display of defiance." Notions of feminine propriety overcame her need to assert her patriotism. "How I wished myself away, and chafed at my folly, and hated myself for being there, and every one for seeing me!" she cried. "I hope it will be a lesson to me always to remember a lady can gain nothing by such displays." Clara Solomon enjoyed making comments about "yellow jack" to passing sentinels, but she too deplored unladylike displays of patriotism. When she returned to school after the fall of New Orleans, fellow students "excited [her] displeasure by wearing upon their shoulders black crepe bows." "How silly!" she commented. "All know that our hearts are in mourning, but why make any outward demonstration."[25]

As Sarah Morgan and Clara Solomon both knew, "outward demonstrations" of patriotism were not taken lightly by Federal authorities.
Hurrahing for Jefferson Davis or showing disrespect toward a Union
soldier carried with it the threat of a prison sentence. While there is no
evidence to suggest that any of the young women in this study were ever
reprimanded for their behavior, all would have been well aware of the
sensational cases of women imprisoned for their flagrant conduct. In
July 1862, Clara Solomon was shocked to read that her friend's mother
had suffered the indignity and humiliation of a prison sentence. "By the
evening paper we saw that Mrs. Phillips (Beauty's Ma) has been sentence[d] to *Ship* [Island]," she wrote in her diary. "Is to be *there confined*;
with one servant; soldiers rations; and to have no communication, verbal
or written, will be allowed her. The charge against her is 'she was found
on the balcony of her house during the passage of the funeral of De Kay,
laughing and mocking at his remains.'"[26]

Such cases served as a stark reminder to all young women that the
boundaries governing feminine behavior could be stretched but not broken. In occupied cities like New Orleans, Clara Solomon and Martha
Josephine Moore found themselves in a delicate situation. On one hand,
Confederate patriotism was tied to family honor and had become a
mechanism through which to affirm social worth. On the other hand,
defiant expressions of patriotism could lead to prosecution by the occupying commander, and even a term of imprisonment. Young ladies—
whose behavior had always been shaped by the presence of Southern men
and notions of reciprocity—now found themselves walking a tightrope:
weighing propriety against patriotism and trying to obtain the approval
of their peers without cultivating the disapproval of their captors.

For some women in New Orleans, the choice was far less problematic,
and many pushed the limits of "patriotism" to include physical abuse.
Federal soldiers out on their regular patrols were often spat on or drenched
in the contents of bedpans strategically hurled from balconies across the
city. As these acts increased in frequency and severity, Butler responded angrily to this challenge against the authority of his command. In May
1862, he outlawed such forms of "patriotism" by issuing the infamous
General Order No. 28:

> As the soldiers of the U.S. have been subject to insults offered
> to them by the women (calling themselves ladies) of N.O., I here-
> by order that should any female treat with contempt, or insult in
> word, gesture, or movement any officer and private under my com-

mand, she shall be liable to be treated as a woman of the town, ply-
ing her avocation.

Clara Solomon was infuriated by the news and fantasized about ways
to torture "The Beast." "Old Butler!" she wrote in June 1862. "If he
could only have as many ropes around his neck as there are ladies in
the city and each have a pull! Or if we could fry him! Or give him many
salt things to eat, and have water in sight, and he unable to obtain it!"
Clara's realization that Confederate soldiers had been displaced by a
more powerful enemy prompted her to fantasize about vengeance. In
her fantasy, however, she imagined Southern ladies hanging Butler for
his criminal behavior.[27]

Women across the South were incensed by the order, which, as Drew
Gilpin Faust has noted, "ratified the new public presence of women and
derogated it by involving an equivalence between a woman acting in
public and a prostitute."[28] Still, some young ladies had already drawn
the distinction between their behavior as genteel and honorable Confederates and the antics of "women calling themselves ladies." Sarah
Morgan, who had also engaged in patriotic acts of defiance, still made
the assumption that Order No. 28 was directed toward "common"
women of lower social standing. In a world where visible class lines had
been obscured by the ravages of war, Butler's order gave Sarah a rare
opportunity to assert her status and honor, even if it was to denounce
the actions of fellow Confederates. "Do I consider the female who could
spit in a gentleman's face merely because he wore United States buttons,
as a fit associate for me?" she wrote. "Such things are enough to disgust
anyone. 'Loud' women, what contempt I have for you! How I despise
your vulgarity!"[29]

FEMININITY TURNED UPSIDE DOWN

By seizing upon the image of the unlawful Yankee invader, young
ladies tried to subsume their antebellum socialization and remodel their
understanding of Confederate womanhood in an attempt to preserve
family honor. They carried knives and guns in self-defense and engaged
in acts of political resistance. Yet as young women encountered Federal
soldiers on the streets and in their homes, they increasingly found themselves waging war on individual Northern men rather than a nameless,
faceless enemy. This shift from the abstract to the personal exposed the

growing tension between antebellum feminine ideals and wartime reality. Regarding Yankees as barbarous devils, young women had to decide if they would extend benevolence to the wounded enemy or offer some assistance to dying Northern men. By dehumanizing Federal soldiers, many young women prayed for God to send yellow fever to the Yankees. Some young ladies, however, struggled between their role as defenders of home and hearth and their socialization as women. They could justify their feelings in patriotic terms, but their failure to extend care to Federal soldiers challenged the very foundations of Victorian femininity, and with it, the ideal of the Southern lady and belle.[30]

After witnessing the horrors of war, some young ladies willingly discarded feminine virtue in their desire for retribution. Sarah Lois Wadley cried for "retributive justice" for the "wicked men who have sent their myrmidons to bathe our land in the blood of its children." Martha Josephine Moore agreed. "Nothing evil could befall any one of them at which I would not rejoice," she wrote bitterly. New Orleans belle Clara Solomon prayed for yellow fever to descend upon the Union troops camping in Lafayette Square. She was not alone. "The papers speak in equivocal terms of a visit from 'yellow Jack,'" she wrote. While the Crescent City had not experienced an epidemic for some time, Clara believed that this was cause for optimism. "His [yellow fever's] appetite will be whetted by abstinence," she declared, "and how many subjects will he fix upon. Why N.O. won't be large enough to bury them." Clara ended her "prayer" by making excuses for her malicious comments. "The times justify profanity," she added.[31]

While Amanda Worthington was incensed to read about a Northern woman wishing for Confederate soldiers to die, young Southern women voiced the same sentiments about the Union army. Lise Mitchell believed it was unpatriotic to possess good will toward the enemy. "How can we at such a time pray for those who persecute us and despitefully use us?" she questioned. Clara Solomon fantasized about torturing "Beast Butler," while Kate Stone hoped for his demise by more conventional means. "Why can he not fall of the scourge of New Orleans, yellow fever?" she wrote. Months later, they were not disappointed. Upon hearing that "the Yankees are dying by the hundreds in New Orleans," Sarah Lois Wadley admitted she was relieved by the news. "[It] is an awful thing to rejoice over, and yet such [is] the fate of a bloody war and such are the feelings which it engenders, even in the merciful heart of a woman."[32]

In Holly Springs, Mississippi, Cordelia Lewis Scales was forced to nurse wounded Federal soldiers after occupying troops turned her father's room into a makeshift hospital. Outwardly, Cordelia performed her duty, but in a letter to her friend, she recorded her delight at being present to witness the suffering and misery of the "blue devils." "Sis Lue said she was trying to look serious to keep them from knowing how much delighted she was, when she happened to look at me, and that there was such a placid smile on my countenance, she had to bite her lips to keep from laughing," she wrote. "I did feel so happy when I looked on the suffering and heard the groans of those blue devils."[33]

By dehumanizing the enemy, Cordelia justified her "patriotic" feelings. Other young ladies recognized the gulf between their antebellum socialization and the wartime reality. In Natchez, Elizabeth Christie Brown struggled to reconcile her feelings of humanity and vengeance after a Federal guard beseeched her for medical attention. "I felt sorry for him, but debated some time whether I should get Ma to do anything for him. I felt that if we cured him, it would just be keeping a soldier in the field to fight against us." She finally attended to the soldier, conceding that she would be "grateful" to a Northern woman who did the same for "our boys." On another occasion, Elizabeth believed that she had developed a severe headache as "punishment for my having such wicked wishes about my country's enemies." "I cannot help praying that they may be defeated and annihilated," she added with guilt. Kate Stone hated the Yankees but could not pray for their demise. "I am not yet so hardened that I can pray even for a Yankee's death," she conceded, while Sarah Lois Wadley lamented the loss of "humanity" among Confederate women.[34]

Sarah Morgan was shocked by the "patriotism" of some of her acquaintances. "This war has brought out wicked, malignant feelings that I did not believe could dwell in woman's heart," she wrote. "I see some with the holiest eyes, so holy one would think the very spirit of Charity lived in them and all Christian meekness, go off in a mad tirade of abuse and say with the holy eyes wondrously changed 'I hope God will send down plague, Yellow fever, famine, on these vile Yankees, and that not one will escape death.' O what unutterable horror that remark causes me as often as I hear it!" After receiving the news that "more than a hundred sick [Union] soldiers" lay unattended in a theater in Baton Rouge, Sarah asked, "What woman has stretched out her hand to save them, to give them a cup of cold water?" When she and her mother tried to help by sending a custard to a sick soldier, they received fierce public censure for their actions. Patriotism had become an important component of family honor, forcing young Confederate women to "look outward as well as inward." "It wont do in the present state to act as we please," Sarah wrote. "Mob governs." In the end, Sarah was forced to concede that service and sacrifice were of little use in a wartime world made up of Confederate women, Union men, and the Southern codes of patriotism and honor.[35]

"Crazy for Plunder"

Encountering Federal soldiers in a public place was one thing; confronting them within the confines of the household was another. The unpredictability of the Federal raid—and the conduct of the soldiers involved—led all women to dread this form of interaction with the enemy. Federal raids occurred at schools, in stores, and on private homes in occupied cities. Urban areas were frequently targeted during the initial stages of occupation, when recently abandoned houses became prime targets for pillaging and wanton destruction. The plantation landscape, however, remained the Union army's greatest resource: a place where they could replenish their supplies of food, horses, livestock, and other provisions. Households situated near a battlefield or encampment could expect regular visits from groups of soldiers temporarily free from the influence of higher command and willing to exercise their power, through violence if necessary. By taking possession of communities and households, Federal soldiers exposed the failure of Southern men to protect their property and their families.

Confederate civilians often spent their days waiting in nervous anticipation, knowing that at any moment their livestock, provisions, furniture, clothes, or keepsakes could be stolen or destroyed by groups of passing soldiers. Those households that still contained men were just as helpless as those that did not. In this desperate wartime landscape, Southern men were forced to relinquish honor in the name of survival. With the arrival of Yankee troops, elite men often ran and hid from the enemy, emasculating themselves by submitting to Northern soldiers and relying on their so called "dependents" for protection.

This new and unpredictable Federal presence was especially confronting to young women who had always relied on the support, guidance, and protection of their male kin. As Kate Stone and her mother awaited the arrival of the enemy, she described their existence as "miserable." The sight of a Federal boat traveling upriver was enough to send the household into a state of confusion. Anticipating that the gunboat was about to land, the Stone family "rushed around the house, each person picking up any valuable in the way of silver, jewelry, or fancy things he could find, and away we ran through the hot, dusty quarter lot, making for the only refuge we could see, the tall, thick cornfield just beyond the fence."[36]

Near Vicksburg, Ida Barlow Trotter's grandmother thought of ingenious places to hide her valuables. "She had a few shingles taken from the roof, and had many things put in on the ceiling," Ida recalled. "She had all the silver and jewelry buried in boxes under the house and to keep some meat where we could eat it, she put two mattresses on a bed and placed a layer of bacon [and] ham, between them." After hiding all their valuables, Emma Stroud and her daughter were more concerned about their vulnerability in a region swarming with "desperados," while Elizabeth Christie Brown was utterly terrified by the news that "the Yankee cavalry were on their way to Natchez." "Of course the expectation was that we would all be swallowed up alive."[37]

When the Yankees finally arrived, there was little relief. Amanda Worthington and her family locked themselves in their home. "We shut up all the shutters and locked every door about the house and not one of us showed ourselves," she wrote. "They . . . drank all the butter milk that was there and ate up all the butter we had churned today—then sent word to Mother they wanted the keys to the meat house and the dairy." After a number of similar raids, the Worthington family lost hundreds of slaves, "the remainder of our mules and a good many of our ploughs," as well as other livestock and provisions. They were not alone. In Vicksburg, the Shannon sisters described the "destitute condition" of their family and community after a period of intense raiding. "Father had laid in $250 worth of corn, that they fed to their horses as soon as they got in. His vegetable garden that he had taken so much pains with, was trampled and ridden over until there is not a thing left in it." As the "trembling" women peeped through the shutters, they saw raiding soldiers "bringing all kinds of plunder, showing around silverware and jewelry they had stolen." "All were crazy for plunder," they added, "and when officers were opposed to such wholesale thieving, they were unable to control their men."[38]

In Natchez, the Brown family's sawmill was stripped of all its lumber, horses, and saddles. Elizabeth's beloved collection of chickens suffered the same fate. "We were aroused from our sleep last night by the chickens crying aloud for assistance and soon discovered that there was someone in the coop," she wrote. "They left it double quick . . . but managed to relieve us from the necessity of feeding several of our fowls, among others a very venerable old Gobler—who was Sultan of the Yard . . . Pa saw the Provost Marshall about getting a gun to protect ourselves with, but was told he could not have it, for the life of one of their soldiers was worth more than all the property." When General Thomas Ransom finally agreed to assign a Yankee guard to protect the sawmill, Elizabeth continued to report the loss of food, horses, and provisions, including "the four oxen that we expected to have for our winter food."[39]

Sarah Morgan's home was completely ransacked when Federal troops reached Baton Rouge. "I stood in the parlor in silent amazement," she wrote. "As I looked for each well known article, I could hardly believe that Abraham Lincoln's officers had really come so low down as to steal in such a wholesale manner. The paper maché workbox Miriam had given me, was gone. The baby sacque I was crocheting, with all knitting needles and wool, gone also. . . . Not a book remained in the parlor, except Idylls of the King, that contained my name also, and which, together with the door plate, was the only case in which the name of Morgan was spared. . . . I stood in mother's room before the shattered armoir, which I could hardly believe the same that I had smoothed my hair before, as I left home three weeks previously."[40]

Without brothers or fathers to protect their honor, young women's shifting conception of patriotism and political resistance prompted many to abandon their socialization in submission. Stripped of the ability to express their patriotism in domestic terms, Federal occupation compelled young ladies to act in assertive ways and to exercise their temper, an attribute that was strongly discouraged in the grooming of Southern belles. For many, the heartbreak of losing family, friends, homes, and possessions was given voice as young ladies made the giant leap from "protected" women to become "protectors" of individual and familial honor. Young women's image of the barbarous Yankee legitimized this shift in femininity without acknowledging the deficiencies of Southern men.

Amanda Worthington's initial fear of Union soldiers turned to rage when she witnessed the plundering of her family's home and possessions. While she could do little to stop them, Amanda and her family refused to submit their patriotic honor and "talked strong secession talk" with a Federal captain while some soldiers "commenced slaughtering" the chickens she had been given by her aunt Pollie. When a Yankee sergeant rode up to Wayside and "wondered if one of the young

ladies wouldn't sing 'The Bonnie Blue Flag' for him," Amanda was outraged when her "mother thought as it was one of *our* songs there could
be no harm in singing it." After her sister failed in the attempt, Amanda
chose to perform "The Stars of Our Banner," "as it was real patriotic."
"I marched myself in never even speaking to the man and seated myself
at the piano," she related, "my face was burning like fire and I was so
agitated and mad that I could hardly sing; when I came to the words
'The foe must be silenced forever tho' millions in battle may bleed' I
looked right at the man. . . . As soon as I finished I got up and stalked
out without saying a word." In Amanda's eyes, submitting to a Yankee's
request did not mean relinquishing one's honor as well.[41]

Near Holly Springs, Cordelia Lewis Scales's ardent patriotism earned
her a reputation among Union soldiers as "the right bower of the Rebel
army." When a passing band of Yankee soldiers began to raid Oakland
for food and provisions, an enraged Cordelia confronted the men. "Just
as I got out in the yard, two Cavalry men and six infantry came up and
surrounded me. Pa was not at home. Ma and Sis Lucy were looking on and
were frightened very much for they knew I would speak my mind to
them if they provoked me," she related. After lauding the bravery of Confederate soldiers to the band of raiders, one gentleman probed Cordelia
on the courage of its women. "The Lt. then said to me, 'Now, Miss, you
southern ladies would not fight, you are too good natured.' I said we
were very good natured but when our soil was invaded and by such creatures as they were it was enough to arouse any one." Her outburst produced unanticipated results. "He then told me that such bravery should
be rewarded—that nothing on the place should be touched," she wrote
proudly. "He made all the men march before him and did not let them
trouble anything."[42]

Kate Stone endured raid after Federal raid with resignation until
Yankee soldiers decided to take her beloved horse, "Wonka": a "lovely
. . . spirited . . . blood bay." After begging two "villainous-looking"
Yankees to leave the horse alone, Kate could not control her rage when
one of the soldiers "bluntly" refused to oblige, and "galloped off to catch
the horse." "I called to one of the Negroes to open the gate, thinking it
would give Wonka a chance to escape, but as they seemed afraid I ran
to do it myself," she wrote. "When the wretch called to me impudently
to stop, I did not notice him but threw the gate open. He then dashed
up with the pistol pointed at my head (I thought I had never seen such
bright caps) and demanded in the most insolent tone how I dared to
open a gate when he ordered it shut. I looked at him and ran on to open

the other gate. Just then Mamma called to me that they had caught the horse, and as I turned to go in the house the man cursed and said, 'I had just as soon kill you as a hoppergrass.' I was not frightened but I was furiously angry and would have been glad to have seen him lying dead." Kate may have affirmed her bravery and her honor, but she had been unable to save her horse. "I cried the rest of the day and half of the night," she added, only later coming to a full realization of how risky this resistance had been.[43]

Ida Barlow Trotter's cousin Elizabeth Reed also "spent her time doing all she could to aggravate the Yankees." Ida admitted that her actions "kept the older members of the family in a constant state of uneasiness for fear they would kill us or burn the house as a result of our cousin's attacks upon the enemy with her tongue." Parental concern did little to deter Elizabeth, who would not tolerate insolence from occupying soldiers. "One night a little servant girl came in and said, 'Miss Bettie, dem dar Yankees is a sleeping on your piano,' where upon she bounced in the parlor and demanded them to dismount, for several great fellows had stretched themselves upon a great square piano for a comfortable nap." Unable to physically prevent the occupation or destruction of their homes, Elizabeth Reed and other young women shifted the boundaries of feminine behavior to preserve their understanding of honor and the values upon which their lives rested. None of these young ladies donned a soldier's uniform and went off to fight. They did, however, hold true to their beliefs and used every opportunity available to them to express their resistance and their bravery. By crossing the street at the sight of a Union soldier or screaming Confederate rhetoric down the barrel of a loaded gun, young women affirmed their self-worth and courage, regardless of the outcome. By doing so, they upheld family honor and the honor of the Confederate cause.[44]

HONORABLE YANKEES?

The arrival of the Northern army confirmed young women's fears about ultimate Confederate victory, but unlike other Southern women, it did not leave them feeling abandoned or betrayed by their men. Ironically, the widespread occupation of Mississippi and Louisiana provided some young ladies with the opportunity of further enhancing their understanding of honorable Confederate manhood. While the Shannon sisters clung to their belief that Federal soldiers were nothing less than "blue devils," many belles chose to partially revise their depiction of the Yankee in an attempt to reaffirm the honor of the cause and those men who had so bravely defended it. Sarah Morgan continued to express contempt for Federal officers such as Farragut, but changed her opinion of some Union soldiers. "Fine noble looking men they were," she wrote of the soldiers who occupied Baton Rouge, "showing refinement and gentlemanly bearing in every motion; one cannot help but admire such foes. . . . I expected to be in a crowd of ruffian soldiers who would think nothing of cutting your throat. . . . The former is the thing as is believed by the whole country, the latter is the true state of affairs." Even after a group of Federal soldiers pillaged her home, Sarah incensed a neighbor by disagreeing with her that "there was no such thing as a gentleman in the Yankee army." "I know Major Drum for one," she wrote, "and that Capt. Clark must be two, and Mr Biddle is three, and Gen. Williams—God bless him where ever he is!"[45]

After exhibiting great animosity toward the Federal soldiers who occupied Natchez, Annie Harper and the township were also quick to reconcile with the enemy. Annie described Union general Marcellus Monroe Crocker as "a whole-souled, big-hearted man," whose staff of "handsome accommodating officers became great favorites with the Natchez people." After some discussion as to whether loyal Confederate citizens should invite Federal soldiers into their homes, "many decided that we could not be less generous than our foe, and having accepted so many sorely needed favors and so many kindnesses," they concluded that "the best return we could make was to treat them hospitably." By doing so, Annie complimented the honor of the Southern people. "Only people of the highest culture and dignity can sustain themselves honorably in such an anomalous position," she wrote, "and Natchez was just the place to find such people."[46]

Elizabeth Christie Brown, also of Natchez, was relieved to "find some gentlemen among the enemy." When Union general Thomas Ransom granted her father protection for his "dwelling and grounds," she "blessed the Gen. from my heart" and wrote of her plans to send him a "handsome" bouquet "as a slight acknowledgement for his protection to us." She later became good friends with a Federal guard and unashamedly entertained him on the balcony of the family home. Kate Foster was similarly impressed by the conduct of a select number of Union soldiers. While she was perfectly shocked to hear that "some of the young ladies around Natchez are receiving attention from the Yankees," she objected on patriotic grounds—not on the grounds that "the Yankees are not gentlemen enough to visit here." "When the Federals first came I was disposed to think there was not a gentleman among them," Kate admitted, "[but] I have had kindness shown me and politeness most assuredly. . . . I have seen three or four Lieuts. who are perfect gentlemen, two I do not know, the name of the other is Lieut. Furlong. If they only wore our uniform how happy I should be to entertain them." Kate, however, did not extend her compliment to the entire Union army, and still referred to the nameless, dirty privates as "blue devils." In the same entry she scorned the "hateful blue coats" who had attended church that day. "I cannot bear to be nearer than three or four pews," she scoffed in disgust. "They are such dirty creatures."[47]

Even Cordelia Lewis Scales, "the right bower of the Rebel army," was prepared to acknowledge the gallantry of Federal captain Flynn, who had protected her family and home on a number of occasions. On the eve of Flynn's departure from Holly Springs, Cordelia swallowed her Confederate pride and fulfilled his request by performing a rendition of "My Maryland." By granting some Yankee soldiers respectability, young ladies preserved their belief in the Southern gentleman and the cause he went to war to defend. "I will not say we were conquered by cowards," Sarah Morgan declared, "for where would that place us? . . . These women may acknowledge that *cowards* have won battles in which their brothers were engaged, but I, I will ever say *mine* fought against brave men, and won the day. Which is most honorable?"[48]

By reworking the boundaries that governed their understanding of themselves and others, young ladies were able to maintain their belief in the cause and the honorable Confederate soldier at a time when other Southern women had lost all faith in their men. Their task was not an easy one, and young women often struggled to accommodate wartime demands that sharply contradicted their own sense of self. As the conflict wore on, Federal occupation further unraveled the Southern social fabric, stripping young women of their assumptions about their slaves. As the peculiar institution slowly crumbled before their very eyes, young ladies were faced with the even greater challenge of maintaining their honor and gentility without slavery.

CHAPTER SEVEN

"Our Slaves Are Gone"

Every thing looked quite desolate at the plantation and it made me
have a feeling of sadness to look at the deserted houses and to think I'd
never see the darkies that lived there again.

Amanda Worthington, May 4, 1863

In May 1863, Amanda Worthington came to the realization that she
had sacrificed her long-anticipated bellehood for the Confederate war.
Piano lessons in New Orleans and leisurely afternoons of reading or
visiting had been replaced with "mighty tiresome" days churning butter, skimming milk, sweeping porches, cleaning, cooking, and mending clothes. Her home, affectionately called Wayside because of the
Worthington family's famous hospitality, had been raided and ransacked
by passing soldiers. Amanda's father, Samuel, who had been one of the
wealthiest and most influential planters in Washington County, Mississippi, now plummeted into debt and desperation. When Northern soldiers liberated more than 160 Worthington slaves, Amanda and her
parents were dumbfounded by their absolute loss of wealth and power.

On the eve of yet another raid, Amanda anticipated that the Yankees
would "leave us bare enough this time, for they have taken the remainder of our mules and a good many cattle." Powerless to change the
situation, Amanda retreated to her room to dream of the gallant Confederate soldiers who were incapable of saving the day. "I wanted something to distract my mind from the wretches so I came in here and drew
a Confederate soldier," she remarked, "thinking as I couldn't see any
real ones I'd make one." By the time Amanda finished her sketch, the
party of Yankees had almost completed its mission—taking abundant
supplies of food, cattle, and provisions and placing Samuel under house

arrest until they were able to move his slaves to a safe Union location. Confined to her room, Amanda was left to ponder her family's destitution. "I wouldn't mind it for myself at all," she wrote in an effort to convince herself, "but it seems hard that my dear Father and Mother should be deprived of every luxury and almost every necessity of life in their old age." As Amanda knew, the loss of slaves represented far more than an inconvenience. At its most profound level, it eroded an elite family's power, dominance, and honor while also stripping them of their source of labor and wealth. It also served as a stark reminder that not all patriotic sacrifices were temporary ones. As slaves ran away, they took with them young women's assurance of their status. Honor and gentility could no longer be assumed; they were notions to which to cling.[1]

Running to Freedom

The pervasive Federal presence in Mississippi and Louisiana opened the doors to black liberation. Southern plantations and elite urban households, once dominated by the master, had been left weak and vulnerable with his departure to war. Without his physical presence in the fields, the quarters, or the Big House, the master's position was challenged as slaves questioned the authority of the mistress to oversee the management of the household or plantation. The arrival of Northern soldiers shattered the already fragile state of domestic affairs. Slaves, who had been bought and sold at the master's whim, who had been unable to own their time or property, who had been prohibited from reading or writing, entering into legally recognized marriages, making contracts, or traveling alone without written authorization, now saw an opportunity for freedom. And they took it.[2]

As Southern mistresses struggled with their new responsibilities and the challenges of wartime, they watched helplessly as slaves fled to the safety of Federal military camps. Some slaves packed up their belongings and left the household in the dead of night. In Louisiana, Sarah Lois Wadley described the plight of her neighbor, Mrs. Tucker, who awoke one morning to find that all her servants had left the household. "[They] did not leave until Monday night," she wrote, "and left everything prepared for breakfast." Kate Stone's neighbor, Mr. Watson, was not so lucky when he rose one morning to find "every Negro gone, about seventy-five, only three little girls left." "The ladies actually had to get up and get breakfast," she exclaimed, adding that "it was funny to see their first attempt at milking." Other slaves left defiantly in the middle of the day, or chose to come and go from the household as they pleased.[3]

For young ladies, this wartime picture of slavery was perplexing when they reflected on their perception of the antebellum household as a place of relative order and harmony. Neither responsible for supervising slaves nor exposed to the daily realities of life in the quarters or the fields, young ladies had been raised with a picture of slavery that grew out of the restrictions placed on their access to certain areas of the household or plantation.[4] These invisible boundaries differed for each member of the Southern family and profoundly influenced the ways in which men and women viewed and interacted with the "peculiar institution."

Only elite men had unreserved access to their plantations and the public world of business and politics. A planter's worth as a businessman, a gentleman, a slave owner, and a patriarch was measured by his ability to assert his influence in every physical sphere of the landscape while limiting his dependents access to space.[5] The plantation mistress's physical sphere of influence, for example, was restricted to the household, the smokehouse, and the vegetable patch. She rarely visited the fields, except to accompany her husband, and made visits to the slave quarters primarily to extend benevolence to sick servants. Her authority, then, was directly linked to the physical space that the master permitted her to inhabit.

In accordance with family hierarchy, young ladies' access to space was further restricted. As children, they often mingled and "shared games" with black playmates, but as they grew, these childhood friendships quickly gave way to the rigid division of black and white. Elite parents often held great reservations about the influence of slaves on their children, and young women were protected, as far as possible, from the culture, folklore, and customs that defined the black community. As a young child, Mississippian Annie Jacobs relished the times when she was left to sew "on the shady back porch with old Aunt Mary Pine and Aunt Martha" and could listen to the "guarded talk of plantation affairs." While she was permitted to move freely throughout the household, Annie, and her urban counterparts, were forbidden from visiting the slave quarters without a parent or older brother. Planter belles also rarely visited the fields, and when they did so, it was only from a distance and under parental supervision.[6]

These invisible boundaries of authority sustained the power and dominance of the master. They also shaped the ways in which each member of the household perceived slaves and slavery. In accordance with his wider view, a master's understanding of slavery reached far beyond the boundaries of the household or plantation and into the world of business and politics. He thought of slaves in economic terms and drew upon his political influence to ensure the maintenance of a legal structure that strengthened his authority as a master and a patriarch.[7] The mistress, whose authority was relegated to the household, most often thought of and understood slavery in terms of her domestic role: the time she spent instructing slaves, attending to sick or old slaves, reprimanding behavior or complimenting on a job well done.

Young women, who had been raised to become the guardians of Southern gentility, thought of slavery as a mechanism through which to assert their elite identities. The fruits of slave labor provided young women with the opportunity to receive an education and dress in the finest attire. Slavery also afforded them the leisure time to pursue social occasions, reading, or embroidery. It was slaves, not the belles' mothers, who attended to the demanding requirements of belles, shampooing their hair, washing and ironing their clothes, and fetching ruffles and bows at the young ladies' insistence. Yet in their diaries and letters, young women referred to their "servants" as nothing more than "punctuations" in daily life: helping them dress, fixing their rooms, doing the laundry, or cooking a delicious dinner. They may have heard about the mistress's daily battle to exert control over one or two "disagreeable" servants, but these ongoing problems were not yet their own. While their elite status was grounded in slave ownership, young women viewed the institution as a part of the landscape, central and fundamental, but assumed.[8]

Young planter women carried this set of assumptions into the wider plantation landscape. Unlike their mothers, they had no reason to venture into the quarters, and only observed many of the family's slaves when they attended celebrations such as Christmas, and watched slave dancing and festivities from the comfortable realms of a porch or piazza. Shielded from the harsh realities of life in the fields or the culture of the quarters, Sarah Lois Wadley's perception of slavery was partly shaped by her attendance at happy Yuletide celebrations, when she heard "the sounds of fiddle, tambourine and 'bones' mingled with the shuffling and pounding of [black] feet." Esther Wright of Rapides Parish, Louisiana, and Annie Jacobs of Doro plantation in Mississippi also observed slave dancing at Christmas. Ester recalled that Alfred was the "star dancer," as he commanded "solo dances with great energy." The celebration of a slave wedding also exposed young ladies to images of happy and contented slaves. Ellen Louise Power and her friends had an enjoyable time when they attended a "Darky's wedding." Ellen made garlands of flowers for the bride. "It is very amusing to see them dance," she remarked. "We sat up till 11 o'clock." At these times, young women saw slavery "at an immediate, personal level, and in its happiest form." This perspective also shaped young women's rather idealized picture of slavery, which drew upon the image of "Sambo"—the contented, docile, childlike slave—to affirm the "civilizing" effect of bondage and the honor and gentility of the slaveholding South.[9]

In wartime, young Confederate women drew upon their antebellum perception of slaves and slavery in an attempt to make sense of the previously incomprehensible state of race relations. While the mistress loomed large in her wartime role as acting master, she continued to anchor her personal struggles with slavery in the daily routine of the household or plantation. As a result, she regarded the departure of slaves as an assault on her role as Southern mistress. Confederate belles experienced a very different identity crisis as the trickle of runaways turned into a flood.[10] While young women were also a part of this domestic landscape, the loss of slaves challenged a Confederate belle's elite identity far more than her role as a budding mistress. Amid the devastation of war, young ladies were forced into the realization that they could no longer rely on slavery to assert their status or their gentility.

"THE NEGROES ARE EAGER TO GO"

The sight of "contented" slaves running to the "Yankee invaders" provoked a crisis in the minds of young ladies, who, unlike their mothers, had not been fully exposed to the inner workings (and tensions) of the master-slave relationship. They responded to the news that "their" slaves had chosen freedom over family loyalty with a mixture of shock and disbelief. "The Negroes are eager to go, leaving wife and children and all for freedom promised them," Kate Stone wrote excitedly in July 1862. Eight months later she recorded the loss of slaves as a common daily event. "A great number of Negroes have gone to the Yankees from this section," she reported in March 1863. "Mr. Matt Johnson has lost every Negro off one place and a number from the other places. Keene Richards has lost 160 from Translyvania."[11]

In New Orleans also, Federal occupation prompted a massive slave exodus. "I hear the Custom House and boats are being crowded with daily arrivals," remarked Clara Solomon. The occupation of Natchez produced similar results. "The Negroes are flocking to the enemy in town," exclaimed Kate Foster. "At any time we can look up the street and see crowds of Negroes on their way to Natchez," added Emily Caroline Douglas. "Old men bent over with age, young men, women, children, wagons, mules, carts, horses." Watching the demise of slavery from her window, Emily was still shocked to hear that "Sister Sallie's house servants packed up their bundles . . . and took their departure without saying 'good bye.'" Emily, like other young women, continued to make a distinction between her "black family" and the other slaves on the road to freedom.[12]

While the loss of field hands could be attributed to an unruly Yankee influence, the departure of trusted house servants and "mammy" figures evoked feelings of bitterness and betrayal and shook young women's belief in paternalism to its very core. It also proved to be the most inconvenient loss because these were the slaves who attended to the daily needs of the household and the demanding requirements of young ladies. Besieged by an array of domestic duties, Sarah Lois Wadley responded angrily to the news that eight more "trusted" servants had departed for Yankee lines. "It was unexpected that the negroes should run away," she wrote. "One of them was one in whom Father placed great confidence, and he had sacrificed so much time and care to them all, that it seems very ungrateful." Natchez belle Elizabeth Christie Brown voiced similar sentiments when "Maria," a house servant, chose the freedom offered by a party of Federal raiders over her mother's kindness. At the first sight of the Yankees, "Cora and Maria had a fuss and Ma tried to stop it. M. gave her a great deal of impudence, and packed up her clothes and left." "Poor Ma was very much deceived in her," she sighed. "She thought better of Maria, after she had been so kind to her,—and done so much for her." Lemuella Brickell was also enraged by the loss of "Ellen Jones and her child Nellie, Yulema and Donelson." "I hope they will be put on a cotton plantation and made to work," she declared bitterly.[13]

Other young ladies mourned the loss of individual slaves—and the loss of yet another symbol of their honor and status. After Federal soldiers "took about 106" slaves from her family's plantation, Amanda Worthington felt "miserably depressed all day, not so much on account of our losses." "It made me feel bad to see so many of the servants that I had known all my life and liked leave us," she wrote. Later, she accepted that the "desolate" appearance of the slave quarters might remain that way. Without the means to recapture runaway slaves, Amanda realized that possible emancipation rendered even this alternative obsolete. "It made me have a feeling of sadness to look at the deserted houses and to think I'd never see the darkies that lived there again," she added.[14]

Kate Stone recorded similar feelings when she inspected the abandoned quarters at Brokenburn. "The place looks deserted now with its empty cabins and neglected fields," she commented, "and the scene is the same wherever we go." In New Orleans, Emma Walton resigned herself to the fact that her family's servants would soon leave. Still, she felt their imminent departure would relieve the unhappy suspense that gripped their wartime household. "It will perhaps be a relief after they go," she wrote her father, "for we will then no longer anticipate their departure." Clara Solomon also predicted that the occupation of New Orleans—and the proximity of Union troops—would prove an irresistible lure to even the most loyal slaves. With only one house servant to oversee, Emma Solomon blamed her constant battles with Lucy on the Federal soldiers who tempted her "property" with freedom. "Ma is quite troubled about her [Lucy]," Clara conceded, "as so many (her acquaintances some) have run away and sought the protection of the Yankees. . . . There are many instances in which house-servants, those who have been raised by people, have deserted them, though they have received the kindest treatment at their hands; but they imagine no sacrifice too great with which to purchase freedom. L. is very weak-minded, and is as a tool in the hands of anyone and yet I sometimes think that she would not act so, yet—the most *faithful* have betrayed."[15]

The loss of slaves was not only a shock and an inconvenience. It also brought family honor into question. In the antebellum South, the willingness of slaves to submit to the master established and accentuated family honor by highlighting the power and dominance of the head of household. During the war, flagrant acts of resistance, including running away, challenged the authority of the elite male and dishonored his family by exposing the true extent to which a slave's submission had been an enforced one. The loss of slaves also stripped Southern families of their leisure time. Without servants to attend to their every need, young ladies were forced to sacrifice their bellehood for an active role in the household. They also faced the daunting prospect of how to define their gentility in a world where the racial hierarchy had been turned upside down.[16]

After assuming the role of housekeeper, Sarah Morgan felt as if she had swapped roles with one of her domestic servants. When she heard rumors that the Yankees had raided elite homes for clothing and given it to the contrabands, Sarah was outraged at the thought of her dresses "doing active duty on the sylph like form of some negro woman" while she wore a patched dress and an old sunbonnet. Unlike Sarah, fellow Baton Rouge belle "Miss Jones" confronted the reality firsthand when a group of Federal soldiers ransacked her home along with a black "Madame." "She had the pleasure of having four officers in her house, men who sported épaulets and red sashes, accompanied by a negro woman, at whose disposal all articles were placed," Sarah related. "The worthy companion of these 'gentlemen' walked around selecting things with the most natural airs and graces, . . . the 'gentlemen' assuring her she only had to cho[o]se what she wanted, and that they would have them removed immediately." Sarah conceded that her elaborate wardrobe had probably met with a similar fate. "Wicked as it may seem, I would rather have all I own burned, than in the possession of the negroes," she cried angrily. "Fancy my magenta organdie on a dark beauty! Bah! I think the sight would enrage me!" As she spent every waking moment washing, knitting, scouring, spinning, working in the vegetable patch, and warping thread, Sallie McRae only had time to dream of such "atrocities." She indulged in a bout of crying after having a dream in which her mother gave all her homespun dresses to the "niggers."[17]

As trusted slaves left urban households and rural plantations, the young ladies of Mississippi and Louisiana experienced an identity crisis. In wartime, their perception of happy and contented slaves had been contradicted by the behavior of servants who refused to work or ran away. Sallie McRae's dreams and Sarah Morgan's outburst indicate that young ladies struggled to accommodate these challenges to deeply rooted conceptions. Expressing their fears about former slaves donning their finest attire, young ladies revealed their fears about the demise of slavery and its impact on their identity and their position in Southern society. As elite ideas about race and slavery were challenged and overthrown, young women floundered in a world where class, gender, reciprocity, and honor lost their footing in a hierarchy that had founded itself on the "peculiar institution."

LOYAL AND DISLOYAL SLAVES

In the face of military defeat and Federal occupation, young ladies had reworked their position in society to preserve family honor. But as the Southern hierarchy began to dissolve before their very eyes, women could do little to contain the challenge from within their own households. As slaves ran to freedom, they exposed their owners to the most dishonorable loss of all. While young women struggled to come to terms with their antebellum perception of slaves and the wartime reality, they clung to notions of patriotism in an attempt to understand the previously unthinkable state of race relations.

After the Federal occupation of Natchez, Kate Foster and her family watched their antebellum world crumble before them. In the days following the surrender, the trickle of runaway slaves turned into a flood as house servants, drivers, cooks, and field hands packed up their belongings and headed for Union lines. It was not long before the Foster slaves joined this exodus to freedom. "When we awakened . . . yesterday morning Billy had returned to the Yankees," Kate wrote on July 16, 1863. "A good riddance, I say, as he is too lazy to work for himself and the biggest liar I ever knew." As droves of runaways passed the Foster plantation, Kate took comfort in the fact that "none of ours have gone from here yet but Billy and I hope they will all prove faithful to the end." Within days, her hopes were dashed. "Pa's boy Allen has gone, fooled off by some old fool. Fred the carriage driver has gone to what they all think a better place but poor deluded creatures they will find out too late who are their best friends, Master or Massa."

Three days later, Kate wrote of more Foster runaways. "Old May and Rizze left Sunday morning and that night old Sally decamped with all her 'traps.' Yesterday morning Jim and Frank left. I think the latter was persuaded off by some of the older negroes. Florence told us yesterday that her Mother was packing up to go to the Yankees. We are in a delightful state of expectancy not knowing exactly what time his honor and wife will leave." By the end of July, "Ned and Mary" were still on the plantation, but Matilda had gone. "We think all will go whensoever it pleases their majesties," Kate wrote bitterly. Compelled to help "Sarah" with the ironing "as she has so much to do with Matilda's work," Kate hoped that her assistance might persuade Sarah to stay a little longer. "I do hope some of them will be faithful," she added, "for if they are not, I shall lose entire faith in the whole race." By losing her faith, Kate may have feared losing part of her identity, which was grounded in slave ownership and the lifestyle it afforded her.[18]

Preserving this elite identity became even harder for young ladies like Kate. Wartime sacrifice had taken their men, their fashionable clothing, their bellehoods, and often their homes and possessions. Now it threatened to take their last symbol of status: their slaves. The only thing left was patriotism, and Kate seized upon this theme in an effort to salvage the vestiges of her elite identity. Just as Emma Walton had justified her status as an "old maid" by regarding it as a patriotic sacrifice, Kate drew upon notions of sacrificial patriotism to absolve her family of the dishonorable loss and to reaffirm her identity, not as a slaveholding woman, but as a true Confederate belle.

In July 1863, she declared that the Confederacy was better off without its slaves. "Grandma does not seem to care at all about the negroes leaving," she commented, "—she is right too for if they go let them reap the benefit of it too." Within her own household, Kate tried to view her new domestic work, not as a tiresome and unwelcome burden, but as a positive and patriotic contribution to her family and the cause. When "Celia" departed "with her two children" in tow, Kate felt powerless and most indignant at the way in which the Fosters' favorite cook chose to leave the plantation. "She was very cool about it, had a wagon to come out for her things," she wrote angrily. "I wish that I had ordered the man away and then made her go, but I was fearful I should bring trouble upon Aunt Jenny." While Kate knew she was powerless to stop Celia leaving, she soon realized that she was in control of the way she reacted to the loss. "She is gone," Kate continued, "and I have been helping old Emmeline to cook. I like it well." By taking on additional chores and describing them as easy and even enjoyable, Kate negated the loss of Celia and other slaves by minimizing the impact of their absence on the household. "Taking *all* the negroes is not whipping us as the enemy will see," she declared triumphantly with a broom and dustpan in hand.[19]

As she prepared dinner and did the washing, Kate soon abandoned her feelings of disillusionment about black "loyalty" and welcomed the departure of her family's slaves, whom she now regarded as "a lot of ingrates, and God punishes us for ingratitude as much as for any other sin." "Let the foe take all the negroes," she proclaimed, "they are welcome to them and the sooner we are rid of them the quicker we will whip our enemy." By placing the loss of slaves within the larger framework of Confederate patriotism, Kate Foster preserved her family's honor and asserted it by viewing their departure as a positive sacrifice for the cause.[20]

Elizabeth Christie Brown, also of Natchez, drew upon a complex mix of antebellum proslavery ideology and popular wartime ideas to understand her family's loss. Unlike Kate, Elizabeth's unreserved hatred for the "Yankee devils" now incorporated "impudent Negroes," who, by transgressing the physical boundaries of the plantation, were physically and psychologically separated from the elite sphere of influence. At no time did Elizabeth question the inability of Confederate forces to protect her region and its institutions. Instead, she became enraged by the actions of former slaves who frequently stole from the Brown family's woodpile or garden. "I felt very rebelious this morning when I saw the impudent niggers stealing the wood," she wrote in August 1863. "I had the will to tell them to go to the d—l," but regained her composure to instruct a soldier to "drive off the vile creatures who think themselves equal to the whites." In the following days, Elizabeth spoke "imprudently . . . to an impudent colored *lady*, who had stolen wood" and wrote of her outrage when her father was arrested "because he threatened to strike a nigger who was in the garden stealing." Elizabeth reported that after discussions with the provost marshall, her father "was told he could set dogs on the darkies but must not strike them." This challenge to her father's authority as master, and ultimately her family's elite status, culminated in another outburst of anger and frustration. "What a fuss the hateful thing made," Elizabeth wrote. "I felt it would do me good to see them all get a drubbing. I hope they will be made to suffer."[21]

Andrew Brown's loss of power was even more apparent when a former slave, accompanied by a Federal soldier, made a visit to the mill to confront his master. "Old Alfred came with an officer—after his clothes. The mean old scamp behaved shamefully towards his master," Elizabeth declared. "I had no good wishes for his future welfare, and perhaps I am very wicked, for I called him some ugly names, I hope we will get even with him yet." By transgressing both the physical boundaries of the plantation and her father's patriarchal authority, Elizabeth rhetorically turned Old Alfred and the other runaways from "Negroes" or "servants" into "niggers." In so doing, she drew upon the proslavery rhetoric of theorists such as Thomas Dew, who had argued that the Negro was a "savage brute" who had been "civilized" by the institution of slavery. Dew had assured Southerners that the slave would remain "docile" under the protection and guidance of his master, but if this authority was removed or weakened in any way, he would revert to "a blood thirsty savage." In her diary, Elizabeth used the image of the "black brute" and the Yankee devil to describe this new "partnership" between soldiers and contrabands. After watching a Federal soldier help a slave to freedom, she exclaimed, "What a magnificent sight to see a U.S. officer in splendid uniform hold out his hands to assist his 'brother', a darky, . . . to carry him away from his Master."[22]

Elizabeth was shocked to see the Southern social order overturned by

Federal occupation. By describing the Union soldier and the runaway slave as "brothers," she elevated herself above these "inferiors" and preserved family honor by asserting that the loss of a beast was no loss at all. Despite this, she still wished that all evidence of "disloyalty" could be banished from her view. "Tis a pity all that have left their homes couldn't be sent away from here," she declared, hinting that the loss of a "beast" was nevertheless a bitter pill for a young lady to swallow.[23]

Elizabeth Christie Brown and Kate Foster only reworked their perception of slaves and slavery because they were forced to do so. As they helplessly watched the Southern hierarchy slipping away from them, many other young women clung steadfastly to any hint of slave loyalty. They showed no desire to contemplate the ways in which external factors such as geography, climate, the proximity of enemy troops, and the availability of food and shelter determined whether slaves would stay or go. Instead, young women seized upon the image of loyalty, which provided them with assurance that those servants who remained with their masters also remained loyal to the institution itself. For many Confederate belles, the loyal slave was the last physical representation of their status and gentility and became a symbol of honor to which to cling.[24]

Despite the loss of her home and possessions to the enemy, Sarah Morgan was proud to record that her family's slaves remained loyal to their status and the Confederacy, even when tempted with freedom. After fleeing her home in Baton Rouge, Sarah was delighted to record the conduct of Aunt Ann Barker's servant, Charles, who "tried his best to defend the [Morgan] property." "'Aint you 'shamed to destroy all dis here, that belongs to a poor widow lady who's got two daughters to support?' he asked of an officer who was foremost in the destruction. 'Poor? Damn them! I dont know when I have seen a house furnished like this! look at that furniture! *they* poor!' was the retort, and thereupon the work went bravely on, of making us poor indeed." Sarah was happy to note that Charles had not watched silently as the troops carried off furniture and other household items, but had "caught a Captain Clark, in the streets, when the work was almost over, and begged him to put an end to it."[25]

Charles Barker not only remained loyal to the Morgan women in the midst of the attack. To Sarah's great relief, he also rejected the freedom offered to him by a passing Yankee soldier. "During the fight, or flight, rather, a fleeing officer stopped to throw a musket in Charles Barker's hands, and bade him fight for his liberty," she wrote. "Charles drew himself up, saying 'I am only a slave, but I am a secesh nigger, and wont fight in such a d—crew!' Exit Yankee, continuing his flight down the river-side." Sarah described the conduct of her family's slaves as "beyond praise." "Five thousand negroes followed their Yankee brothers, from the town and neighborhood, but ours remained," she boasted with pride. In retelling this story, Sarah drew upon Charles's behavior to celebrate her family's honor and gentility. While other slaves had fled to the Yankees, Charles remained loyal to the Morgan women. Under their elite influence, he was able to discern the difference between Southern gentility and a "d—crew." His willing submission, even when tempted with freedom, reaffirmed the true nature of their honor. By publicly denouncing the enemy, Charles had publicly affirmed the Morgan family's honor.[26]

Eliza Lucy Irion also wrote with pride about her family's "faithful" and "obedient" servants, who prayed for Confederate soldiers and the cause. Emily Caroline Douglas commented on her "Mammy's" joy when her brother, Kirtland, arrived home in May 1863. Elizabeth described the emotional scene in her diary where Mammy "fell upon the floor at his feet hugging and kissing him, 'My Massa come, My Massa come.'" "I would be so glad if some of our northern friends could see her!" she added smugly. In occupied New Orleans, Emma Walton even regarded half-hearted loyalty as a symbol of family honor. In a letter to her father, Emma conceded that "Rhody" and another slave would soon leave. Yet "when we consider the influences which surround them," she wrote, "we can but be astonished that they may have remained here so long." Kate Stone declared that overall "the Negroes have behaved well," adding that in "many cases they have been the only mainstay of their owners." In March 1863, she was proud to record the behavior of their servants during a Union raid. "Most of them hid, and the others did not show the slightest disposition to go with them, though the Yankees asked them to go," she wrote. Kate was particularly proud that William had "refused most positively" to go with them, even when the soldiers held a pistol to his head.[27]

The notion of the loyal slave, however, was a weak foundation upon which to build one's honor and identity. Young ladies were well aware that those "loyal" slaves who remained were not always submissive or obedient. Many capitalized on the absence of the master and the repercussions of war to challenge the antebellum structures of power. Some refused to work. Others informed raiding troops on the whereabouts of provisions or shattered the physical boundaries of power by coming and going at will. Each act of defiance chipped away at young women's faith in the "loyal" slave, their antebellum perception of slavery, and their assurance of their place in the elite South. As early as 1861, Clara Solomon commented that their house servant, "Lucy," had become "very impudent, and entirely fearless of Ma." Kate Stone recorded that "barrels of pork" had been taken by slaves and were later found in the cotton fields. Such acts of "disobedience" were not restricted to the field hands. "The house servants have been giving a lot of trouble lately—lazy and disobedient," she wrote in June 1861. "Will have to send one or two to the field and replace them from the quarters if they do not settle down."[28]

Two years later, planter families had lost the ability to swap house servants with field hands. After all but a few slaves had run away, Amanda Worthington commented, "Our servants are very much demoralized by yankee influence." As a result, she and her mother were compelled to do "most of the housework . . . all the time." Sallie McRae remarked that her family's slaves refused to work in the fields, while the servants in Kate Foster's household spent more time in town than performing their duties. Elizabeth Christie Brown was also familiar with "loyal" slaves who remained within the boundaries of the household or plantation but refused to work. Sarah Morgan maintained her belief in the complete loyalty of her family's slaves, but for many other young ladies, the small daily acts that challenged slavery and the authority of the absent master chipped away at this perception. The image of the loyal slave became nothing more than a bandage over a festering wound, temporarily preventing a total reassessment of Southern ideology and self-identity.[29]

INSURRECTION AND BLACK YANKEES

Young ladies' fears about insurrection and black soldiers reveal the extent to which the war had challenged and dismantled the foundations of the Southern hierarchy. In antebellum Mississippi and Louisiana, Southerners had always feared that slaves might one day band together to overthrow the ruling class. A successful insurrection at Santo Domingo, the failed Nat Turner rebellion, and John Brown's stand at Harper's Ferry had placed an innate fear in the hearts of all Southerners. While a student at boarding school, Esther Boyd remembered nights when she and the other girls "would gather in my room" to talk over frightening reports of insurrection.[30]

Secession and war exacerbated these fears, and groups of Confederate women left alone and outnumbered by slaves were constantly plagued by rumors of violence. Not only was Kate Stone terrified by the thought of roaming bands of Negroes, but she also feared the slaves who remained "loyal" to her household. After a nasty quarrel occurred between her aunt Laura's cook, Jane, and the Stones' slave, Aunt Lucy, Kate grew anxious when tense domestic relations erupted in violence. "Jane cut a great gash in Lucy's face with a blow from a chair and hurt her severely. Mamma had Jane called up to interview her on the subject, and she came with a big carving knife in her hand and fire in her eyes." Kate drew on the image of the wild, beastly slave to understand this previously unthinkable incident. "She scared me," she added. "She is nearly six feet tall and powerful in proportion, as black as night and with a fearful temper."[31]

When Jane packed up her children and belongings and left the house that night, Kate expressed the family's relief. "We are all glad she is gone," she sighed. "We would not have been surprised to have her slip up and stick any of us in the back." A year later, Kate reflected upon her family's inability to control their slaves or prevent an insurrection. "We would be practically helpless should the Negroes rise, since there are so few men left at home," she wrote. "It is only because the Negroes do not want to kill us that we are still alive."[32]

Such fears were not limited to planter women in remote parts of Mississippi and Louisiana. In New Orleans, Clara Solomon also worried about the prospect of an insurrection. "Mrs. N. told us that she heard from a reliable source that Butler had opened the prison and allowed all the negroes to be released," she wrote anxiously in May 1862. "It is this fear which alarms me. I fear more from the negroes than Yankees and an insurrection is my continual horror." These fears revealed the underlying crisis in young ladies' perception of slavery and, further, its challenge to the masculinity and honor of Southern men. Both Kate Stone and Clara Solomon believed themselves to be helpless against an uprising. Slave disobedience revealed that masters had less than ultimate control over their dependents. Confederate men were unable to win the war; nor did their authority over their slaves extend from beyond the physical boundaries of the household or plantation. The master's authority and honor was challenged through slave disobedience. It was also challenged indirectly by young ladies, who revealed their fears about slaves and slavery in their diaries.[33]

Perhaps more than anything else, the image of the black Yankee soldier vividly captured the altered state of race relations and the disintegration of the master-slave relationship. Unable to protect their women's honor or purity from black Yankees, Confederate men and their families were subjected to an ultimate "assault on their honor." In Mississippi, Amanda Worthington and Ellen Louise Power were enraged to hear the news that Federal soldiers had armed groups of former slaves in an effort to quash the Southern rebellion. "I think thats horrible," wrote Amanda. "I never had such feelings as I did," commented Ellen after hearing that "400 black Yankee negroes and 100 white Yankees marched in Jackson about dark." Her anger, however, was exacerbated by what she regarded as a challenge to her honor. "To think that we must be ruled by a set of black negroes," she wrote in disgust. In Natchez, Elizabeth Christie Brown was perturbed when she discovered that her family's slaves were among those who "had joined a Co. to fight against their masters." Hereafter, the arrival of Federal troops made her "very much alarmed." After hearing reports that "armed men (I cannot call them Soldiers) of African *descent*" had arrived at their plantation, she was "very much relieved when I found they were Yankees." "Of the two evils I think I would rather have the latter," she conceded.[34]

Kate Stone experienced the wrath of black soldiers firsthand. In her diary, she described the terror that gripped her family as she sat "petrified" in a corner with her "little sister" as a group of "beasts" raiding the plantation forced their way into the house. "One came bursting into our room, a big black wretch, with the most insolent swagger, talking all the time in a most insulting manner," she wrote. Kate described her terror as the soldier "came right up to us standing on the hem of my dress while he looked me slowly over, gesticulating and snapping his pistol." "He stood there about a minute, I suppose," she added. "It seemed to me like an age. I felt like I would die should he touch me. I did not look up or move, and Little Sister was as still as if petrified." While he terrified Kate and her family, other black soldiers "ransacked" the house and sprinkled "a white powder into the cisterns and over everything they left." "We never knew whether it was poison or not," she wrote after the encounter.[35]

Kate's fears of insurrection had been turned into a frightening reality. In wartime Mississippi and Louisiana, the household was no longer a place of safety and refuge. Instead, the arrival of black troops challenged elite white masculinity at its very core. For masters who had used the submission of their slaves to affirm their honor, the violation of their homes by black troops shattered these illusions. Kate Stone admitted "the Yankees know they make it ten times worse for us by sending Negroes to commit these atrocities." Black troops represented an elite Southerner's worst fear: Not only had former slaves transgressed the boundaries of the plantation or household to become "beasts," they had empowered themselves to exert authority over their former owners. No longer a symbol of status or gentility, "black Yankees" were all the more terrifying to young ladies because they were a sign of what defeat might bring with the downfall of the plantation South. With servants, possessions, homes, and family members lost, young ladies in wartime Mississippi and Louisiana could no longer use race as a continuing symbol of their honor and status. Instead, they were left to wonder what "elite womanhood" really meant in a world where every physical symbol of this privileged position had become just another casualty of war.[36]

The Confederate Belle in Defeat, 1865-1870

> January 25, 1868: Pruning, working in the yard and reading.
> February 14, 1868: Putting the cloth in the loom in morn. Planted
> cabbage, lettus, radishes, mustard, onion and English peas in eve.
> February 20, 1868: Spinning all the day.
>
> *Lula Thompson diary*

Lula Thompson had just turned eighteen when General Robert E. Lee surrendered his army at Appomattox Courthouse in April 1865. As a young Confederate woman, she had experienced firsthand the turmoil and anguish that had gripped the South through four long years of war. Living in the small community of Phoenix Mills, Mississippi, Lula had sewed and prayed for Confederate soldiers and had anxiously waited for news of her uncles, who had served in the 6th Georgia Regiment. In 1861 she had been socialized to believe in the Southern feminine ideal. Yet the war had made her a Confederate belle. Instead of parties and visiting, Lula had learned the art of spinning and sewing uniforms. Without slaves, she had been forced to cook, wash, clean, and care for her invalid mother and sister. Her years of struggle and hardship did not end with defeat. In the postwar South, Lula's days were spent washing, ironing, cooking, cleaning, spinning, and gardening. Her diary became a testimony to her new and difficult life. With little time for reflection, Lula used her journal to jot down the weather and list the completion of an array of domestic tasks:

> Feb. 3rd [1868]: Sewing on an old dress. Cloudy.
> 4: Spinning stocking thread. Rain.
> 5: Spinning, making a bonnet and knitting. Cloudy.

6: Finished my bonnet, planting shrubbery and knitting. Cloudy.

7: Washing, carding and knitting.

8: Cooking for Sunday. Knitting.

9: Attend preaching at Liberty C. Cloudy.

10: Spinning warp to weave cloth for pants.

11: Spinning.

12. Spinning, digging grass nuts and spooling thread.

13: Washing scouring and doing divers things.[1]

Lula gained no respite from her household chores, except perhaps on a Sunday afternoon, if she had had the opportunity to prepare the family's dinner on Saturday night. By 1870, she felt overwhelmed by her responsibilities. "I fear I shall not find much to write in my diary this year," she wrote on January 15, 1870. "It seems so dull now, its cold and rainy most all the time, and nothing but work, work from morning till night. Well I've been spinning some stocking thread, and knitting, patching the boys clothes, picked my ducks, . . . and washed the pork and hung it in the smoke house to dry, besides helped to do the cooking. Planted English peas in the garden on the 8th on 11th planted onions, collard and mustard seed." Taking care of her mother, maintaining the household, smokehouse, and vegetable patch, and ensuring that all family members possessed clean yet plain attire did little to restore Lula's self-worth or honor, nor did it provide her with a foundation upon which to build a new, postwar identity. Instead, she knitted, sewed, and baked, all the while lamenting her current predicament and dreading a future filled with "work from morning till night."[2]

"Nothing Is Left but to Endure"

By April 1865, Southern women of all ages had made profound sacrifices for the cause. They had sent their men away in fine uniforms and fine spirits. Those who returned came home in tattered, worn clothing and bare feet, some without arms or legs. Their wounds ran far deeper than the physical scars, and many soldiers were maimed forever by what they had seen and what they had done on the bloody battlefield. Their fields, once filled with bountiful crops of cotton and sugar, had been reduced to a ravaged wasteland. Their slaves, once a source of honor and status, had been freed by the powerful Northern enemy. Their pantries, once stocked with an array of culinary delights, were now bare of even the most basic provisions. Clothed in homespun or secondhand dresses, young ladies could scarcely believe the emotional and physical cost of the war effort.

Kate Stone and her family had paid dearly for their belief in Confederate liberty and freedom. Forced to flee Brokenburn in the wake of advancing Federal troops, the Stones had lost all their slaves, along with crops, furniture, clothing, animals, and provisions. Kate's brother Walter had also sacrificed his life for a lost cause. "Our glorious struggle of the last four years, our hardships, our sacrifices, and worst of all, the torrents of noble blood that have been shed for our loved Country—all, all in vain," Kate cried bitterly. "The best and bravest of the South sacrificed—and for nothing. Yes, worse than nothing. Only to rivet more firmly the chains that bind us. The bitterness of death is in the thought. We could bear the loss of my brave little brothers when we thought that they had fallen at the post of duty defending their Country, but now to know that those glad, bright spirits suffered and toiled in vain, that the end is overwhelming defeat, the thought is unendurable. . . . Truly our punishment is greater than we can bear." Overcome by grief, Kate only wanted to forget. "I cannot bear to think of it all," she wrote, "—forget when I can." Eliza Lucy Irion agreed. "Four years of hard fighting; millions of dollars of treasure lost, and perfect seas of precious blood spilt, all—for what? Subjugation, humiliation and degradation. Three horrid words! And their experience, I fear, will be worse than war!"[3]

In New Orleans, Sarah Morgan dreaded the sight of recently paroled Confederate soldiers, knowing that her brothers, George and Gibbes, would not be among the tired and dejected band of men. "While praying for the return of those who have fought so nobly for us, how I have dreaded their first days at home!" she conceded tearfully. "Since the boys died I have constantly thought of what pain it would bring to see their comrades return without them—to see families reunited, and know that ours never could be again, save in heaven. Last Saturday the 29th of April, seven hundred and fifty paroled Louisianians from Lee's army were brought here—the sole survivors of ten regiments who left four years ago so full of hope and determination. On the 29th of April 1861, George left New Orleans with his regiment. On the fourth anniversary of that day, they came back; but George and Gibbes have long been lying in their graves—George far away in desolated Virginia."[4]

In Natchez, Kate Foster also experienced feelings of heartache and bitterness as she mourned the loss of two brothers and the cause for which they had fought, and died. "Both of my noble brothers sacrificed upon our country's altar as far as I can see for nothing," she wrote in despair. "God grant that I may some day feel they were taken for *some* good." Grief-stricken and alone, Kate conceded that she had "too much heart and am too sensitive" for the "heartless" postwar world. "I *must* overcome such tender feelings or I shall never be able to battle with the life that is before me," she added. In Monroe, Sarah Lois Wadley refused to admit that defeat had reduced the loss of millions of "noble" lives to nothing more than a futile endeavor. Clinging to the tenets of the code of honor, Sarah proclaimed that to fight and die for one's cause was a sacred act, regardless of the outcome. "I cannot regret our course, better die protesting for our liberty than tamely submit." "The bitterness," she added, "is that we might have won."[5]

Young ladies now confronted a defeated world dominated by hardship and necessity. In Mississippi and Louisiana, poverty shaped the existence of all former Confederates. In 1860, Mississippi's true combined estate had been calculated at $607 million. By 1870, the ravages of war and the effects of emancipation saw this total plummet to $209 million. Louisiana's true combined estate had also suffered, going from $602 million in 1860 to $323 million in 1870.[6]

While all Southerners encountered hardship on some level, the nature and extent of this poverty depended largely on a family's wartime experience. Sarah Morgan's family, for example, had lived in an elegant house in Baton Rouge and had owned at least eight slaves who worked as domestic servants. The Federal occupation of the city in early 1862 had led to the abandonment of their home, which fell into a "general state of dilapidation" and was not recovered at the end of the war. In 1866, Sarah and her mother were forced to rely on the financial support of Sarah's stepbrother, Philip Hicky Morgan. The Morgan family's desperate economic plight was in contrast to Clara Solomon's family, who had spent the war in occupied New Orleans. As a result, they entered 1866 with their home and possessions intact. Clara's father, Solomon Solomon, was a merchant and so did not confront the same postwar challenges that faced the Worthington family, whose plantation had been all but destroyed by Northern troops. By 1866, the Worthingtons had lost their wealth (most of which had been tied up in slaves), amassed a sizable wartime debt, and now faced the overwhelming prospect of beginning anew.[7]

While most elite Southerners never experienced the destitution suffered by their poorer neighbors, relief associations were no longer patronized only by the lower class. In New Orleans, the *Daily Picayune* reported that the Relief Association of Louisiana had "noted a change in the character of its applicants." "Many persons who were, not long since, not merely independent, but moving in high circles have applied for assistance," it reported, "which goes to show that the present epidemic of poverty is widespread, and has its ramifications extending into every sphere of life in the city."[8]

Poverty and desperation confronted refugees such as Emma Stroud, who returned to Vicksburg with her daughter to find blackened ruins where her home had once stood. "I cannot describe my emotions when we reached what had once been our home," she wrote. "Tall weeds grew in the yard, and only the fallen brick remained to mark the ruins. Not a home of any kind was to be seen—all had been destroyed." Without timber or any money to purchase building materials, her family, including her adolescent daughter, were forced to pitch a tent, "hoping and trusting in the same God who had so often cared for us." A young Annie Jacobs returned to Doro plantation to discover that her family was also destitute. All that remained were "a few old mahogany or rosewood beds and wardrobes too heavy to move away." "Such desolation!" she cried. "Like Nehemiah when he went back to Jerusalem, everything gone to rack and ruin."[9]

Kate Stone was luckier, and returned to Louisiana to find Brokenburn still standing. "It does not seem the same place," she remarked solemnly. "The bare echoing rooms, the neglect and defacement of all—though the place is in better repair than most—and the stately oaks and the green grass make it look pleasant and cheerful, though gardens, orchards and fences are mostly swept away." The immense task of rebuilding their lives, however, seemed insurmountable when Kate reflected on her family's meager resources. "Our future is appalling," she admitted, "no money, no credit, heavily in debt. . . . No wonder Mamma is so discouraged." With only the "bare necessaries for the table and the plainest clothes for the family," all funds were devoted to cotton crops, which yielded so little money that Amanda Stone could not afford to send her daughter to school. By 1867, Kate's brothers had lost so much money that they resorted to farming, "and having nothing to do pulled off their coats and rolled up their sleeves and went to work to raise a crop of corn and potatoes." To her delight, their venture succeeded, and for the first time in years Kate and her sister were "jubilant at the prospect of new dresses and bonnets."[10]

Kate Stone's postwar existence was common to that of a generation of young women. Up until 1865, Mary Wright had regarded Greenwood plantation—her home in Rapides Parish—as a source of pride and honor. "A simple yet commodious one story and a half frame house, painted white, with large dormer windows in the roof," Greenwood was encircled by "porches or galleries around the four sides of the house." Flanked by a bountiful vegetable patch on one side and a formal garden on the other, the Wright home was a fine example of the status and gentility of Louisiana's planter elite. The Confederate War, however, had turned a pristine tribute to planter society into an insurmountable burden— and one that exacerbated the Wright family's already desperate plight. "We never lived so near out of every thing before, and money never was so scarce," Mary admitted. "We have felt the difference since the negroes were all set free and all the stock driven off or killed. We cannot carry on the place, nor rent it because we have not the capital to make repairs and stock it." Like the Wright family, the Worthingtons had been prominent slave owners in Mississippi. By the end of the war, Amanda noted in her diary that her father was "constantly bothered by persons he owes." "None of us can realize that we are no longer wealthy," she conceded, "yet thanks to the yankees the cause of all unhappiness, such is the case."[11]

Confronting poverty, hardship, and few prospects of a brighter future, young ladies possessed neither the strength nor the courage to look outward to a desolate world turned upside down. Race and politics—which formed the staple of life in the postwar South—received only a rare mention in their diaries and letters. Just as Elizabeth Christie Brown had called for the banishment of all disloyal slaves as a way to remove the constant reminder of her family's loss of power, young ladies tried to shut out a world that had become an all-too-painful reminder of defeat. Considering their circumstances, this was understandable. Early in the war, Sarah Lois Wadley had vowed, "I would rather die than see our armies humiliated by flight, our country ruined by submission." "Victory or death is our only alternative," she added, "worse than death would be our conquest by the Yankees." In 1865 she admitted, "My country has been my great love, my pride, my life," and had to face the harsh reality that the Confederacy had failed in its bid for independence.[12]

While they could shut race and politics out of their diaries, young women could not shut the vast postbellum changes out of their lives. In 1865, the Southern hierarchy was temporarily overthrown. The passage of the Thirteenth and Fourteenth Amendments abolished slavery and granted freedpeople civil rights, including the right to marry, to sue, to purchase and hold property, and for men, the right to vote. These

Amendments were followed quickly by the Reconstruction Acts, which allowed freedmen to stand for public office. For the first time in their history, white Southerners encountered black judges, civic officials, and politicians. Race and class no longer ensured an elite white monopoly on power.[13]

This erosion of power and status extended itself to the plantation and the Big House. Paternalism, which had governed the antebellum relationship between master and slave, was now replaced by capital. Those who could afford to hire free labor often struggled to make the transition from "slave holder" to "employer," and relations between freedpeople and their former masters were often tense, even volatile. As active members of their households and communities, young ladies must have watched or even participated in these postwar relations. Certainly, they would have had strong opinions on this profound challenge to their race and class. Yet only Kate Stone commented briefly on the "trouble" her mother encountered trying to instruct "Negroes in a state of insubordination, insolent and refusing to work."[14]

Just as young women chose to shut out the changed state of race relations from their diaries and letters, many also abandoned any interest in politics. At the same time that President Andrew Johnson pursued an aggressive policy to dismantle the power and authority of the elite South, Amanda Worthington commented that her interest in politics had died with defeat. "I take no interest in any election now . . . for I feel that I have no country," she wrote, "and the affairs of the United States Government will never have power to interest me."[15]

Instead, Amanda turned her half-hearted attention to a local election in which two former Confederate soldiers were campaigning for the office of sheriff and county clerk. "I find I take some interest in this election as all the candidates have been in our dear Confederate army and I know them all," she remarked. "I am bent on Hal Yerger's being Sheriff as he was such a good soldier." Amanda's renewed interest in politics was quashed when her favorite candidates were not elected. "I am so provoked at the result of the election I dont know what to do," she wrote angrily. "My two favorite candidates, Mr Yerger and Mr Carter, were both defeated and by men who have never been soldiers too, and I am perfectly disgusted with the people who voted for those 'stay-at-homes.'" Amanda perceived the election not as a political contest between opposing candidates but as an opportunity for defeated Confederates to affirm their loyalty to the lost cause. Her interest in the affair died as soon as politics won out over patriotism. While abandoning the idea of immediate political retribution, Amanda could not turn her back on the ideals of her lost cause. "The spirit is not subdued though the body is forced to yield," she added defiantly. Sarah Morgan agreed, praying "never to be otherwise than what I am this instant—a Rebel in heart and soul."[16]

Bowed down by grief and unprecedented hardship, Kate Stone believed that "nothing is left but to endure." While the Confederacy had fought Lincoln's Republican politics, Kate and the other members of the elite South had no alternative but to submit to "the detested" President Johnson in 1865. After a long, bloody war, the bitterness of defeat and the humiliation of Reconstruction politics, Kate regarded endurance as the only honorable alternative.[17]

Without their Confederate nation, young women struggled to define their place in this bleak world without wealth or slaves. Lacking homes, possessions, finery, or men for courting, young women also felt that they had been stripped of their status, which in the Deep South had always rested on wealth rather than family lineage. Young ladies were unable to resume their genteel life as elegant Southern belles. Defeat had also rendered the ideal of patriotic womanhood equally useless. Sacrifice and struggle were no longer made in the name of the cause; in postwar Mississippi and Louisiana, they were made in the name of survival.

"To Come Down to the Level of a Servant"

In April 1865, Confederate defeat transformed patriotic housekeepers into postwar servants. In wartime, and under the banner of patriotism, young ladies had sewed for the soldiers and taken on an expanded role in the household. In the wake of defeat, poverty and necessity required them to continue this domestic role. Mistresses across the South legitimized their postbellum plight by fashioning an ideal of domesticity and using it as a mechanism through which to assert their status. By attending to the needs of their husbands and children, "putting well prepared meals on the table, banishing dirt and dust, selecting tasteful interior decorations and maintaining a cheerful, supportive atmosphere," Southern ladies were able to reconstruct their identities as "worthy women." They used this framework to distinguish themselves from African-American and poor white women, whose economic status prevented them from attaining the exalted domestic ideal.[18]

Confederate belles could have embraced this ideal, but they did not.

After sacrificing their long-anticipated "coming out" for the cause, most young ladies did not have the heart—or the inclination—to suffer an endless round of domestic chores in silence and submission. Many grew disillusioned and frustrated. To sacrifice for the cause was one thing. To be forced into a permanent and difficult domestic role because of poverty was another. Young women who had taken on additional responsibilities during the war grew increasingly frustrated at the gulf between their antebellum lives as privileged belles and their postwar lives as "servants."

In defeated Natchez, Kate Foster was so absorbed in her domestic routine that she was forced to abandon her beloved pastime of "journalizing." "My time is so occupied," she explained, "that a few moments cannot be allowed to write in my diary." Besieged by an array of monotonous household chores, Kate mourned the loss of her leisure time and her elite status. "I hope I may work more willingly but it is so hard to come down to a level with a servant," she admitted. Mary Wright was also familiar with a busy domestic schedule. At times, she felt overwhelmed by her responsibilities. "We are without a driver, gardener, cook and house servants," she cried in January 1866, "if we go without much longer—I shall give up housekeeping in despair."[19]

Other young women resigned themselves to this permanent yet arduous role. Sarah Lois Wadley set aside Saturdays to attend to the housework and also "turned over and dusted beds," packed trunks, washed dishes, and completed other chores. By late 1865, she accepted this as the norm. "Our servants have all left us and we have now only one hired woman and one little girl," she remarked. "We have all the housework to do but we are now so accustomed to this that it does not trouble us much." Kate Stone and her friends also adapted to the rigors of domestic life. Like countless other young ladies, she too kept her days busy by housekeeping and "scrubbing" rooms to make them inhabitable.[20]

Eliza Lucy Irion was one of the few young ladies who still took pride in her domestic accomplishments. "Well in earnest I am astonished at my own self," she declared. "I never imagined I should feel real pleasure in housekeeping, but, wonderful to relate, I do. I have never been late for breakfast since I assumed the responsibility of the coffee pot." "Keeping house is so much easier to me now that I have fully made up my mind to do it with all my might," she added. "Things which used to be so dreadfully hard are now done with resolution and decision." Despite the presence of a number of house servants, Eliza exhibited a willingness to extend these duties whenever necessary. "As soon as I get up courage enough I am going among the horny occupants and learn to milk," she resolved. Eliza also did the washing, tied up clothes to dry, made winter clothes, and participated in the less-than-genteel task of hog killing. "Oh! hog killing was such a brand new experience," she remarked in December 1867, "but I now know every item. Why I believe I could dissect a hog with as much ease as Aunt Hayden ever could." Eliza's attitude toward housekeeping was the exception, not the rule. For most young ladies in Mississippi and Louisiana, the postwar reality was hard to bear. They had sacrificed for the cause. But defeat, poverty, and necessity had turned a "temporary" wartime role into a painful reminder of the lifestyle and comforts they had lost.[21]

Young ladies' frustration over domestic chores paled in comparison to their revulsion for paid employment. During the war, many Confederate belles had entertained the possibility that reduced circumstances might propel them into the workforce. In defeated Mississippi and Louisiana, however, young ladies were presented with few employment opportunities. In a desperate attempt to supplement the family income, women often baked or took in sewing.[22] For elite young ladies, the despised life of a governess loomed before them as the only respectable form of employment, a life that Sarah Morgan and many other young women described as "a hopeless, thankless task." "I think of all the nameless, numberless, insults and trials she is forced to submit to," wrote Sarah, "and I cry, Heaven help a governess! my heart bleeds for them."[23]

Unlike many Confederate belles, Lula Thompson recovered her sense of self-worth and honor though teaching. Amid days of spinning, cleaning, sewing, and working in the vegetable patch, Lula established a home school, where she devoted her spare time to instructing her siblings, Woodard and Elie. Much to her surprise, she met with immediate success. "Washing and scouring some but don't neglect my school," Lula remarked in February 1869. "We study so many hours every day, even if we have to borrow a little from the night." "My studies embrace reading, writing and spelling, also arithmetic, geography, grammar and philosophy," she added the next day. "We review every friday what we have learned during the week. Are making better progress than we ever did at a regular school."

Lula's efforts soon became a point of discussion among neighbors and friends, and after some hesitation, Lula finally consented to expand her school to include the other children of Phoenix Mills, Mississippi. "At the request of several of our neighbors, but against my own will, I commenced teaching school at Liberty Chapel on Monday morning. It being a cold rainy day had but few scholars, but they keep coming in," she wrote. "Feel the responsibility of the position and hope that by closely observing my duties to win the confidence and respect of both scholars and patrons." Lula's day was filled with teaching, lessons, and examinations—in addition to her already onerous schedule at home—but she reveled in her new achievements and restored her honor by earning the admiration and respect of scholars and parents. "The children and I have become very much attached to each other," Lula remarked with delight. "One little boy cried the first day because he had to come to school, and now he cries if he has to stay away." While the drudgery of the domestic landscape had weighed down Lula's spirits, her teaching—and the "splendid" progress of her students—became a cause for rejoicing and a foundation upon which to build a new, postwar identity.[24]

Lula Thompson was the exception, not the rule. For most, teaching was rendered intolerable by the long hours, willful children, and the threat of downward social mobility that had long been associated with gainful employment in the South. In Natchez, Kate Foster was reluctant to undertake teaching, even when she was confronted with financial hardship. While Aunt Jenny was always "worrying herself about future finances," Kate felt there was no way that she could alleviate the family's postwar burden. "I wish that I was able to help her," she wrote in November 1865, but concluded that she was "not able to teach." "The confinements of a school room would soon kill me," she added. The prospect of teaching was rendered even less attractive to Kate as she watched her sister struggle to adapt to a lifestyle that was so antithetical to the belle ideal. "Sis Lizzie whose head and heart were made for something else has to drag her life away teaching," she wrote in disgust, "and who thanks her for it."[25]

Some young ladies were unable to sustain their positions, even in the face of financial hardship. Ann Lewis Hardeman's nieces, Adelaide and Bettie, were forced out of economic necessity to utilize the genteel education they had obtained at Saint Mary's school in Burlington, New Jersey. Adelaide successfully took charge of five pupils, but her sister, Bettie, found the task intolerable. In the end, she was "excused . . . from practical duties." Although Adelaide maintained her position, Ann secretly feared that teaching was "not suitable" for either of her beloved girls, who had been raised for a life of gentility, not the thankless life of a governess. "O how much I do desire that they may be relieved from teaching as I fear it does not suit them," she recorded in her diary, finally resigning their fate to the will of "our Heavenly Father." For Bettie, the life of a governess was so alien to all she had known; the sacrifice was too great. Even defeat and poverty could not force some young ladies into a life that revoked every fiber of their status and gentility.[26]

POSTWAR BELLES

Instead of resigning themselves to a new existence without wealth or slaves, the young women of Mississippi and Louisiana clung to every last vestige of their pre-war lives as belles. After completing her household chores, Kate Stone regularly "made [her] afternoon toilet," even though she regarded it as a fruitless endeavor. "[It is] a habit of old that I may as well forget now that evening visiting is a thing of the past," she concluded. Mary Wright managed to make time for "reading" in a day full of housework, while Kate Foster set aside what spare time she had for educational pursuits. In Washington County, Amanda Worthington played the piano in between washing corsets and mending her father's shirts. On other days she devoted time to visiting after completing her chores. Such modest assertions of gentility helped to remind young ladies of who they were and, in a powerful way, affirmed their sense of self in a world where most representations of elite culture had been lost with the devastation of war.[27]

Still, a pretty dress or a good book did little to mask the painful reality of postbellum life. For most Confederate belles, the pleasures of youth were gone, never to return. While Amanda Worthington continued to read and visit, she struggled with her passage into womanhood and an existence that scarcely resembled her intended life as a belle. In October 1865, she grew anxious that her "youth [was] vanishing," even though she did not consider herself a "fully grown young lady." Unable to dress in fashionable attire and without the social occasions that provided the opportunity for courting, Amanda admitted that her "manners [were] not at all matured"—nor was her recognized feminine status. Instead of indulging in the delights of bellehood, she had to be content with building "'castles in the air'—about things that I know never can and never will take place."[28]

Kate Foster also found it difficult to reconcile her antebellum dreams and desires with her difficult postwar existence. "When I retire to my room thoughts of what has been and what might have been are almost too much for my calmness and I nearly give way to the tears which fill my eyes." Like Amanda, Kate found some solace in her dreams, or what she described as her "drama of 'Bygones.'" "The future looks in my 'castles in Spain' like it would be one long long rest of happiness secure in the love of some *chosen one* to whom I shall look for protection and guidance in the vicissitudes of this life." "It may be this will turn out *all* a dream," she admitted, "but pleasant it is thus to while an hour or two away." Sarah Lois Wadley's dreams only made her miserable. "[I] woke this morning very sorrowful," she wrote tearfully in November 1865, "woke to find that my vivid dreams were only dreams of the past which can never return."[29]

Other young ladies were so weighed down by grief that they were unable or unwilling to assume the façade of carefree young womanhood. Sarah Morgan admitted that her life was "sad and dreary." "Within and without, it is unutterably gloomy," she wrote, wondering how she would find the strength to bear her miserable, lonely life. Still grieving the death of her brother, Amanda Worthington remarked that "life itself seems a disappointment and there seems to be nothing on earth to look forward to." Mary Wright also hated her bleak postbellum existence. "I am so tired, so tired of this way of living," she sighed. "The world presents no happiness to me compared to the joys of Heaven. When I am prepared, I want to die soon." Kate Foster agreed. "If I could only die and be with my darling brothers," she sobbed. At Brokenburn, Kate Stone experienced similar bouts of depression and was unwilling to participate in the "visiting and various picnics and fish frys" after the war. "I felt like I did not want to see anybody or ever dance again," she wrote. In Monroe County, Mississippi, Anna Shaw also refrained from participating in rare social occasions. She refused to attend a Christmas party in 1866 and was enraged when her visiting cousins disregarded her family's "respect for the dead" and "danced in spite of all creation."[30]

A WOMAN ALONE

Depression, grief, and anxiety reached a crisis point when young ladies contemplated their limited prospects of marriage. Many potential suitors had died on the battlefield. Others returned home maimed in body or spirit. From this band of poor, dejected, sometimes dependent soldiers, young ladies often searched in vain for a suitable husband while "subjected to the same pressure to marry" from family and friends.[31]

In November 1865, Kate Foster grew increasingly worried about the prospect of spinsterhood. "My old friends are all leaving me behind in the lottery 'marriage,'" she wrote anxiously. "I must hurry to find *some one* on whom to lavish my wealth of love and tenderness. . . . I know I would make a faithful, obedient wife, loving with *all* my heart, yielding entire trust in my husband and his acts. But I am getting sentimental in this age of frivolity and heartlessness. I must curb all such sentiments or be called a fool." By 1871, Kate lamented the loss of her youth and resigned herself to a single, melancholy existence. "An old maid's life and one of struggle presents no allurements to a woman who feels that a woman's life is incomplete without Man's sustaining influence, each needing the other to create that soul music which is the result of a happy union," she wrote. "A woman alone, in this cold world, how sad it is—no eye in which to see the reflection of her own love."[32]

She was not alone. When Mary Wright's sister, Esther, announced her engagement to David F. Boyd, Mary felt as if her sister was "to be buried instead of married." Mourning the loss of the one "who is all the world to me," Mary also regarded the event as a sign that she would spend the rest of her life single and alone. "I was never born to see a happy life, but I am so long in feeling resigned to it," she cried. "Home will never seem like home when she is gone. No one will come to see us—young people, I mean. They never come to see me because I am not lively like Ettie, and cannot play or sing. I cannot bear to look at my life as it will hence forth. . . . I can see no green spot in it for me."[33]

Like Mary Wright, Katherine McGehee Burrus and Florence Louisa Burrus of Egypt Ridge, Mississippi, were young ladies in 1861. Both had watched their suitors go off to war to defend the South. Neither of the men returned, and Katherine and Florence never married. Kate Stone took what she described as a "dreadful risk" and wed Henry Bry Holmes at Walton Bend plantation on December 8, 1869. At Wayside plantation, the Worthington family's postwar burden was lightened considerably by the delightful double wedding of Amanda and her sister, Mamie. In contrast, Sarah Morgan moved to South Carolina, where she was forced to support herself as a writer for the *Charleston News and Courier*. At thirty-one years of age, she married her editor, Captain Francis Warrington Dawson, and retreated to the domestic sphere to become a consummate wife and mother. Sarah Lois Wadley and Mary Wright never married. In antebellum times, single women had often been regarded as social failures. In postwar Mississippi and Louisiana, an increasing number of women confronted the prospect of a single life. They did not perceive this reality as a reason to reconstruct the Southern feminine ideal.

Instead they lamented their existence and used their diaries to recall the glorious past.[34]

For other elite families, marriage was used as a tool for concentrating wealth and facilitating economic gain. While young ladies had always been encouraged to make a good social and economic match, the financial benefits of matrimony assumed even greater importance in postwar Mississippi and Louisiana. In 1866, Anna Shaw confided in her aunt that "Pa is very anxious for some of us to marry but woe is me." "I do not think I shall ever marry indeed I am quite certain I shall not," she added. "I am not one of those who marry for wealth or position. I have heard it said that very few people marry those they love best and I believe it is quite true." Anna remained adamant that if she did not "marry the one I love best I shall never marry at all." While Clara Solomon had spent 1862 dreaming of romantic flirtations and dashing gentlemen, her nuptials to her father's business partner—a man twenty years her senior—indicate that in the difficult postwar environment, money and the quest for survival often won out over love.[35]

For young ladies, survival in a defeated, war-ravaged land posed a new set of struggles and hardships. During the war, sacrifices had been made for the good of the cause, and endurance had become a patriotic badge of honor. In defeat, the harsh reality that they had sacrificed all for nothing evoked feelings of bitterness, sorrow, and bewilderment in the young ladies of Mississippi and Louisiana. They mourned the loss of the Confederate nation. They also mourned the loss of their lives as belles of the American South.

Still, by focusing on all they had lost, young women were yet to realize what they had, in fact, gained by coming of age during the Civil War. Hardships and runaway slaves had forced them to become true "mothers of invention" who could manage households without relying on an unlimited budget or a bevy of servants to complete the work. The skills they had acquired sewing for the soldiers—not to mention patching and remodeling their own attire—proved invaluable to the frugal postwar family trying to "keep up appearances." And their commitment to education provided belles with a means of self-support while also affirming their role as the true intellectual guardians of a lost culture and a lost cause.

But perhaps the most important gift that belles had given themselves was the ability to maintain a belief in their self-worth by adapting the principles of Southern honor to the ever-changing contingencies of war. In 1865, their belief in their own elitism was battered, but not broken. Their slaves may have gone, their homes and possessions lost, but young ladies could still assure themselves that something set them apart—and above—others, irrespective of the law or their immediate conditions. This powerful sense of self-worth had provided Confederate belles with a compass to negotiate their way through a difficult wartime world and would ultimately aid them in their quest to resurrect the tenets of their old life in the New South.

Notes

ABBREVIATIONS

DSU	Charles W. Capps Jr. Archives and Museum Building, Delta State University, Cleveland, Mississippi
DUKE	Rare Book, Manuscript, and Special Collections Library, Duke University, Durham, North Carolina
LSU	Louisiana and Lower Mississippi Valley Collections, Hill Memorial Library, Louisiana State University, Baton Rouge, Louisiana
MC	Eleanor S. Brockenbrough Library, Museum of the Confederacy, Richmond, Virginia
MDAH	Mississippi Department of Archives and History, Jackson, Mississippi
MSU	Mitchell Memorial Library, Mississippi State University, Mississippi State, Mississippi
TSL	Tennessee State Library and Archives, Nashville, Tennessee
TU	Howard-Tilton Memorial Library, Tulane University, New Orleans, Louisiana
UM	John Davis Williams Library, University of Mississippi, University, Mississippi
UNC	Southern Historical Collection, University of North Carolina Library, Chapel Hill, North Carolina
USM	William D. McCain Library and Archives, University of Southern Mississippi, Hattiesburg, Mississippi
WRC	Williams Research Center, New Orleans, Louisiana

INTRODUCTION

1. For a description of Scarlett see Margaret Mitchell, *Gone with the Wind*, 1. For critiques of Mitchell's book see Elizabeth Fox-Genovese, "Scarlett O'Hara: The Southern Lady as New Woman"; Drew Gilpin Faust et al., "Coming to Terms with Scarlett: A Southern Cultures Forum." On the Southern belle in literature see Kathryn Lee Siedel, *The Southern Belle in the American Novel*; Elizabeth Morrow Nix, "An Exuberant Flow of Spirits: Antebellum Adolescent Girls in the Writing of Southern Women."

2. These historians deconstructed the image of the Southern lady and argue that the mistress was integral to the successful operation of the plantation. See Anne Firor

Scott, *The Southern Lady: From Pedestal to Politics, 1830-1930;* Catherine Clinton, *The Plantation Mistress: Women's World in the Old South;* Elizabeth Fox-Genovese, *Within the Plantation Household: Black and White Women in the Old South;* Marli F. Weiner, *Mistresses and Slaves: Plantation Women in South Carolina, 1830-1880.*

3. For earlier interpretations that regard the Civil War as a watershed for women see Scott, *The Southern Lady;* Francis Butler Simkins and James Welch Patton, *The Women of the Confederacy;* Mary Elizabeth Massey, *Bonnet Brigades.* For more recent interpretations see George C. Rable, *Civil Wars: Women and the Crisis of Southern Nationalism;* Drew Gilpin Faust, *Mothers of Invention: Women of the Slaveholding South in the American Civil War;* Lee Ann Whites, *The Civil War as a Crisis in Gender: Augusta, Georgia, 1860-1890;* Laura F. Edwards, *Scarlett Doesn't Live Here Anymore: Southern Women in the Civil War Era.* For a more general examination of the survival of the planter class and the resurrection of their social values see Michael Wayne, *The Reshaping of Plantation Society: The Natchez District, 1860-1880;* Laura F. Edwards, *Gendered Strife and Confusion: The Political Culture of Reconstruction.*

4. For definitions of honor see Edward L. Ayers, "Honor," 1483-84; Bertram Wyatt-Brown, *Southern Honor: Ethics and Behavior in the Old South,* 14; Bertram Wyatt-Brown, *The Shaping of Southern Culture: Honor, Grace, and War, 1760s–1880s,* 56-57; Julian Pitt-Rivers, "Honour," 6:503-10. This type of honor was not exclusive to the American South. Julian Pitt-Rivers argues that these criteria also defined honor in Spain. See "Honour and Social Status," 21-22. On honor in the antebellum South (general) see Wyatt-Brown, *Southern Honor;* Rollin G. Osterweis, *Romanticism and Nationalism in the Old South;* Kenneth S. Greenberg, *Honor and Slavery: Lies, Duels, Noses, Masks, Dressing as a Woman, Gifts, Strangers, Humanitarianism, Death, Slave Rebellions, the Proslavery Argument, Baseball, Hunting, and Gambling in the Old South;* Edward L. Ayers, *Vengeance and Justice: Crime and Punishment in the 19th-Century American South;* Christopher J. Olsen, *Political Culture of Secession in Mississippi: Masculinity, Honor, and the Antiparty Tradition, 1830-1860.* Many historians argue that Southern honor was embraced by all classes and was firmly entrenched in the family unit, the community, and the political spheres of the South. See Wyatt-Brown, *Southern Honor,* xv; Ayers, "Honor," 1483; Orville Vernon Burton, *In My Father's House Are Many Mansions: Family and Community in Edgefield, South Carolina,* 47.

5. For an examination of male youth and their socialization in honor see Wyatt-Brown, *Southern Honor,* 149-74. On dueling see Steven M. Stowe, *Intimacy and Power in the Old South: Ritual in the Lives of the Planters,* 5-49; Wyatt-Brown, *Southern Honor,* 350-61; Kenneth S. Greenberg, *Masters and Statesmen: The Political Culture of American Slavery,* 23-41; Burton, *In My Father's House,* 90-95. Perhaps dueling emerged as the cornerstone of Southern honor because of the plantation economy: Slavery ensured that business and politics were inextricably linked to the household. In her study of honor in Germany, Ute Frevert argues that the growing distinction between personal and professional honor diminished the utilization of the duel as the only means of dispute resolution. If a doctor or lawyer "attempted to eliminate a rival by unfair means" he was brought before a "disciplinary court." In the American South, the plantation economy ensured that professional honor was linked to personal and familial honor. This connection helped strengthen the use of the duel as a mechanism for regulating social behavior. See Ute Frevert, *Men of Honour: A Social and Cultural History of the Duel,* 142.

6. Ayers, *Vengeance and Justice,* 13-14.

7. Wyatt-Brown, *Southern Honor,* 227.

8. On women's honor as passive or nonexistent see Ayers, *Vengeance and Justice,* 13; Ayers, "Honor," 1483; Brenda E. Stevenson, *Life in Black and White: Family and Community in the Slave South,* 152; Catherine Clinton, "'Southern Dishonor': Flesh, Blood, Race, and Bondage," 282 n 17. Sarah Morgan noted the presence of female honor by commenting on her sister's honor. See Sarah Morgan, *Sarah Morgan: The Civil War Diary of a Southern Woman,* 362. See also Eliza Lucy Irion-Neilson diary, June 17, 1865, Irion-Neilson Family Papers, MDAH, book 5.

9. Most academic studies on Southern honor place great emphasis on Southern men. See, for example, Wyatt-Brown, *Southern Honor;* Wyatt-Brown, *The Shaping of Southern Culture;* Ayers, *Vengeance and Justice;* Greenberg, *Masters and Statesmen;* Olsen, *Political Culture of Secession.*

10. While I have defined *planter ideology* as the linkage of elite ideas about race, class, and gender, this ideology did not dominate the cultural life of just the planters: It also formed the basis of urban upper-middle-class and upper-class life. See Clement Eaton, *The Growth of Southern Civilization, 1790-1860,* 98. Planter ideology embodied many contradictions. It required an uneasy dose of paternalism and patriarchy, elitism and egalitarianism. The elite white male, as head of household, was required to work his way through these contradictions, to strike a balance that reinforced his status and the status of his dependents and social inferiors.

11. See Mary Ann Sternberg, *Along the River Road: Past and Present on Louisiana's Historic Byway.*

12. Douglas C. North, *The Economic Growth of the United States, 1790-1860,* 130. For an understanding of western migration see James Oakes, *The Ruling Race: A History of American Slaveholders;* Joan E. Cashin, *A Family Venture: Men and Women on the Southern Frontier;* James David Miller, "South by Southwest: Planter Emigration and Elite Ideology in the Deep South, 1815-1861."

13. Charles L. Dufour, *Ten Flags in the Wind: The Story of Louisiana,* 156; Charles S. Sydnor, *Slavery in Mississippi,* 187-88. For an examination of slavery in Mississippi see Sydnor, *Slavery in Mississippi.* For an examination of slavery in Louisiana see V. Alton Moody, *Slavery on Louisiana Sugar Plantations;* Ann Patton Malone, *Sweet Chariot: Slave Family and Household Structure in Nineteenth-Century Louisiana;* Roderick A. McDonald, *The Economy and Material Culture of Slaves: Goods and Chattels on the Sugar Plantations of Jamaica and Louisiana.*

14. Erik F. Haites, James Mak, and Gary M. Walton, *Western River Transportation: The Era of Early Internal Development, 1810-1860;* John Hebron Moore, *The Emergence of the Cotton Kingdom in the Old Southwest: Mississippi, 1770-1860,* 156-64.

15. Cashin, *A Family Venture,* 97; Moore, *Emergence of the Cotton Kingdom,* 116.

16. The Federal Census for 1860 recorded the white population of Louisiana at 357,456, with 22,033 slaveholders and 70,994 slaveholding families. In Mississippi, the white population was listed at 353,899, with 30,943 slaveholders and 62,882 slaveholding families. For the purposes of this study, it is assumed that a slaveholder is the head of a family. In 1860, the total number of slaveholders with 20 slaves or more was 5,895 in Mississippi and 3,923 in Louisiana. Statistics taken from the federal Census for 1860, *United States Historical Census Data Browser* (http://fisher.lib.virginia.edu/census/). Many historians also note the problems with defining the planter class as those who owned 20 slaves or more. See Mary Johnston-Miller, "Heirs to Paternalism: Elite Women and Their Servants in Alabama and Georgia, 1861-1874," 4; Edwards, *Scarlett Doesn't Live Here Anymore,* 16.

17. In this way, I follow Edwards's framework of analysis. See *Scarlett Doesn't Live Here Anymore*, 7.

18. Arthur M. Ponsonby, *English Diaries: A Review of English Diaries from the Sixteenth to the Twentieth Century with an Introduction on Diary Writing*, 2-3.

19. For an overview of the theoretical literature on diaries, letters, and memoirs see Cinthia Gannett, *Gender and the Journal: Diaries and Academic Discourse;* Jane H. Hunter, "Inscribing the Self in the Heart of the Family: Diaries and Girlhood in Late-Victorian America"; Margo Culley, ed., *A Day at a Time: The Diary Literature of American Women from 1764 to the Present;* Suzanne L. Bunkers and Cynthia A. Huff, eds., *Inscribing the Daily: Critical Essays on Women's Diaries;* Amy L. Wink, *She Left Nothing in Particular: The Autobiographical Legacy of Nineteenth-Century Women's Diaries.* Sarah Elizabeth Gardner notes the particular issues surrounding Southern women's memoirs. See "Blood and Irony: Southern Women's Narratives of the Civil War, 1861-1915." On the silences in women's diaries see Nell Irvin Painter, *Southern History across the Color Line*, 40-92.

CHAPTER ONE

"When I Am Grown": The Southern Belle in Mississippi and Louisiana

1. Lemuella Brickell diary, January 7, 1859, Edward Fontaine Papers, MSU.

2. Mother to Mary Bertron, February 13, 1851, in Mary Bertron Hughes Letters, MDAH. See also Annie E. Jacobs, "The Master of Doro Plantation: An Epic of the Old South," manuscript in Annie E. Clark Jacobs Papers, MDAH, 23; Leonora Bisland diary, essay entitled "Youth," April 9, 1857, Bisland-Shields Family Papers, MDAH; Brickell diary, January 7, February 10, March 6, 1859, Edward Fontaine Papers, MSU. See also Christie Ann Farnham, *The Education of the Southern Belle: Higher Education and Student Socialization in the Antebellum South*, 174-75; Stevenson, *Life in Black and White*, 41.

3. Brickell diary, March 30, 1861, Edward Fontaine Papers, MSU; Clara Solomon, *The Civil War Diary of Clara Solomon: Growing Up in New Orleans, 1861-1862*, 130. See also Maria Dyer Davies diary, September 25, 1855, DUKE.

4. Clinton, *The Plantation Mistress*, 85. Lee Virginia Chambers-Schiller's study of northeastern spinsters uncovers a different perception of single women in the North. See *Liberty, A Better Husband: Single Women in America: The Generations of 1780-1840.*

5. Michael O'Brien, ed., *An Evening when Alone: Four Journals of Single Women in the South, 1827-67*, 18. On the position of single women in the South see Scott, *The Southern Lady*, 35-36; Stevenson, *Life in Black and White*, 55, 324; Wyatt-Brown, *Southern Honor*, 238-39; Victoria E. Bynum, *Unruly Women: The Politics of Social and Sexual Control in the Old South*, 44-45. Suzanne Lebsock provides a different perspective. Examining single and widowed women's access to the law, she concludes that the women of Petersburg "became increasingly active in exercising these [legal] options." She contends that their choices were often different from men's, indicating the presence of a "distinct female value system" with personalism at its core. See *The Free Women of Petersburg: Status and Culture in a Southern Town, 1784-1860*, 112-33. See also Joyce Linda Broussard, "Female Solitaires: Women Alone on the Lifeworld of Mid-Century Natchez, Mississippi, 1850-1880."

6. O'Brien, ed., *An Evening when Alone*, 109-10, 135, 145. See also Virginia Owen to "Molly," October 26, 1853, in Effie Robinson Drane Papers, MSU.

7. Caroline Seabury, *The Diary of Caroline Seabury, 1854-1863*, 28, 46.

8. See Jane Turner Censer, *North Carolina Planters and Their Children, 1800-1860*, 65-67, 72; Stevenson, *Life in Black and White*, 45-47; Wyatt-Brown, *Southern Honor*, 199; Fox-Genovese, *Within the Plantation Household*, 207; Stowe, *Intimacy and Power in the Old South*, 84.

9. Morgan, *Civil War Diary*, 60-63.

10. Brickell diary, May 4, January 22, 1859, Edward Fontaine Papers, MSU; Sophie Collins to Mollie Collins, April 11, 1858, October 21, 1859, in Emmett Lloyd Ross Papers, MSU.

11. Morgan, *Civil War Diary*, 60, 62. See also Edwards, *Scarlett Doesn't Live Here Anymore*, 15.

12. Cashin, *A Family Venture*, 15; Joan E. Cashin, ed., *Our Common Affairs: Texts from Women in the Old South*, 10; Joan E. Cashin, "Into the Trackless Wilderness: The Refugee Experience in the Civil War," 32; Burton, *In My Father's House*, 128; Faust, *Mothers of Invention*, 6.

13. "The Women of a Nation," *Godey's Lady's Book*, December 1862, 566. See also Deborah Gorham, *The Victorian Girl and the Feminine Ideal*, 38-47; Lebsock, *The Free Women of Petersburg*, 51; Lori D. Ginzberg, *Women and the Work of Benevolence: Morality, Politics, and Class in the Nineteenth-Century United States*, 12; Barbara J. Berg, *The Remembered Gate: Origins of American Feminism: The Woman and the City, 1800-1860*, 68. Marli Weiner argues that ideas about the moral superiority of women were rooted in the separation of spheres, which developed as a result of the industrialization of the Northern middle class. She argues that this ideology was still accepted in the rural South because of the cultural domination of the North and because the ideology was also supported by biological arguments. See *Mistresses and Slaves*, 55-56. Stevenson argues that Southern women's moral superiority (together with the ideal image of Southern manhood) served as counterimages to the abolitionist image of the corrupt "slaveocracy." See *Life in Black and White*, 41.

14. "Evenings at Home," scrapbook, Annie Jeter Carmouche Papers, TU. Marli Weiner argues that Southern writers infused domestic ideology with ideas about race as well as gender, charging that slavery "kept women from menial duties" and the "debasing influences" that may result in the "rash equality" of mistress and servant. Weiner argues that the "presence of slaves added a racial dimension to justifications for white women's proper place," and thus heavily influenced their role on the plantation and their role in Southern society. See *Mistresses and Slaves*, 60-62, 71. See also Stevenson, *Life in Black and White*, 42; Fox-Genovese, *Within the Plantation Household*, 197-98.

15. For the role of Southern women in the church see Anne M. Boylan, "Evangelical Womanhood in the Nineteenth Century: The Role of Women in Sunday Schools"; Lebsock, *The Free Women of Petersburg*, 215-16; Jean E. Friedman, *The Enclosed Garden: Women and Community in the Evangelical South, 1830-1900*; Edwards, *Scarlett Doesn't Live Here Anymore*, 19; Stevenson, *Life in Black and White*, 120-22.

16. Davies Diary, April 25, August 28, 1853, DUKE. See also November 27, 1850, February 11, 1851, October 13, 15, 1853, December 16, 1854. See also Eliza L. Magruder Diary, July 14, September 4, 1856, LSU; Brickell diary, January 6, 21,

December 19, 1859, January 2, 1860, Edward Fontaine Papers, MSU.

17. Davies Diary, November 24, 1850, April 17, 1853, November 8, 25, 1854, DUKE.

18. Clinton, *The Plantation Mistress*, 124; Censer, *North Carolina Planters*, 42-64. For analysis of the idea that women should be educated to be more companionable see Gorham, *The Victorian Girl*, 104-5.

19. Trey Berry, "A History of Women's Higher Education in Mississippi, 1819-1882"; Julia Huston Nguyen, "The Value of Learning: Education and Class in Antebellum Natchez"; Stowe, *Intimacy and Power in the Old South*, 133.

20. Eudora Hobbs, school records, 1857-1858, B. T. Hobbs Papers, MSU; Laura Hyde Moss Journal, July 31, September 1, 1851, July 5, 1852, WRC. See also Ellen Howe to Julia and Chiliab Howe, February 14, 1854, in Chiliab Smith Howe Papers, UNC; Bisland diary, Bisland-Shields Family Papers, MDAH; Cornelia Thornton to Aunt, June 18, 1852, in Randolph and Yates Family Papers, UNC; Sophie Collins to Mary Collins, August 13, 1854, in Emmett Lloyd Ross Papers, MSU. Emma Shannon and Eudora Hobbs were also supplied with additional reading material by their parents. See Emma Shannon to Levina Morris Shannon, November 6, 1857, in Crutcher-Shannon Family Papers, MDAH; Howell Hobbs to Eudora Hobbs, November 17, December 23, 1860, in B. T. Hobbs Papers, MSU. See also Clifford C. Norse, "School Life of Amanda Worthington of Washington County, 1857-1862"; Rable, *Civil Wars*, 21.

21. Bisland diary, Bisland-Shields Family Papers, MDAH. See also Mary Beth Norton, *Liberty's Daughters: The Revolutionary Experience of American Women, 1750-1800*, 256-94; Linda K. Kerber, *Women of the Republic: Intellect and Ideology in Revolutionary America*, 189-231; Sally G. McMillen, *Southern Women: Black and White in the Old South*, 78, 83; Farnham, *The Education of the Southern Belle*, 16, 128-29; Censer, *North Carolina Planters*, 44-47. Anya Jabour has examined the education of the Wirt daughters in the first three decades of the nineteenth century. She argues that William and Elizabeth Wirt developed an educational program for their six daughters that meshed a formal classical curriculum with an "informal curriculum" based upon "domesticity, piety and charity." In this way, the Wirts and other Southern families developed a "template" of female education in the early nineteenth century that would be widely adopted by Southern educational institutions in the antebellum period. See "'Grown Girls, Highly Cultivated': Female Education in an Antebellum Southern Family."

22. Eliza Lucy Irion-Neilson diary, Irion-Neilson Family Papers, MDAH, book 2, 3; Cornelia Thornton to Aunt, June 18, 1852, in Randolph and Yates Family Papers, UNC. See also Laura Howe to Julia Howe, September 19 [undated], in Chiliab Smith Howe Papers, UNC; Farnham, *The Education of the Southern Belle*, 70-71.

23. Louisiana Gibson to Tobias Gibson, May 15, 1857, in Gibson and Humphreys Family Papers, UNC; Emma Shannon to Levina Morris Shannon, October 27, 1857, in Crutcher-Shannon Family Papers, MDAH. Many young ladies experienced feelings of homesickness while away at school. See Laura Howe to Julia Howe, March 16, 1857, Laura Howe to Ellen Howe, November 25, 1856, January 17, 1857, in Chiliab Smith Howe Papers, UNC; "Cousin" to Eudora Hobbs, August 12, 1860, B. T. Hobbs Papers, MSU; Florence Chapman to mother, November 25, 1859, in Chapman Family Papers, MDAH.

24. Chiliab Smith Howe to Ellen Howe, October 5, 1851, in Chiliab Smith Howe Papers, UNC; B. T. Hobbs to Eudora Hobbs, July 31, September 6, 1860,

May 8, 1861, in B. T. Hobbs Papers, MSU. See also Anna Mary Girault Farrar to her daughter, August 26, 1860, in Richardson and Farrar Family Papers, UNC; Margaret Snodgrass to Emma Snodgrass, October 2, 1858, in John Snodgrass and Family Papers, MDAH; Martha Davenport to daughter, March 17, 1861, in Davenport Family Letters, MDAH.

25. H. B. Trist to Mary W. Trist, [undated] 1855, January 28, 1853, in Trist Wood Papers, UNC.

26. Ellen Howe to Julia Howe, July 12, 1851, in Chiliab Smith Howe Papers, UNC.

27. Julia Howe to Ellen Howe, July 12, 15, 1851, ibid.

28. Chiliab Smith Howe to Ellen Howe, August 4, 30, 1851, ibid.

29. Elizabeth C. Irion diary, September 10, 1852, January 9, 1853, Irion-Neilson Family Papers, MDAH. See also September 6, 22, 24, 1852.

30. Morgan, *Civil War Diary*, 290.

31. On young women being groomed to attract a husband see Scott, *The Southern Lady*, 23-27; Siedel, *The Southern Belle in the American Novel*, 6; Clinton, *The Plantation Mistress*, 59; Friedman, *The Enclosed Garden*, 32; Weiner, *Mistresses and Slaves*, 29; Cashin, *A Family Venture*, 25.

32. For an understanding of the household or plantation as the cultural foundation of Southern society see Fox-Genovese, *Within the Plantation Household*; Clinton, *The Plantation Mistress*; Stowe, *Intimacy and Power in the Old South*; Stevenson, *Life in Black and White*; Weiner, *Mistresses and Slaves*; Nancy Dunlap Bercaw, "Politics of Household during the Transition from Slavery to Freedom in the Yazoo-Mississippi Delta, 1861-1876."

33. Joan Cashin argues that men in the Southwest adopted the notion of "manly independence" and that this changed their attitudes toward paternalism. She does note, however, that women in the Southwest continued to practice the "female version" of paternalism. See *A Family Venture*, 112-18. I would like to note, however, that some diarists in this study came from families who drew heavily on paternalism in their relations to each other and to their slaves. Sarah Lois Wadley's father, for example, drew upon this ideology in his role as a master of slaves. See Sarah Lois Wadley diary, Sarah Lois Wadley Papers, UNC. See also Edwina Burnley Memoir, UNC, 3; Morgan, *Civil War Diray*, 80-81. Paternalism also served as a powerful justification for the right to govern slaves. See Greenberg, *Masters and Statesmen*, 3. For Eugene D. Genovese's examination of paternalism see *Roll, Jordan, Roll: The World the Slaves Made*, 3-7.

34. For an examination of the plantation household and the role of the mistress see Scott, *The Southern Lady*, 28-34; Clinton, *The Plantation Mistress*, 18-35; Friedman, *The Enclosed Garden*, 21-32; Lebsock, *The Free Women of Petersburg*, 147-59; Fox-Genovese, *Within the Plantation Household*, 115-30; Weiner, *Mistresses and Slaves*, 23-49. Joan Cashin notes that women who lived in the Southwest confronted a more difficult domestic environment than did their eastern counterparts. See *A Family Venture*, 109. For an understanding of the role of slaves on a plantation, or the influence of the institution on the political and cultural institutions of the South, see, for example, Kenneth M. Stampp, *The Peculiar Institution: Slavery in the Ante-Bellum South*; Genovese, *Roll, Jordan, Roll*; Charles W. Joyner, *Down by the Riverside: A South Carolina Slave Community*; Peter Kolchin, *American Slavery, 1619-1877*. Kolchin's book also contains an excellent bibliographical essay. See 257-91.

35. Jacobs manuscript, Annie E. Clark Jacobs Papers, MDAH, 26; Kate Stone,

Brokenburn: The Journal of Kate Stone, 1861-1868, 70; Mary Carson Warfield, "The Antebellum Woman," undated essay, Mary Carson Warfield Papers, DSU. See also Louisa Russell Conner Memoirs, MDAH, 6. Rable notes that some mistresses failed to exemplify this image. See *Civil Wars,* 34-35.

36. Fox-Genovese, *Within the Plantation Household,* 110-14; Clinton, *The Plantation Mistress,* 19; McMillen, *Southern Women,* 109; Michael P. Johnson, "Planters and Patriarchy: Charleston, 1800-1860," 66; Edwards, *Scarlett Doesn't Live Here Anymore,* 21. Some young ladies played a vital role in the household, but this was often because of their unique place within the family unit. For example, Elizabeth Irion's domestic obligations came about as a result of her mother's death and her position as the eldest female in the household. See Irion diary, Irion-Neilson Family Papers, MDAH; Davies Diary, DUKE. Historians vary in their interpretation of this issue. Rable argues that young ladies "learned to be women and slaveholders at the same time" through their daily observance of the plantation household. See *Civil Wars,* 33. Weiner contends that while young women did not make "significant contributions" to the household, they did learn many skills in adolescence. Still, she acknowledges that "the daughter of a well-to-do planter probably enjoyed more leisure than any other person in the antebellum South." See *Mistresses and Slaves,* 28-29. Cashin disagrees, and argues that young ladies "learned the skills of household management from mothers and other female kin" and by their early twenties were capable enough "to run establishments on their own." See *A Family Venture,* 24.

37. Stone, *Brokenburn,* 13.

38. Annie Rosalie Quitman diary, February 4, March 2, 27, 1852, September 18, November 27, December 5, 1857, Quitman Family Papers, UNC. See also Eliza Lucy Irion-Neilson, *Lucy's Journal,* 18-19; Irion-Neilson diary, January 1, 1861, Irion-Neilson Family Papers, MDAH; Jacobs manuscript, Annie E. Clark Jacobs Papers, MDAH, 19-20; Elizabeth Christie Brown Diary, January 1853, UM.

39. Wadley diary, January 4, 1860, February 21, 1861, April 16, November 10, 1860, Sarah Lois Wadley Papers, UNC. On Northern tour see August 8, 23, 24, 26-28, 31, September 2, 4, 14, 20, 1859, ibid. See also August 9, 14, December 8, 1860, ibid.; Susan Hobbs to Eudora Hobbs, September 29, 1860, in B. T. Hobbs Papers, MSU; Lise Mitchell diary, July 1862, (Lise) Elizabeth Mitchell Papers, TU; Moss Journal, July 29, 1851, July 9, 1852, WRC; Stone, *Brokenburn,* 15, 22, 23, 25, 56, 65; Esther G. Wright Boyd Memoir, TSL, 9; Emma Finley, *Our Pen Is Time: The Diary of Emma Finley,* 55, 65, 81.

40. Brickell diary, February 3, 15, 1861, Edward Fontaine Papers, MSU. See also January 29, March 6, 1859, ibid.; Morgan, *Civil War Diary,* 33. Many historians argue that Southern belles found it difficult to adapt to the domestic responsibilities of married life, indicating how little they had participated in household affairs. See Catherine Clinton, *Tara Revisited: Women, War, and the Plantation Legend,* 43; Scott, *The Southern Lady,* 27-28; Friedman, *The Enclosed Garden,* 32; Fox-Genovese, *Within the Plantation Household,* 113.

41. Leonore Davidoff, *The Best Circles: Society, Etiquette, and the Season,* 93; Fox-Genovese, *Within the Plantation Household,* 213.

42. Eliza Lucy Irion to family, March 16, 1858, in Irion-Neilson Family Papers, MDAH; Emma Shannon to Levina Morris Shannon, October 31, 1857, in Crutcher-Shannon Family Papers, MDAH. See also Farnham, *The Education of the Southern Belle,* 133-34.

43. Farnham, *The Education of the Southern Belle*, 133; Berry, "A History of Women's Higher Education," 306; Laura Howe to Julia Howe, September 19 [undated], Julia Howe to Ellen Howe, July 12, 1851, in Chiliab Smith Howe Papers, UNC.

44. Florence Chapman to mother, December 2, 1859, in Chapman Family Papers, MDAH. See also Stevenson, *Life in Black and White*, 50-51; Farnham, *The Education of the Southern Belle*, 133-34; Fox-Genovese, *Within the Plantation Household*, 213.

45. Brickell diary, February 9, 1860, Edward Fontaine Papers, MSU; Mary Shannon to Emma Shannon, January 9, 1858, in Crutcher-Shannon Family Papers, MDAH. See also Davies Diary, March 23, 1853, DUKE.

46. Morgan, *Civil War Diary*, 5, 32, 125; Stone, *Brokenburn*, 65; Annie Jeter Carmouche memoir, Annie Jeter Carmouche Papers, TU, 15. See also Brickell diary, December 9, 1860, Edward Fontaine Papers, MSU; Mitchell diary, July 1862, (Lise) Elizabeth Mitchell Papers, TU; Mary Estelle Rountree to Charlotte Davis, December 28, 1855, August 28, 1856, in Mary Estelle Rountree Letters, LSU; Robert E. May, "Southern Elite Women, Sectional Extremism, and the Male Political Sphere: The Case of John A. Quitman's Wife and Female Descendants, 1847-1931," 259.

47. Sophie Collins to E. J. Stone, March 2, 1858, Sophie Collins to Mary Collins, October 18, 1857, in Emmett Lloyd Ross Papers, MSU. See also Sophie Collins to Mary Collins, January 14, October 17, 1855, September 12, 1858, ibid.

48. Farnham, *The Education of the Southern Belle*, 180; McMillen, *Southern Women*, 19. Censer argues that this emphasis on a belle's power "yielded a dual image of females." The first image of an "innocent unworldly charmer" was "supplemented by that of the coldly conniving, heartless belle." See *North Carolina Planters*, 78. See also Virginia Jeans Laas, *Love and Power in the Nineteenth Century: The Marriage of Violet Blair*, 37. It is important to note, however, that patriarchal authority tempered a belle's "power." On antebellum courtship rituals see Censer, *North Carolina Planters*, 68-72; Stowe, *Intimacy and Power in the Old South*, 50-121; Stevenson, *Life in Black and White*, 51-58. Stowe compares the courtship process to the "affair of honor" (or duel). See 89.

49. On the transition from belle to wife and mistress see Clinton, *Tara Revisited*, 43; Scott, *The Southern Lady*, 27-28; Friedman, *The Enclosed Garden*, 32; Fox-Genovese, *Within the Plantation Household*, 113. For statistics that compare the ages of Southern and Northern women at the time of marriage see Wyatt-Brown, *Southern Honor*, 203.

50. Quitman diary, June 29, 1858, Quitman Family Papers, UNC.

CHAPTER TWO

The Trumpet of War Is Sounding: Young Ladies Respond to the Cause

1. Howell Hobbs to Eudora Hobbs, August 25, 1860, in B. T. Hobbs Papers, MSU.

2. Howell Hobbs to Eudora Hobbs, November 17, 1860, ibid.

3. Howell Hobbs to Eudora Hobbs, January 15, 1861, ibid.

4. Howell Hobbs to Eudora Hobbs, February 8, 25, May 8, 1861, ibid.

5. Annie Harper, *Annie Harper's Journal: A Southern Mother's Legacy*, 7-8;

Dwight Lowell Dumond, ed., *Southern Editorials on Secession*, 338.

6. Seabury, *Diary of Caroline Seabury*, 60; Columbus Chapter UDC, eds., *War Reminiscences of Columbus, Mississippi, and Elsewhere, 1861-1865*, 3.

7. Drew Gilpin Faust, *The Creation of Confederate Nationalism: Ideology and Identity in the Civil War South*, 6. Historians have widely debated the presence or strength of nationalism in the Confederate South. In his thorough historiographical overview, Gary W. Gallagher argues that the debate has focused on structural factors (such as political or military structures) and ideology. Gallagher notes that those who argue that there was "little evidence of true Confederate nationalism" usually draw upon the absence of will thesis, noting class conflict, "doubts about slavery," and the "absence of unique cultural bonds." See *The Confederate War*, 63-71. For examples of the "weak nationalism" thesis see Richard E. Beringer et al., eds., *Why the South Lost the Civil War*, 64-81. Beringer, Hattaway, Jones, and Still Jr. argue that Confederate men went to war for varied and sometimes incompatible reasons, and thus the Confederacy did not "possess a feeling of oneness" or a "mystical sense of nationhood." Lack of will, they contend, "constituted the decisive deficiency in the Confederate arsenal" and culminated in Confederate defeat. Kenneth M. Stampp also contends that "behavioral problems" such as "the failure of political leadership, the absurd lengths to which states rights was carried, the reluctance of Southerners to accept the discipline that war demanded and the internal conflicts among the southern people" all point to a "weakness of morale." See *The Imperiled Union: Essays on the Background of the Civil War*, 246-69.

Faust examines the ideological framework of nationalism, with particular emphasis on religion, which, she argues, became the "transcendent framework" for Confederate ideology. Faust contends that the "substance of Confederate nationalism, rather than the quantity or quality of its adherents' faith, was the ultimate source of its disintegration." See *The Creation of Confederate Nationalism*. Paul D. Escott also notes the presence of nationalism, but contends that Davis failed to create "internal unity and the spirit essential for the growth of Confederate nationalism." See *After Secession: Jefferson Davis and the Failure of Confederate Nationalism*. Finally, Gallagher regards General Robert E. Lee and the Army of Northern Virginia as the most powerful rallying point of nationalist feeling. See *The Confederate War*, 63-111. For David M. Potter's valuable examination of the theoretical problems of nationalism in the Southern context see *The South and the Sectional Conflict*, 34-83.

8. Robert May argues Quitman domesticity included a "political component" that culminated in the transmission of regional political thought to future generations. See "Southern Elite Women," 261, 285. See also Eugene D. Genovese, "Toward a Kinder and Gentler America: The Southern Lady in the Greening of the Politics of the Old South," 129-30.

9. Chiliab Smith Howe to Ellen Howe, August 30, 1851, Laura Howe to Ellen Howe, October 20, 1856, in Chiliab Smith Howe Papers, UNC.

10. Many historians argue that women were politically articulate and actively participated in antebellum Southern politics. See, for example, Genovese, "Toward a Kinder and Gentler America"; Elizabeth R. Varon, "Tippecanoe and the Ladies, Too: White Women and Party Politics in Antebellum Virginia"; Christopher J. Olsen, "Respecting 'The Wise Allotment of Our Sphere': White Women and Politics in Mississippi, 1840-1860"; John M. Sacher, "'The Ladies Are Moving Everywhere': Louisiana Women and Antebellum Politics." As I have indicated, the age of the young ladies in this study influenced their political understanding.

11. Mollie Whitley to Eudora Hobbs, January 14, 1861, in B. T. Hobbs Papers, MSU.

12. Morgan, *Civil War Diary*, 73-74, 142-43. See also ibid., 121; Kathryn Reinhart Schuler, "Women in Public Affairs in Louisiana during Reconstruction," 675.

13. Jacobs manuscript, Annie E. Clark Jacobs Papers, MDAH, 25; Irion-Neilson, *Lucy's Journal*, 14-15, 18; Worthington diary, January 29, 1862, May 26, 1863, Amanda Dougherty Worthington Papers, UNC; Ella Pegues, "Recollections of the Civil War Lafayette County," Maud Morrow Brown Papers, MDAH; Wadley diary, July 12, 1863, April 18, 21, 1861, Sarah Lois Wadley Papers, UNC.

14. Stone, *Brokenburn*, 19, 85.

15. Richard B. Harwell, ed., *The Confederate Reader: How the South Saw the War*, 55-56. On the use of religion in proslavery and secession rhetoric see Donald G. Mathews, *Religion in the Old South*; Faust, *The Creation of Confederate Nationalism*. Bertram Wyatt-Brown has examined what he describes as the "significant minority" of clergymen who did not support secession. See *The Shaping of Southern Culture*, 154-74. On the importance of religion to Confederate women see Faust, *Mothers of Invention*, 179-95; Marlene Hunt Rikard and Elizabeth Crabtree Wells, "'From It Begins a New Era': Women and the Civil War."

16. Stone, *Brokenburn*, 24-25, 31, 36, 79, 230; Mary Wright diary, January 4, 1861, Wright-Boyd Family Papers, LSU. See also Wadley diary, November 15, 1861, Sarah Lois Wadley Papers, UNC; Emma Walton to James B. Walton, April 2, 22, July 15, 1863, in Walton-Glenny Family Papers, WRC; Solomon, *Diary of Clara Solomon*, 58; Cordelia Lewis Scales, "Notes and Documents: The Civil War Letters of Cordelia Lewis Scales," 174; Harper, *Annie Harper's Journal*, 12. See also Rable, *Civil Wars*, 203. Confederate president Jefferson Davis often proclaimed days of prayer and fasting. See Elizabeth Christie Brown Diary, March 27, 1863, UM; Wadley diary, November 15, 1861, March 2, 1862, March 30, 1863, Sarah Lois Wadley Papers, UNC; Solomon, *Diary of Clara Solomon*, 259, 370. See also Rable, *Civil Wars*, 206-7; Faust, *The Creation of Confederate Nationalism*, 26-27.

17. Stone, *Brokenburn*, 79, 31; Wadley diary, April 18, 1861, Sarah Lois Wadley Papers, UNC; Kate D. Foster Diary, July 30, 14, 1863, DUKE; Brickell diary, April 25, 1861, February 26, 1862, Edward Fontaine Papers, MSU; Morgan, *Civil War Diary*, 438. See also Florence Cooney Tompkins, "Women of the Sixties," 283; Wadley diary, April 21, July 22, November 15, 1861, June 1, 1862, Sarah Lois Wadley Papers, UNC. Elizabeth Christie Brown wrote about a sermon she heard in which the minister regarded Confederate success as a sign of God's blessing. See Brown diary, March 4, 1863, UM. For those women who prayed for Confederate victory see Ellen Louise Power Diary, May 6, 1862, UNC; Wadley diary, February 17, 1862, August 3, 1864, Sarah Lois Wadley Papers, UNC; Morgan, *Civil War Diary*, 438. See also Faust, *Mothers of Invention*, 180-81.

18. Harper, *Annie Harper's Journal*, 10.

19. Stone, *Brokenburn*, 17-18.

20. Brickell diary, May 5, November 22, 25, 1861, Edward Fontaine Papers, MSU. On doubts about the success of the war effort see, for example, Worthington diary, February 2, 11, 25, 27, 1862, Amanda Dougherty Worthington Papers, UNC; Ellen Louise Power Diary, February 24, 1862, UNC; Solomon, *Diary of Clara Solomon*, 295, 341; Stone, *Brokenburn*, 90, 91, 94; Wadley diary, February 17, March 2, 16, 1862, Sarah Lois Wadley Papers, UNC; Irion-Neilson, *Lucy's Journal*, 21.

21. David Potter argues that "national loyalty flourishes not by challenging and

overpowering all other loyalties, but by subsuming them all in a mutually support-ive relation to one another." See *The South and the Sectional Conflict,* 48-49. See also Rable, *Civil Wars,* 144-51.

22. On patriotic womanhood see Drew Gilpin Faust, "Altars of Sacrifice: Confed-erate Women and the Narratives of War"; Clinton, *Tara Revisited,* 59, 79. The image of Confederate womanhood was used as one way to unite the South. Faust asserts that the image of the patriotic woman, rich or poor, who gave her son, husband, or brother to the Confederacy highlighted a nationalist image that minimized class division in the overriding theme of sacrifice. See "Altars of Sacrifice," 1201.

23. Greenberg, *Masters and Statesmen,* 144. Greenberg argues that secession was an act that "paralleled the duel," yet was unique because it was not a confrontation between men of equal status. While Southerners were compelled to defend their honor, they regarded Northerners as corrupt, antislavery radicals. On the importance of equality between opponents see Stowe, *Intimacy and Power in the Old South,* 14.

My sources differ from James M. McPherson's, who argues from a selection of soldiers' letters that honor was not "always appreciated by wives," who often felt that "a man's duty to his family was more important than pride in his reputation." See *For Cause and Comrades: Why Men Fought in the Civil War,* 23-24. For exam-ples of women looking to their men to uphold family honor in the antebellum South see Genovese, "Toward a Kinder and Gentler America," 131.

24. Wadley diary, December 18, 9, 1862, Sarah Lois Wadley Papers, UNC.

25. Stone, *Brokenburn,* 21, 135-36. See also 98, 117, 159, 263, 308. See also Morgan, *Civil War Diary,* 39, 182.

26. Scales, "Notes and Documents," 172. See also Worthington diary, April 20, December 6, 1862, May 2, 1863, January 19, 1865, Amanda Dougherty Worthington Papers, UNC.

27. Stone, *Brokenburn,* 121, 167, 217, 247-48. See also Rable, *Civil Wars,* 63.

28. Wadley diary, March 16, 1862, September 12, 1863, Sarah Lois Wadley Papers, UNC.

29. Ibid., October 15, 1863. In his study of Confederate soldiers, Bell Irvin Wiley explains that "when summoned to a camp of instruction, [a conscriptee] might take a substitute with him"; if the proxy passed the medical examination, "the 'princi-pal' was permitted to return home and the substitute accepted in his place." This policy began in 1861 and continued throughout most of the war until it was abol-ished in 1864. See *The Life of Johnny Reb: The Common Soldier of the Confederacy,* 125-27; Albert Burton Moore, *Conscription and Conflict in the Confederacy;* Rable, *Civil Wars,* 73-78. Other women expressed their disgust for men who would not become soldiers or hired substitutes to go to war for them. See Worthington diary, May 26, 1863, Amanda Dougherty Worthington Papers, UNC; Kate D. Foster Diary, June 25, 1863, DUKE; Carmouche memoir, Annie Jeter Carmouche Papers, TU, 17; Stone, *Brokenburn,* 87, 92, 96, 102-3, 113; Morgan, *Civil War Diary,* 183.

30. Wadley diary, November 16, December 10, 1863, Sarah Lois Wadley Papers, UNC. It is unclear if Sarah felt shame because of her belief in honor, or because of the judgment of her brother's honor by the community.

31. Ibid., January 27, March 19, 1864, January 25, February 11, 1865. Kate Stone also regarded it as the "duty" of Southern men to enter the army. See Stone, *Brokenburn,* 131.

32. Harper, *Annie Harper's Journal,* 12. On the importance of women manufac-

turing supplies for the Confederate army see Wiley, *The Life of Johnny Reb*, 19; Rable, *Civil Wars*, 140; Clea Lutz Bunch, "Confederate Women of Arkansas Face the 'Fiends in Human Shape,'" 176; Faust, *Mothers of Invention*, 24.

33. Ellen Louise Power Diary, December 29, 1862, January 27, March 28, 1863, UNC. See also June 4, August 9, October 20, 21, 23, November 11, December 2, 6, 1862.

34. The Civil War became the catalyst for Southern women to organize in groups outside the home for the benefit of the soldiers. See Rable, *Civil Wars*, 139-44. Faust contends that while sewing societies affirmed women's "traditional" role, the mere existence of these groups "defined and empowered women as women, independent of men." See *Mothers of Invention*, 24.

35. Wadley diary, July 14, August 28, 1861, Sarah Lois Wadley Papers, UNC. See also August 21, September 21, 1861, April 27, August 31, November 17, 1862, June 19, 1863. On Sarah's attendance at the sewing society see July 9, 14, August 8, 16, October 7, 19, December 7, 1861. Other young ladies wrote about their attendance at sewing societies and sewing for the soldiers. See Irion-Neilson, *Lucy's Journal*, 18; Stone, *Brokenburn*, 50, 53, 55, 57, 59, 61; Harper, *Annie Harper's Journal*, 11-12; Ellen Louise Power Diary, November 10, 1862, UNC; Elizabeth Christie Brown Diary, April 6, 1863, UM; Jacobs manuscript, Annie E. Clark Jacobs Papers, MDAH, 58; Mary C. Wright diary, May 15, 1861, January 6, 1863, Wright-Boyd Family Papers, LSU; Emily Caroline Douglas diary, October 8, 9, 11, December 8, 1862, Emily Caroline Douglas Papers, LSU; Emily Caroline Douglas memoir, Emily Caroline Douglas Papers, LSU, 124, 126; Morgan, *Civil War Diary*, 256-57.

36. Stone, *Brokenburn*, 47, 51, 144. Kate's diary contains regular entries on the work she and her family completed for the soldiers. See 18, 45, 49, 51-52, 54-56, 58, 61, 95, 102, 106, 161-62, 294, 312-13, 324. Kate also mentioned that her mother "taught so many people" how to knit socks. See 54. See also Worthington diary, May 8, 1863, Amanda Dougherty Worthington Papers, UNC; Harper, *Annie Harper's Journal*, 12; Wadley diary, August 21, 1861, June 19, 1863, Sarah Lois Wadley Papers, UNC; Sallie B. McRae diary, May 8, 1862, Sallie B. McRae Papers, MSU.

37. Mary C. Wright diary, May 15, 1861, Wright-Boyd Family Papers, LSU; Elizabeth Christie Brown Diary, April 6, February 18, February 2, 1863, UM. See also January 26, February 3, 6, 17, March 20, April 10, 11, 1863; Sidney Harding Diary, November 19, August 24, 27, 1863, LSU; Tompkins, "Women of the Sixties," 283.

38. Morgan, *Civil War Diary*, 411. See also 115, 170, 192, 202, 256, 258, 318, 414, 439; Mary C. Wright diary, January 21, 1863, Wright-Boyd Family Papers, LSU; Mathilda Todd DeVan Memorial Volume, TU, 22-25; J. L. Underwood, ed., *The Women of the Confederacy*, 97; Mary Carol Miller, *Lost Mansions of Mississippi*, 54.

39. Solomon, *Diary of Clara Solomon*, 149.

40. Ibid., 182. See also Rable, *Civil Wars*, 141-42; Faust, *Mothers of Invention*, 27.

41. Worthington diary, January 11, 1862, Amanda Dougherty Worthington Papers, UNC; Harper, *Annie Harper's Journal*, 8; Brickell diary, July 21, 1861, Edward Fontaine Papers, MSU.

42. Stone, *Brokenburn*, 52.

43. Scales, "Notes and Documents," 172.

CHAPTER THREE

Keeping House: The Southern Belle in the Confederate Household

1. Stone, *Brokenburn*, 14, 3. For an examination of Kate's diary see Edmund Wilson, *Patriotic Gore: Studies in the Literature of the American Civil War*, 258-63.

2. Stone, *Brokenburn*, 8.

3. Ibid., 33, 32.

4. For an examination of the mistress's wartime role see Simkins and Patton, *The Women of the Confederacy*, 111-16; Drew Gilpin Faust, "Trying To Do a Man's Business: Slavery, Violence, and Gender in the American Civil War"; Rable, *Civil Wars*, 112-21; Edwards, *Scarlett Doesn't Live Here Anymore*, 77-79.

5. Stone, *Brokenburn*, 11, 3-4.

6. Ibid., 17. A small minority of women operated plantations in the antebellum South, one of the most notable being Rachel O'Conner. See O'Conner, *Mistress of Evergreen Plantation: Rachel O'Conner's Legacy of Letters, 1823-1845*; Friedman, *The Enclosed Garden*, 31.

On agricultural adjustment see James L. Roark, *Masters without Slaves: Southern Planters in the Civil War and Reconstruction*, 39-41; Armstead Louis Robinson, "Day of Jubilo: Civil War and the Demise of Slavery in the Mississippi Valley, 1861-1865," 127-29.

7. Stone, *Brokenburn*, 18.

8. Ibid., 33, 35. See also Julia to Haller Nutt, [undated] 1863, in Nutt Family Papers, MDAH. Faust notes that the master's failure to uphold his reciprocal obligations to his dependents "undermined" not only the institution of slavery but also the legitimacy of his power as an elite white male. Ultimately, this "slackening of authority" was exacerbated by Federal occupation, which exposed slaves to unprecedented opportunities for freedom. See *Mothers of Invention*, 53-79; Roark, *Masters without Slaves*, 85; Clarence L. Mohr, *On the Threshold of Freedom: Masters and Slaves in Civil War Georgia*, 221, 223; Leon F. Litwack, *Been in the Storm So Long: The Aftermath of Slavery*, 4, 11-12. Armstead Robinson argues that wartime conditions, including the "collapse of white solidarity," the use of slaves in the Confederate war effort, and the debate between planters and the government over agricultural adjustment, also contributed to the dismantling of planter authority. See "Day of Jubilo," 241.

9. Solomon, *Diary of Clara Solomon*, 99, 123-24, 121. On the Solomon family's finances see 101, 105, 109, 120, 145, 154, 162.

10. Kate D. Foster Diary, July 14, 16, 24, 1863, DUKE.

11. See Faust, "Trying To Do a Man's Business."

12. Faust has explored the contradictions inherent in women's socialization and their need to embrace violence to control slaves. See ibid.; Faust, *Mothers of Invention*, 65-79.

13. See James M. McPherson, *Battle Cry of Freedom: The American Civil War*, 91-103.

14. Solomon, *Diary of Clara Solomon*, 233, 363, 110, 233. See also 13, 29, 151, 154, 164, 184, 189, 212-13, 221-22, 230, 245, 258, 309, 313, 319, 325, 334, 340, 351, 353, 365, 383, 428. On Clara's search for cocoaine see 80-81, 106-7, 112, 164. On the effects of the blockade on women see, for example, Simkins and Patton, *The Women of the Confederacy*, 131-35; Rable, *Civil Wars*, 100-101. On the effect

of the blockade in the Delta region see John D. Winters, *The Civil War in Louisiana*, 44-56; Charles L. Dufour, *The Night the War Was Lost*, 59-70.

15. Ellen Louise Power Diary, September 15, 8, 10, 1862, UNC; Morgan, *Civil War Diary*, 251, 273, 326; Mary C. Wright diary, January 28, 1863, Wright-Boyd Family Papers, LSU; Harper, *Annie Harper's Journal*, 15. Many young ladies also made or purchased "Confederate" items. See Morgan, *Civil War Diary*, 273; Stone, *Brokenburn*, 289, 291, 344; Elizabeth Christie Brown Diary, January 28, March 31, 1863, UM; Sidney Harding Diary, August 28, 1863, LSU; Ellen Louise Power Diary, May 7, 1862, April 23, 1863, UNC; Worthington diary, December 27, 1862, Amanda Dougherty Worthington Papers, UNC.

16. Harper, *Annie Harper's Journal*, 16; Stone, *Brokenburn*, 147; Solomon, *Diary of Clara Solomon*, 151. See chapter 4 herein for a full analysis of the implications of the blockade on women's clothing. On wartime inflation or the scarcity of goods see, for example, "Hinds County Women in Wartime," John Logan Power and Family Papers, MDAH, scrapbook 18, 22; Solomon, *Diary of Clara Solomon*, 67, 148, 154, 184, 233, 374; Ellen Louise Power Diary, September 8, 10, 15, 1862, UNC; Sidney Harding Diary, August 19, 1863, LSU. Faust notes that the plight of Southern women was very different from that of Northern women, who did not endure the "ravages of battle" or acute "material deprivation" caused by a weak economy. See *Mothers of Invention*, 5.

17. Solomon, *Diary of Clara Solomon*, 154; Morgan, *Civil War Diary*, 78, 247, 270, 305.

18. Morgan, *Civil War Diary*, 260-61. Robinson argues that a combination of factors caused food shortages, including the blockade, drought, a business slump, the withdrawal of external credit (upon which the plantation economy depended), and the discontinuance of trade routes. See "Day of Jubilo," 110-11, 116.

19. Stone, *Brokenburn*, 109.

20. Harper, *Annie Harper's Journal*, 15; Solomon, *Diary of Clara Solomon*, 120, 325, 334. See also Letitia Dabney Miller memoir, Letitia Dabney Miller Papers, UNC, 11; Ellen Louise Power Diary, December 25, 1862, UNC; Wadley diary, December 9, 1862, Sarah Lois Wadley Papers, UNC; Stone, *Brokenburn*, 193, 206, 259; Belle Strickland Diary, August 18, 1864, UM.

21. Morgan, *Civil War Diary*, 251, 442.

22. Francis Warrington Dawson, ed., *"Our Women in the War": The Lives They Lived, the Deaths They Died*, 322. See also Stephen V. Ash, *When the Yankees Came: Conflict and Chaos in the Occupied South, 1861-1865*, 79; Elizabeth Joan Doyle, "Civilian Life in Occupied New Orleans," 29-45.

23. Scales, "Notes and Documents," 175, 177. For a description of Oakland see Miller, *Lost Mansions of Mississippi*, 74-76. See also Ellen Louise Power Diary, June 23, 1863, UNC.

24. Miller memoir, Letitia Dabney Miller Papers, UNC, 11. On lack of government assistance see Mary Elizabeth Massey, *Ersatz in the Confederacy: Shortages and Substitutions on the Southern Homefront*, 33; Paul D. Escott, "The Cry of the Sufferers: The Problem of Welfare in the Confederacy"; Escott, *After Secession*, 140-44; Rable, *Civil Wars*, 102-6; William Frank Zornow, "State Aid for Indigent Soldiers and Their Families in Louisiana, 1861-1865." It is important to remember that the financial plight of Southern families was often relative to their class. Yeoman and poor white families often experienced far harder financial circumstances in wartime than the elite. For an example of this see Seabury, *Diary of Caroline Seabury*, 86-87,

90-91. For an examination of the plight of refugees in the Confederacy see Mary Elizabeth Massey, *Refugee Life in the Confederacy;* Friedman, *The Enclosed Garden,* 95-98; Rable, *Civil Wars,* 181-92; Cashin, "Into the Trackless Wilderness." For an examination of the class dimensions of refugee life see Faust, *Mothers of Invention,* 40-45. For primary accounts on the way refugee life reinforced class identity see Wadley diary, June 8, 1864, Sarah Lois Wadley Papers, UNC; Sidney Harding Diary, August 7, 1863, LSU; Morgan, *Civil War Diary,* 478; Stone, *Brokenburn,* 226, 232, 234, 237-38, 249, 275.

25. Stone, *Brokenburn,* 258-59, 193.

26. Morgan, *Civil War Diary,* 439, 449. Sophie Collins also worried about the plight of her family. See Sophie Collins to E. J. Stone, April 26, June 9, 1863, in Emmett Lloyd Ross Papers, MSU.

27. Sidney Harding Diary, May 11, June 28, 1864, November 14, 17, 23, 1863, September 14, 1864, LSU. For other primary accounts of refugee life (general) see Stone, *Brokenburn,* 188-364; Margaret Gooch Memoir, TSL; Sophie Collins to E. J. Stone, September 30, 1863, in Emmett Lloyd Ross Papers, MSU; Louisa Russell Conner Memoirs, MDAH, 19.

28. Solomon, *Diary of Clara Solomon,* 371. See also Simkins and Patton, *The Women of the Confederacy,* 138-59; Massey, *Ersatz in the Confederacy.* Ingenuity was also a part of life in the antebellum South. See, for example, Jo Ann Carrigan, "Nineteenth-Century Rural Self-Sufficiency: A Planter's and Housewife's 'Do-It-Yourself' Encyclopedia."

29. Miller memoir, Letitia Dabney Miller Papers, UNC, 11; Harper, *Annie Harper's Journal,* 15; Stone, *Brokenburn,* 180-81; Ellen Louise Power Diary, May 7, 1862, April 23, 1863, UNC; Stone, *Brokenburn,* 289; Elizabeth Christie Brown Diary, March 31, 1863, UM; Worthington diary, December 27, 1862, Amanda Dougherty Worthington Papers, UNC. For other examples of ingenuity see Margaret Gooch Memoir, TSL, 6-7; Mary C. Wright diary, January 3, 1863, Wright-Boyd Family Papers, LSU.

30. Moore, *Emergence of the Cotton Kingdom,* 286, 230-31; Bradley G. Bond, *Political Culture in the Nineteenth-Century South: Mississippi, 1830-1900,* 54.

31. Wadley diary, November 2, 1861, Sarah Lois Wadley Papers, UNC. Young women often wrote about their efforts to mend and remodel clothes. See Stone, *Brokenburn,* 61, 80, 152, 162, 180, 206, 252, 296; Harper, *Annie Harper's Journal,* 15; Sidney Harding Diary, August 15, October 22, 25, November 2, December 2, 1863, LSU; Morgan, *Civil War Diary,* 137; Solomon, *Diary of Clara Solomon,* 215, 221, 233, 249, 255, 363; Belle Strickland Diary, August 18, 1864, UM; Douglas diary, October 30, 1862, Emily Caroline Douglas Papers, LSU; McRae diary, February 8, May 24, 30, 1862, Sallie B. McRae Papers, MSU; Ellen Louise Power Diary, April 15, 22, October 3, November 4, 24, 1862, UNC; Miller memoir, Letitia Dabney Miller Papers, UNC, 5.

32. Stone, *Brokenburn,* 152, 180; Solomon, *Diary of Clara Solomon,* 90, 221, 80, 123-24, 177, 255, 371, 363; Columbus Chapter UDC, eds., *War Reminiscences of Columbus,* 15. See also Sidney Harding Diary, November 2, 1863, LSU.

33. Elizabeth Christie Brown Diary, January 24, February 21, March 6, 9, 1863, UM.

34. Kate D. Foster Diary, July 7, 1863, DUKE; Wadley diary, November 28, 1863, March 31, 1864, Sarah Lois Wadley Papers, UNC. See also December 4, 1863, January 18, 19, 27, February 29, March 31, April 20, July 9, September 5,

1864; Elizabeth Christie Brown Diary, May 14, March 2, April 6, 18, 1863, UM. See also Sidney Harding Diary, July 26, August 12, October 26, 28, 1863, LSU; Stone, *Brokenburn*, 48, 112, 115, 217. Kate also commented on her mother's millinery skills. See 251; Harper, *Annie Harper's Journal*, 14.

35. Jennie Pendleton diary, June 16, 1864, Mary E. Wilkes Shell Papers, MDAH; Stone, *Brokenburn*, 180-81; Morgan, *Civil War Diary*, 305.

36. "Patriotism of Mississippi Women," *Confederate Veteran* 25 (February 1917): 51. Elizabeth Fox-Genovese documents the antebellum relationship between mistress and slave in the production of cloth and clothing. See *Within the Plantation Household*, 120-28. For an examination of nineteenth-century textile production see Mary Edna Lohrenz and Anita Miller Stamper, *Mississippi Homespun: Nineteenth-Century Textiles and the Women Who Made Them*. Faust notes that Southern newspapers often connected home production with patriotism. One newspaper even connected wearing homespun to Southern honor. Still, Faust argues that the "propaganda effort surrounding homespun . . . succeeded only partially in overcoming the identification of weaving and spinning as degrading physical labor." See *Mothers of Invention*, 46, 48.

37. Stone, *Brokenburn*, 147. By using this imagery, Kate was drawing upon popular Confederate images that drew a parallel between the Southern cause and the American Revolution. See also Wadley diary, March 7, 1865, September 5, 1864, Sarah Lois Wadley Papers, UNC. See also December 7, 1861, August 23, 1864.

38. Ellen Louise Power Diary, April 1, September 1, 11, 1862, July 27, 31, August 1, 12, 1863, UNC; McRae diary, January 1, 2, 14, 29, February 3, 4, 10, 11, 25, 27, March 10, 13, 21, 22, 25, April 8, 21, 24, 25, 26, 30, May 1, 13, 15, 19, 20-23, 28, June 2, 4, 1862, Sallie B. McRae Papers, MSU; Lucy Paxton Scarborough, "So It Was when Her Life Began: Reminiscences of a Louisiana Girlhood," 431; Sophie Collins to E. J. Stone, April 26, September 30, 1863, in Emmett Lloyd Ross Papers, MSU. See also Jacobs manuscript, Annie E. Clark Jacobs Papers, MDAH, 58; Miller memoirs, Letitia Dabney Miller Papers, UNC, 13, 16.

39. The extent of the slave exodus depended on a number of factors, discussed in chapter 7.

40. Worthington diary, April 25, June 12, May 14, 16, 14, 1863, Amanda Dougherty Worthington Papers, UNC. See also April 24, 25, May 15, 18, 22, June 10, 12, 1863; Solomon, *Diary of Clara Solomon*, 81; Stone, *Brokenburn*, 173, 176; Dawson, ed., *"Our Women in the War,"* 20; Kate D. Foster Diary, July 25, 1863, DUKE. See also Rable, *Civil Wars*, 118-19.

41. Stone, *Brokenburn*, 193, 211, 223.

42. Kate D. Foster Diary, July 30, 25, November 15, 1863, DUKE. See also August 23, 1863.

43. Elizabeth Christie Brown Diary, April 14, 1863, UM. For housework see January 20, 21, 22, 23, 29, 30, February 11, March 17, 21, 30, 31, April 4, August 21, 1863.

44. Morgan, *Civil War Diary*, 103.

45. Solomon, *Diary of Clara Solomon*, 160, 225. See also 41, 49, 61, 70, 101, 121, 126, 144, 165, 249, 301, 320, 328, 384; Sidney Harding Diary, September 20, November 18, 1863, LSU; McRae diary, January 25, February 1, 11, 27, March 1, 8, 21, April 4, 18, 19, May 10, 16, 17, 30, June 2, 1862, Sallie B. McRae Papers, MSU. See also Douglas diary, November 1, 1862, Emily Caroline Douglas Papers, LSU; Irion-Neilson diary, March 3, 1865, Irion-Neilson Family Papers, MDAH,

book 5; Ellen Louise Power Diary, January 25, 1863, UNC; Wadley diary, July 14, 1864, Sarah Lois Wadley Papers, UNC; Belle Strickland Diary, August 17, 1864, UM; Morgan, *Civil War Diary*, 103; O'Brien, ed., *An Evening when Alone*, 344.

46. Stone, *Brokenburn*, 155, 210. See also 32, 82, 244, 277, 311.

47. Wadley diary, October 20, 1863, July 19, 1864, Sarah Lois Wadley Papers, UNC. See also July 7, December 9, 17, 1861, June 16, July 14, 1864.

48. Solomon, *Diary of Clara Solomon*, 61, 82, 203; Scales, "Notes and Documents," 172; Mitchell diary, February 19, 1863, (Lise) Elizabeth Mitchell Papers, TU; Morgan, *Civil War Diary*, 605. Sarah's sister, Miriam, also undertook the role of acting mistress in her brother's household. See 500-501. See also Kate D. Foster Diary, July 25, 1863, DUKE; Elizabeth Christie Brown Diary, March 25, 1863, UM.

49. In her analysis of the postwar experiences of elite women in North Carolina, Jane Turner Censer found that the young woman's experience in the wartime household helped her to adapt more easily to the conditions of postwar domesticity. See "A Changing World of Work: North Carolina Elite Women, 1865-1895."

<h2 style="text-align:center">CHAPTER FOUR</h2>
The Confederate Belle

1. William Bisland to Caroline Pride, August 11, 1862, in Bisland-Shields Family Papers, MDAH.

2. Ibid., February, 9, 1863. Faust argues that in the latter stages of the war, more and more women voiced their dissent and urged their soldier kin to desert. She contends that women rejected their public wartime role in preference for their private, traditional role. Further, women's failing patriotism signified their realization that in the Confederacy, "the public interest did not encompass their own." See *Mothers of Invention*, 234-47; Rable, *Civil Wars*, 73-90. I have found no evidence to suggest that this group of young women urged their kin to desert at any time during the war. It is possible that wives and mothers had more pressing financial or managerial problems than young women, who remained in a subordinate position within the family and household.

3. Emma Walton diary, Walton-Glenny Family Papers, WRC.

4. Emma Walton to James B. Walton, July 27, 1862, April 2, 1863, Walton-Glenny Family Papers, WRC. Many women in New Orleans and the surrounding area expressed feelings of despondency about the war during this period. See Worthington diary, February 2, 11, 25, 27, 1862, Amanda Dougherty Worthington Papers, UNC; Ellen Louise Power Diary, February 24, April 26, 1862, UNC; Harper, *Annie Harper's Journal*, 18; Brickell diary, November 22, 25, 1861, Edward Fontaine Papers, MSU; Wadley diary, June 1, 1862, Sarah Lois Wadley Papers, UNC; Solomon, *Diary of Clara Solomon*, 343. Other older women also recorded their despondency after the fall of New Orleans. See Katherine Jones, ed., *Heroines of Dixie: Confederate Women Tell Their Stories of the War*, 125; Margaret Johnson Erwin, *Like Some Green Laurel: Letters of Margaret Johnson Erwin, 1821-1863*, 117.

5. Emma Walton to James B. Walton, July 11, 15, 1863, January 30, June 20, 1864, in Walton-Glenny Family Papers, WRC.

6. On patriotic womanhood see Faust, "Altars of Sacrifice"; Clinton, *Tara Revisited*, 58-59; H. E. Sterkx, *Partners in Rebellion: Alabama Women in the Civil*

War, 54-55. Jörg Nagler notes the importance of loyalty on the home front. See "Loyalty and Dissent: The Home Front in the American Civil War." See also Morgan, *Civil War Diary*, 411. While scholars have examined the Confederate model of womanhood, they have placed far less emphasis on the extent to which women of different age groups, particularly young women, were able to adapt to and fulfill the requirements of the wartime feminine ideal. Faust is one of few historians to devote a chapter in her book to the wartime plight of young Confederate women. See *Mothers of Invention*, 139-52.

7. Lizzie Cary Daniel, ed., *Confederate Scrap Book Copied from a Scrap-book Kept by a Young Girl during and Immediately after the War, with Additions from War Copies of the "Southern Literary Messenger" and "Illustrated News" Loaned by Friends and Other Sections as Accredited. Published for the Benefit of the Memorial Bazaar, Held in Richmond, April 11, 1893*, 213-14.

8. "Hinds County Women in Wartime," John Logan Power and Family Papers, MDAH, scrapbook 18, 22. See also Solomon, *Diary of Clara Solomon*, 67, 148, 151, 154, 184, 233, 374; Ellen Louise Power Diary, September 15, 1862, UNC; Wadley diary, November 28, 1863, Sarah Lois Wadley Papers, UNC; Sidney Harding Diary, August 19, 1863, LSU; Stone, *Brokenburn*, 147, 232, 267; Harper, *Annie Harper's Journal*, 14. For an analysis of the currency problems and their effect on Southern women see Rable, *Civil Wars*, 93-94, 102-3. On women's inability to achieve antebellum standards of fashion see 92-96.

9. Stone, *Brokenburn*, 231, 86, 189.

10. Ibid., 206-7.

11. Ibid., 281-82. See also 147, 161, 231. Kate also noted a change in the Southern gentleman's appearance. See 109-10; Harper, *Annie Harper's Journal*, 14. See also Wadley diary, August 3, 1864, Sarah Lois Wadley Papers, UNC.

12. Morgan, *Civil War Diary*, 140, 262, 240, 286. See also Sophie Collins to E. J. Stone, February 22, June 9, 1863, in Emmett Lloyd Ross Papers, MSU.

13. Solomon, *Diary of Clara Solomon*, 155, 172, 371. See also 267, 317; Wadley diary, July 17, 1861, Sarah Lois Wadley Papers, UNC.

14. Sophie Collins to E. J. Stone, September 30, 1863, in Emmett Lloyd Ross Papers, MSU; Harper, *Annie Harper's Journal*, 12, 14; James Silver, ed., *Mississippi in the Confederacy: As Seen in Retrospect*, 170; Morgan, *Civil War Diary*, 503. See also Edwina Burnley Memoir, UNC, 17; Columbus Chapter UDC, eds., *War Reminiscences of Columbus*, 15; McRae diary, January 14, 1862, Sallie B. McRae Papers, MSU.

15. Elizabeth Christie Brown Diary, April 11, 1863, UM; Irion-Neilson diary, Irion-Neilson Family Papers, MDAH, book 2, 16; Irion-Neilson, *Lucy's Journal*, 42. The availability of mourning clothes also altered mourning rituals during the war. Patricia R. Loughridge and Edward D. C. Campbell Jr. argue that women who had lost kin had to "make do [with their attire] by dying fabric or borrowing clothes from friends." See *Women in Mourning: A Catalog of the Museum of the Confederacy's Corollary Exhibition Held November 14, 1984, Through January 6, 1986*, 20. See also Faust, *Mothers of Invention*, 188-91; Stone, *Brokenburn*, 189, 240, 277.

16. Stone, *Brokenburn*, 225, 231. See also Sidney Harding Diary, November 11, 1863, LSU; Edwards, *Scarlett Doesn't Live Here Anymore*, 76.

17. Stone, *Brokenburn*, 39, 50-51, 52-53, 55, 57, 59, 61, 65, 162; Wadley diary, July 14, August 16, October 19, 1861, Sarah Lois Wadley Papers, UNC; Mary C. Wright diary, May 15, 1861, January 6, 1863, Wright-Boyd Family Papers, LSU;

Carmouche memoir, Annie Jeter Carmouche Papers, TU, 17. See also Douglas memoir, Emily Caroline Douglas Papers, LSU, 126; Ellen Louise Power Diary, July 9, 1863, UNC; Irion-Neilson, *Lucy's Journal*, 18. On young women entertaining or nursing Confederate soldiers, see, for example, Ellen Louise Power Diary, May 31, June 15, July 14, August 3, 1863, UNC; Morgan, *Civil War Diary*, 317-18, 451; Sidney Harding Diary, April 10, 1864, LSU; Worthington diary, June 24, December 6, 1862, May 2, 12, November 19, 1863, Amanda Dougherty Worthington Papers, UNC; Wadley diary, May 16, July 1, 7, August 13, December 10, 1863, March 7, 1865, Sarah Lois Wadley Papers, UNC.

18. Morgan, *Civil War Diary*, 385-93; William Bisland to Caroline Pride, February 9, 1863, in Bisland-Shields Family Papers, MDAH. While Sarah attended the dance, she could not participate in the event because of a back injury. See also Rable, *Civil Wars*, 196-200. Some families, however, continued to hold balls and parties if finances allowed. For examples of extravagant social occasions see Rable, 200-201.

19. Elizabeth Christie Brown Diary, May 1, 1863, UM; Cordelia Lewis Scales to Lulie Irby, August 4, 1861, in Cordelia Lewis Scales Papers, MDAH.

20. Sophie Collins to E. J. Stone, November 30, 1862, in Emmett Lloyd Ross Papers, MSU; Irion-Neilson, *Lucy's Journal*, 27. See also Wadley diary, December 21, 1863, Sarah Lois Wadley Papers, UNC. Some young ladies noted the absence of social occasions. See Morgan, *Civil War Diary*, 385; Ellen Louise Power Diary, April 30, May 1, 1862, UNC.

21. Wadley diary, August 10, 1862, February 16, April 29, 1864, Sarah Lois Wadley Papers, UNC. See also July 16, October 15, 1863, March 27, 1865.

22. Morgan, *Civil War Diary*, 104, 156, 162; Sidney Harding Diary, December 27, 1864, LSU; Brickell diary, March 26, 1864, Edward Fontaine Papers, MSU.

23. Stone, *Brokenburn*, 204; Wadley diary, December 11, 1864, Sarah Lois Wadley Papers, UNC; Mary C. Wright diary, December 14, 29, 1864, January 18, 1865, Wright-Boyd Family Papers, LSU. See also Cordelia Lewis Scales to Lulie Irby, August 4, 1861, in Cordelia Lewis Scales Papers, MDAH; Sidney Harding Diary, September 30, 1864, LSU; Solomon, *Diary of Clara Solomon*, 129.

24. Brickell diary, June 11, 1864, Edward Fontaine Papers, MSU.

25. Jacobs manuscript, Annie E. Clark Jacobs Papers, MDAH, 72; Mary C. Wright diary, December 2, 1864, January 22, February 10, 1865, Wright-Boyd Family Papers, LSU.

26. Kate D. Foster Diary, September 20, 1863, DUKE; Stone, *Brokenburn*, 181, 314. No young lady in this study became romantically involved with a Union soldier.

27. Morgan, *Civil War Diary*, 418, 443.

28. Worthington diary, May 2, 17, September 16, 1863, Amanda Dougherty Worthington Papers, UNC.

29. Elizabeth Christie Brown Diary, April 6, 1863, UM; Irion-Neilson, *Lucy's Journal*, 25-26; Rable, *Civil Wars*, 51-54, 193-94. See also Sterkx, *Partners in Rebellion*, 148-51. While Eliza Lucy Irion entered society during the war, no young lady in this study wrote about a wartime courtship. On antebellum courtship rituals (to compare with wartime courtship) see, for example, Stowe, *Intimacy and Power in the Old South*, 50-121; Stevenson, *Life in Black and White*, 51-58.

30. Stone, *Brokenburn*, 61, 154.

31. Sidney Harding diary, November 7, 1863, May 1, 1864, LSU; Brickell diary, February 26, 1862, March 30, 1861, December 18, 1864, May 13, 1865, Edward

Fontaine Papers, MSU; Solomon, *Diary of Clara Solomon*, 427. Faust argues that young women "deprived of the distractions and excitements of heterosexual courtship and romance turned increasingly to one another for a surrogate interior life." See *Mothers of Invention*, 142-45. For an examination of love between young women see Carroll Smith-Rosenberg, "The Female World of Love and Ritual: Relations between Women in Nineteenth-Century America."

32. Emma Walton to James B. Walton, October 4, 1863, in Walton-Glenny Family Papers, WRC.

33. Morgan, *Civil War Diary*, 217, 548. Just months before Sarah had described her "beau ideal" in detail. See 60-63; Solomon, *Diary of Clara Solomon*, 202-3; Wadley diary, October 2, 1860, Sarah Lois Wadley Papers, UNC; Stone, *Brokenburn*, 301.

34. Worthington diary, April 30, 1863, Amanda Dougherty Worthington Papers, UNC; Brickell diary, March 6, 1864, Edward Fontaine Papers, MSU; Irion-Neilson, *Lucy's Journal*, 62.

35. Solomon, *Diary of Clara Solomon*, 315-16, 393. See also 287, 296-97, 328, 386-87.

36. Pendleton diary, June 15, 1864, Mary E. Wilkes Shell Papers, MDAH; Tompkins, "Women of the Sixties," 284; Morgan, *Civil War Diary*, 153, 217. Sarah Morgan's comment reflects the attitude of many elite young ladies toward teaching. See Rable, *Civil Wars*, 129-30. Sarah Lois Wadley's efforts to teach her siblings hint at the challenges that teaching posed to young ladies. See Wadley diary, June 5, November 16, 1863, January 14, March 25, November 23, 1864, Sarah Lois Wadley Papers, UNC. See also Morgan, *Civil War Diary*, 593-94.

37. See Berry, "A History of Women's Higher Education"; Nguyen, "The Value of Learning."

38. Wadley diary, August 8, 1861, January 15, September 13, 1862, Sarah Lois Wadley Papers, UNC; Emma Walton's letters to James Walton, in Walton-Glenny Family Papers, WRC; Martha Josephine Moore diary, Frank Liddell Richardson Papers, UNC; Solomon, *Diary of Clara Solomon;* "Blanche" to brother, [undated], in Soldiers Letters (Civilians to Combatants), 1861-1865, MC. See also Stone, *Brokenburn*, 256, 316; Alcinda Timberlake memoirs, Alcinda Timberlake Papers, MDAH, 6; Margaret Gooch Memoir, TSL, 2; Sophie Collins to E. J. Stone, April 26, 1863, in Emmett Lloyd Ross Papers, MSU; Carrie Zacharie Composition Book, LSU; O'Brien, ed., *An Evening when Alone*, 348. This commitment to education is consistent with antebellum Southerners' belief in academic training as a means of class distinction. In her study of the plantation mistress, Clinton argues that planters impressed upon their daughters the importance of education. If, for economic reasons, a planter could not provide a dowry for his daughter's marriage, he hoped that her education would attract an appropriate suitor. See *The Plantation Mistress*, 136.

CHAPTER FIVE

"How Has the Mighty Fallen": Defeat in Mississippi and Louisiana

1. Morgan, *Civil War Diary*, 47-48.
2. Ibid., 51.
3. Ibid., 85.

4. Irion-Neilson, *Lucy's Journal*, 21.

5. Ken Burns, *The Civil War*, pt. 2, *1862: A Very Bloody Affair*, documentary (Florentine Films and WETA-TV, 1991); Richard Wheeler, *Voices of the Civil War*, 471-73.

6. Stone, *Brokenburn*, 85. Faust argues that a "touch of realism tempered women's politics and women's patriotism." See *Mothers of Invention*, 13. My analysis confirms these findings for the young ladies of Mississippi and Louisiana.

7. Worthington diary, February 2, 25, 11, 27, 1862, Amanda Dougherty Worthington Papers, UNC; Ellen Louise Power Diary, February 24, 1862, UNC. See also Mary C. Wright diary, January 4, 1863, Wright-Boyd Family Papers, LSU; Solomon, *Diary of Clara Solomon*, 295, 341; Stone, *Brokenburn*, 90, 91, 94; Wadley diary, February 17, March 2, 16, June 1, 1862, Sarah Lois Wadley Papers, UNC; Irion-Neilson, *Lucy's Journal*, 21.

8. Worthington diary, February 2, 1862, Amanda Dougherty Worthington Papers, UNC; Brickell diary, November 25, 22, 1861, Edward Fontaine Papers, MSU; Solomon, *Diary of Clara Solomon*, 129.

9. Wadley diary, August 10, 1862, September 15, April 26, 1861, Sarah Lois Wadley Papers, UNC.

10. Solomon, *Diary of Clara Solomon*, 351, 345. On the fall of New Orleans see Winters, *The Civil War in Louisiana*, 85-102; Dufour, *The Night the War Was Lost*; McPherson, *Battle Cry of Freedom*, 418-22.

11. Solomon, *Diary of Clara Solomon*, 343, 350-51, 354, 351. See also Stone, *Brokenburn*, 105.

12. Ellen Louise Power Diary, April 26, 1862, UNC; Worthington diary, June 24, April 2, 1862, Amanda Dougherty Worthington Papers, UNC; Stone, *Brokenburn*, 100. See also Mitchell diary, July 1862, (Lise) Elizabeth Mitchell Papers, TU; Elizabeth Christie Brown Diary, February 14, 1863, UM; Solomon, *Diary of Clara Solomon*, 354; Wadley diary, August 25, 1863, Sarah Lois Wadley Papers, UNC.

13. Stone, *Brokenburn*, 105; Morgan, *Civil War Diary*, 172-73. On the battle of Baton Rouge see Winters, *The Civil War in Louisiana*, 113-24.

14. Morgan, *Civil War Diary*, 91, 247, 173; Simkins and Patton, *The Women of the Confederacy*, 101. For another account of the war in Baton Rouge see Céline Frémaux Garcia, *Céline: Remembering Louisiana, 1850-1871*, 62-89. See also "Burning of Jackson," John Logan Power and Family Papers, MDAH, scrapbook 17; Stone, *Brokenburn*, 194-202.

15. Stone, *Brokenburn*, 128. Many young women recorded the loss, pain, and humiliation they felt after Federal raids. See, for example, Ellen Louise Power Diary, June 23, 1863, UNC; Morgan, *Civil War Diary*, 212; Scales, "Notes and Documents," 174-78; Worthington diary, April 23, 24, 1863, Amanda Dougherty Worthington Papers, UNC; Ida Barlow Trotter memoir, Ida Barlow Trotter Papers, MDAH, 1-4; Mitchell diary, August 4, 1864, (Lise) Elizabeth Mitchell Papers, TU; Mrs. S. G. McLain, "Some Incidents and a Skirmish Witnessed during the Civil War in my Home Town," manuscript, Southern Women's Collection, box 2, MC; Elizabeth Christie Brown Diary, July 14, 15, UM.

16. Stone, *Brokenburn*, 179, 185. As they watched for Yankees, Kate and her mother worried about the loss of their home and possessions. Amanda Stone must have also worried about potential assaults on her daughter. Kate and her peers remain silent on the issue of rape during the war. This silence is consistent with their antebellum silence on the rape of black women by white men. It is also consis-

tent with Southern honor, which scorned the woman who relinquished her sexual purity, voluntarily or otherwise. See chapter 6 for an examination of the issue of wartime rape.

17. Marilyn Mayer Culpepper, *Trials and Triumphs: Women of the American Civil War*, 96-97; Stone, *Brokenburn*, 14, 88, 185. See also Brickell diary, March 16, 1862, Edward Fontaine Papers, MSU.

18. Wadley diary, March 25, 1864, Sarah Lois Wadley Papers, UNC. See also April 13, 1862, July 1, August 6, 1863, March 19, April 9, 25, August 11, 13, September 7, 24, 1864; Solomon, *Diary of Clara Solomon*, 365, 349, 381.

19. Morgan, *Civil War Diary*, 169, 48, 186, 193; Worthington diary, February 25, March 20, 1862, Amanda Dougherty Worthington Papers, UNC; Elizabeth Christie Brown diary, February 5, 1863, UM. On rumors, contradictory reports, and lack of news see, for example, Mary C. Wright diary, January 5, 1863, Wright-Boyd Family Papers, LSU; Elizabeth Christie Brown Diary, February 14, July 9, 1863, UM; Stone, *Brokenburn*, 20, 52, 108, 137-38, 216, 229, 233; Kate D. Foster Diary, June 25, 1863, DUKE; Sophie Collins to Mary Collins, March 22, 1863, in Emmett Lloyd Ross Papers, MSU; Ellen Louise Power Diary, June 26, 30, July 11, 1863, UNC. Women in occupied cities were forced to read censored newspapers. See Winters, *The Civil War in Louisiana*, 131; Solomon, *Diary of Clara Solomon*, 368, 381; Morgan, *Civil War Diary*, 515.

20. Morgan, *Civil War Diary*, 38-39, 6-11, 25-26, 33-34, 197. See also Frevert, *Men of Honour*, 2-3.

21. Worthington diary, May 2, 1863, January 19, 1865, Amanda Dougherty Worthington Papers, UNC; Stone, *Brokenburn*, 135; Scales, "Notes and Documents," 172.

22. Morgan, *Civil War Diary*, 442, 519; Solomon, *Diary of Clara Solomon*, 429; Wadley diary, December 21, 1863, Sarah Lois Wadley Papers, UNC. See also Scales, "Notes and Documents," 179.

23. Rable argues that because of the Confederacy's smaller population, combined with Northern military success, Confederate women were more likely to experience the loss of a loved one. See *Civil Wars*, 69. See also Faust, *Mothers of Invention*, 5.

24. Wadley diary, April 13, 1862, September 15, 1861, April 25, 1864, Sarah Lois Wadley Papers, UNC; Sidney Harding Diary, April 10, 1864, LSU.

25. Ellen Louise Power Diary, June 29, May 3, 1862, UNC; Wadley diary, August 10, October 15, 1862, May 26, July 16, 1863, April 25, 1864, Sarah Lois Wadley Papers, UNC; Kate D. Foster Diary, September 20, November 15, 1863, DUKE. See also Mary C. Wright diary, November 12, 1864, Wright-Boyd Family Papers, LSU; Stone, *Brokenburn*, 48, 144, 186, 257-58; Harper, *Annie Harper's Journal*, 11; Scales, "Notes and Documents," 174; Irion-Neilson, *Lucy's Journal*, 32; Solomon, *Diary of Clara Solomon*, 62, 89; Brickell diary, May 5, 1861, Edward Fontaine Papers, MSU.

26. Kate D. Foster Diary, September 20, November 15, 1863, DUKE.

27. Stone, *Brokenburn*, 186-88, 264.

28. Worthington diary, October 11, 1864, Amanda Dougherty Worthington Papers, UNC. See also Mary C. Wright diary, November 14, 18, December 2, 1864, January 22, February 10, 1865, Wright-Boyd Family Papers, LSU; Stone, *Brokenburn*, 259-62; Irion-Neilson, *Lucy's Journal*, 29-31; Morgan, *Civil War Diary*, 597-603.

29. Cordelia Lewis Scales to Lulie Irby, August 17, 1862, in Cordelia Lewis Scales Papers, MDAH; Scales, "Notes and Documents," 174; Brickell diary, April 3, 1861, Edward Fontaine Papers, MSU.

30. Mattie Burkett to brother, April 11, 1865, in Soldiers Letters (Civilians to Combatants), Mississippi, MC; Solomon, *Diary of Clara Solomon*, 322-23. Clara also worried about the safety of her father, who was a sutler in Virginia. See 269, 313, 316, 365, 383, 407. See also Worthington diary, January 29, February 12, March 4, 20, 1862, Amanda Dougherty Worthington Papers, UNC; McRae diary, May 3, 1863, Sallie B. McRae Papers, MSU; Stone, *Brokenburn*, 39, 102, 133, 144, 185, 205; Morgan, *Civil War Diary*, 86. It was also common for young women to worry about the moral welfare of their kin. Faust argues that men's religious observance became increasingly important to Southern women because they feared the loss of kin "not just in the world but for all time." See *Mothers of Invention*, 186-87; Rable, *Civil Wars*, 56-57; Wadley diary, March 19, April 15, August 15, 1864, January 14, 1865, Sarah Lois Wadley Papers, UNC; Emmett Lloyd Ross to Mary Collins, June 9, 15, 26, July 24, 1864, in Emmett Lloyd Ross Papers, MSU.

31. Morgan, *Civil War Diary*, 121, 153; Moore diary, April 27, 1863, Frank Liddell Richardson Papers, UNC; Solomon, *Diary of Clara Solomon*, 429. See also Sophie Collins to E. J. Stone, April 26, 1863, in Emmett Lloyd Ross Papers, MSU; Wadley diary, June 1, 1862, Sarah Lois Wadley Papers, UNC; Elizabeth Christie Brown Diary, April 22, 1863, UM.

32. Worthington diary, January 5, March 20, 1862, Amanda Dougherty Worthington Papers, UNC; Elizabeth Christie Brown Diary, August 5, February 4, 1863, UM; Morgan, *Civil War Diary*, 77-78, 260, 442. See also 128, 149, 151, 161; Wadley diary, May 18, July 18, September 29, November 7, 1862, January 14, 1864, Sarah Lois Wadley Papers, UNC; Moore diary, April 23, 1863, Frank Liddell Richardson Papers, UNC; Stone, *Brokenburn*, 180; Brickell diary, December 14, 1862, February 24, 1863, Edward Fontaine Papers, MSU.

33. Ken Burns, *The Civil War*, pt. 3, *1862: Forever Free*, documentary (Florentine Films and WETA-TV, 1991). See also Winters, *The Civil War in Louisiana*, 186-205; James T. Currie, *Enclave: Vicksburg and Her Plantations, 1863-1870*; Peter F. Walker, *Vicksburg: A People at War, 1860-1865*.

34. On the fall of Vicksburg see Winters, *The Civil War in Louisiana*, 186-205; Bond, *Political Culture in the Nineteenth-Century South*, 118. For primary accounts of life in Vicksburg during the siege see, for example, letter by Ann Shannon and finished by Grace or Alice Shannon, June/July 1863, in Crutcher-Shannon Family Papers, MDAH; Terrence J. Winschel, *Alice Shirley and the Story of Wexford Lodge*; Mary Webster Loughborough, *My Cave Life in Vicksburg*; Emilie Riley McKinley, *From the Pen of a She-Rebel: The Civil War Diary of Emilie Riley McKinley*. Unfortunately, I have not been able to locate primary material written by young women living in Vicksburg during the siege, preventing any further analysis other than what is presented here.

35. Elizabeth Christie Brown Diary, July 7, 8, 9, 10, 1863, UM.

36. Worthington diary, July 25, 1863, Amanda Dougherty Worthington Papers, UNC; Stone, *Brokenburn*, 229, 233. See also Wadley diary, July 12, 1863, Sarah Lois Wadley Papers, UNC.

37. Harper, *Annie Harper's Journal*, 18; Kate D. Foster Diary, July 13, 1863, DUKE; Mitchell diary, August 4, 1864, (Lise) Elizabeth Mitchell Papers, TU; Morgan, *Civil War Diary*, 519, 515; Wadley diary, July 12, 1863, Sarah Lois Wadley

```

Papers, UNC. See also Trotter memoir, Ida Barlow Trotter Papers, MDAH, 1, 7.

38. Emma Walton to James Walton, July 15, 1863, in Walton-Glenny Family Papers, WRC; Morgan, *Civil War Diary*, 515.

39. Morgan, *Civil War Diary*, 523.

40. Wadley diary, July 16, 1863, April 5, 1864, Sarah Lois Wadley Papers, UNC. See also September 2, December 21, 1863, March 25, 1864.

41. Many young women had voiced their concerns about Confederate military success. See Worthington diary, February 2, 11, 25, 27, 1862, Amanda Dougherty Worthington Papers, UNC; Ellen Louise Power Diary, February 24, April 26, 1862, UNC; Harper, *Annie Harper's Journal*, 18; Moore diary, April 27, 1863, Frank Liddell Richardson Papers, UNC; Brickell diary, November 22, 25, 1861, Edward Fontaine Papers, MSU; Wadley diary, June 1, 1862, Sarah Lois Wadley Papers, UNC. Other, more mature ladies in Mississippi and Louisiana wrote similar comments in their diaries. See, for example, Julia LeGrand, *The Journal of Julia LeGrand, New Orleans, 1862-1863*; Seabury, *Diary of Caroline Seabury*, 76; Mahala Roach diary, February 7, 10, 21, 1862, Roach and Eggleston Family Papers, UNC.

CHAPTER SIX

"The Yankees Are Coming"

1. Solomon, *Diary of Clara Solomon*, 344, 351, 354. Unlike the other young ladies in this study, Clara Solomon was Jewish. Her family were natives of South Carolina and were "members of an elite group among American Jews in the nineteenth century." Elliott Ashkenazi argues that Clara's "American heritage, decidedly southern," gave her a "comfortable place in the world of New Orleans." Clara attended school with Christian students and mixed with them on an academic and social level. See 4, 7.

2. Trotter memoir, Ida Barlow Trotter Papers, MDAH, 1. On the importance of women's manufacturing of supplies for the Confederate army see Wiley, *The Life of Johnny Reb*, 19; Rable, *Civil Wars*, 140; Faust, *Mothers of Invention*, 24; Bunch, "Confederate Woman of Arkansas," 176.

3. See Bunch, "Confederate Women of Arkansas." In his study of the occupied South, Stephen V. Ash defines three categories of invasion. First, he examines the impact of occupation on garrisoned towns, such as New Orleans. He argues that because they were dependent on commerce, many garrisoned towns were economically debilitated by occupation. Confederate citizens living in garrisoned towns were least likely to instigate forms of armed resistance and were most dependent on the enemy for necessities such as food and provisions. Ash defines the Confederate frontier as the second region and argues that this area was "beyond the limits of the districts that the Union army was able to hold and regularly patrol." This region experienced a labor shortage because of a loss of slaves to the Union army and was susceptible to Federal raids and the destruction and confiscation of property. Ash defines the third region as "No Man's Land." Describing this area as "the zone surrounding the garrisoned towns," Ash argues that this region was "beyond the pale of Confederate authority" and received regular visitations from the Union army but was not subjected to permanent occupation. Because of the regular Federal presence, the citizens of "No Man's Land" frequently lost horses and livestock,
```

fences and slaves. See *When the Yankees Came*, 77-107. The style of the regional commander and the extent of civilian resistance also influenced relations between Southern women and the enemy. In occupied Baton Rouge, Sarah Morgan's inter-action with General Thomas Williams and his troops contrasted sharply with Emma Walton's experience as a loyal Confederate in General Benjamin Butler's New Orleans.

4. Stone, *Brokenburn*, 125. See also Morgan, *Civil War Diary*, 85. On the impor-tance of protecting women see Cashin, *A Family Venture*, 15; Burton, *In My Father's House*, 128; Faust, *Mothers of Invention*, 6. On soldiers' motivations to fight see McPherson, *For Cause and Comrades*; Charles Joyner, paper given to the American Civil War Round Table of Australia, Melbourne, April 11, 1998. On the conflict between familial and patriotic duty see Whites, *The Civil War as a Crisis in Gender*, 64-65; Richard E. Beringer, "Confederate Identity and the Will to Fight," in *On the Road to Total War: The American Civil War and the German Wars of Unification, 1861-1871*, ed. Stig Forster and Jörg Nagler, 92-98. This crisis was more acute for those who did not belong to the Southern elite and lacked the resources to evade service or conscription. Despite possessing the funds to evade service, all the male family members in this study served the Confederacy if phys-ically able.

5. Solomon, *Diary of Clara Solomon*, 340; Worthington diary, November 20, 1863, Amanda Dougherty Worthington Papers, UNC. See also July 25, September 25, 1863.

6. Worthington diary, October 11, 1864, Amanda Dougherty Worthington Papers, UNC; Miller, *Lost Mansions of Mississippi*, 99; Morgan, *Civil War Diary*, 438. See also Wadley diary, February 11, 1865, Sarah Lois Wadley Papers, UNC.

7. Stone, *Brokenburn*, 137, 175; Sidney Harding Diary, July 27, 1863, LSU; Morgan, *Civil War Diary*, 76, 180. See also Wadley diary, January 14, 1864, Sarah Lois Wadley Papers, UNC; Solomon, *Diary of Clara Solomon*, 35.

8. Regarding the low incidence of rape during the Civil War see Susan Brownmiller, *Against Our Will: Men, Women, and Rape*, 88; Faust, *Mothers of Inven-tion*, 198-200. On the rape of black women by Union soldiers see Faust, *Mothers of Invention*, 200; Michael Fellman, *Inside War: The Guerrilla Conflict in Missouri dur-ing the American Civil War*, 210-11; Deborah Gray White, *Ar'n't I a Woman?: Female Slaves in the Plantation South*, 164; Reid Mitchell, *The Vacant Chair: The Northern Soldier Leaves Home*, 104, 106-9. On symbolic rape see Ash, *When the Yankees Came*, 201; Rable, *Civil Wars*, 160-62; Fellman, *Inside War*, 207. Bell Irvin Wiley notes that eighteen Union soldiers were executed for rape. See *The Life of Billy Yank: The Common Soldier of the Union*, 205.

Faust writes that "the safety and purity of young white girls was a particular con-cern in the wartime South" and "many families exerted considerable effort to keep them away from areas of military action and upheaval." This was the reason behind the placement of young ladies in boarding schools during the war. See *Mothers of Invention*, 39. In my study, the overwhelming majority of young ladies remained with the family unit, despite pervasive Federal occupation.

9. Wadley diary, February 15, 1865, Sarah Lois Wadley Papers, UNC; Scales, "Notes and Documents," 175; Morgan, *Civil War Diary*, 240.

10. Morgan, *Civil War Diary*, 234, 213.

11. See Rable, *Civil Wars*, 171; George C. Rable, "Missing in Action: Women of the Confederacy," 145; Faust, "Altars of Sacrifice"; Faust, *Mothers of Invention*, 234-47.

12. Worthington diary, January 19, 1865, Amanda Dougherty Worthington Papers, UNC; Emma Walton to James Walton, July 15, 1863, in Walton-Glenny Family Papers, WRC; Stone, *Brokenburn*, 278, 79, 281. See also Elizabeth Christie Brown Diary, February 25, 1863, UM; Wadley diary, July 13, September 29, 1862, August 3, 1864, Sarah Lois Wadley Papers, UNC; Morgan, *Civil War Diary*, 295, 313, 515, 581; Solomon, *Diary of Clara Solomon*, 271.

13. Emma Walton to James Walton, April 22, 1863, in Walton-Glenny Papers, WRC; Emma Walton diary, May 13-19, 1862, Walton-Glenny Family Papers, WRC; Wadley diary, February 22, 1864, Sarah Lois Wadley Papers, UNC; Mitchell diary, July 1862, (Lise) Elizabeth Mitchell Papers, TU; Solomon, *Diary of Clara Solomon*, 89, 322, 340, 377, 404; letter begun by Ann Shannon and finished by Grace or Alice to [unknown], June/July 1863, in Crutcher-Shannon Family Papers, MDAH. See also Stone, *Brokenburn*, 90, 127, 130, 239; Morgan, *Civil War Diary*, 213. On the contrasting images and ideals of Northern and Southern masculinity see Michael Kimmel, *Manhood in America: A Cultural History*, 16-17; Anthony E. Rotundo, *American Manhood: Transformations in Masculinity from the Revolution to the Modern Era*, 18-20. On the way in which binary constructions of Northern and Southern masculinity emerged as a component of the sectional conflict see Nina Silber, *The Romance of Reunion: Northerners and the South, 1865-1900*. Faust contends that the Yankee soldier became a socially acceptable target for women, who may have otherwise directed their anger "within their own families, households or social order." See *Mothers of Invention*, 204.

14. Morgan, *Civil War Diary*, 67, 94-96, 146, 160, 235. See also Solomon, *Diary of Clara Solomon*, 429-30.

15. Kate D. Foster Diary, July 4, 1863, DUKE; Moore diary, May 7, 1863, Frank Liddell Richardson Papers, UNC; Shannon sisters to [unknown], June/July 1863, in Crutcher-Shannon Family Papers, MDAH; Stone, *Brokenburn*, 175. See also Worthington diary, April 20, 22, 1862, Amanda Dougherty Worthington Papers, UNC; Elizabeth Christie Brown Diary, February 21, March 7, 17, 1863, UM; Brickell diary, March 6, 1864, Edward Fontaine Papers, MSU; Scales, "Notes and Documents," 175-76; Morgan, *Civil War Diary*, 517.

16. Wadley diary, September 6, 1860, Sarah Lois Wadley Papers, UNC; Stone, *Brokenburn*, 43. In the antebellum South, shooting was regarded as one of the most "masculine of activities." See Rable, "Missing in Action," 136. For women's organization of drill teams see Massey, *Bonnet Brigades*, 39.

17. Scales, "Notes and Documents," 175, 178-79; Stone, *Brokenburn*, 172, 183-84.

18. Morgan, *Civil War Diary*, 150, 76-77, 51, 65.

19. Ibid., 77, 166; Cordelia Lewis Scales to Lulie Irby, August 17, 1862, in Cordelia Lewis Scales Papers, MDAH; Stone, *Brokenburn*, 114; Wadley diary, April 21, 1861, August 20, 1863, December 20, 1864, Sarah Lois Wadley Papers, UNC.

20. Worthington diary, January 29, February 11, 1862, April 21, 1863, Amanda Dougherty Worthington Papers, UNC; Morgan, *Civil War Diary*, 65, 166-67. Amanda Worthington's sister also dressed up in men's clothing. See May 8, 1862; Rable, "Missing in Action," 136. Weiner argues that young women were the only Confederates to engage in these wartime fantasies. She attributes this to personal frustration because, unlike their mothers, they "did not share increased responsibilities." See *Mistresses and Slaves*, 162. I reject this claim on the basis of the evidence I have presented in chapter 3, which describes young women's expanded role in the wartime household.

A small minority of Southern women disguised themselves as men and became soldiers. See Massey, *Bonnet Brigades,* 78-86; Janet Kaufman, "Under the Petticoat Flag: Women in the Confederate Army"; Faust, *Mothers of Invention,* 202-4; Clinton, *Tara Revisited,* 98-100.

21. Morgan, *Civil War Diary,* 65.

22. Ash, *When the Yankees Came,* 41-42; Rable, "Missing in Action," 141.

23. Solomon, *Diary of Clara Solomon,* 355-56, 395, 412. See also 388, 425. Mitchell notes that some Northern soldiers regarded Confederate women as more "vicious" than their men. See *The Vacant Chair,* 97.

24. Moore diary, May 7, April 7, 12, 1863, Frank Liddell Richardson Papers, UNC.

25. Morgan, *Civil War Diary,* 64-65, 68-69, 122, 142-43; Solomon, *Diary of Clara Solomon,* 354.

26. Solomon, *Diary of Clara Solomon,* 429-30.

27. Ibid., 369-70, 419-20. Mary P. Ryan contends that while Federal occupation of the city "turned gender symbolism topsy-turvy, it did not dislodge patriarchy. Rather, women fought the Yankees from their customary informal and symbolic places on the margins of public life, using their feminine weaponry of etiquette and attire, snubs and handkerchiefs." See *Women in Public: Between Banners and Ballots, 1825-1880,* 143-47. Still, this kind of political action marked a strong departure from women's participation in antebellum politics. See also Massey, *Bonnet Brigades,* 228-30; Winters, *The Civil War in Louisiana,* 125-48; Rable, "Missing in Action." On Butler (general) see Dick Nolan, *Benjamin Franklin Butler: The Damnedest Yankee;* Joy J. Jackson, "Keeping Law and Order in New Orleans under General Butler, 1862." For young ladies' derogatory descriptions of General Butler see Stone, *Brokenburn,* 111, 126; Morgan, *Civil War Diary,* 64, 140, 141; Solomon, *Diary of Clara Solomon,* 367; Wadley diary, June 1, November 30, 1862, Sarah Lois Wadley Papers, UNC.

28. Faust, *Mothers of Invention,* 210-12.

29. Morgan, *Civil War Diary,* 122.

30. See Carol Dyhouse, *Girls Growing Up in Late Victorian and Edwardian England,* 2; Gorham, *The Victorian Girl,* 47.

31. Wadley diary, April 13, July 18, 1862, Sarah Lois Wadley Papers, UNC; Moore diary, May 7, 1863, Frank Liddell Richardson Papers, UNC; Solomon, *Diary of Clara Solomon,* 350.

32. Worthington diary, April 20, 1862, Amanda Dougherty Worthington Papers, UNC; Mitchell diary, July 1862, (Lise) Elizabeth Mitchell Papers, TU; Solomon, *Diary of Clara Solomon,* 419-20; Stone, *Brokenburn,* 126; Wadley diary, September 18, 1862, Sarah Lois Wadley Papers, UNC.

33. Scales, "Notes and Documents," 178.

34. Elizabeth Christie Brown Diary, August 18, February 16, 1863, UM; Stone, *Brokenburn,* 115; Wadley diary, July 18, 1862, Sarah Lois Wadley Papers, UNC.

35. Morgan, *Civil War Diary,* 122-24, 108, 112-13. Sarah also noted that accepting assistance from Federal soldiers could result in censure from the Confederate government. While still living in Baton Rouge in 1862, she wrote that if her family asked for Federal protection "against our own men" and the Confederate forces won, they would be regarded as "traitors and our property confiscated by our own government." See 106. Other young ladies scorned fellow Southerners who associated in any way with the Union army. See Stone, *Brokenburn,* 181, 314; Wadley

diary, October 31, 1863, February 3, 1865, Sarah Lois Wadley Papers, UNC; "Blanche" to brother, March 29, [undated], in Soldiers Letters (Civilians to Combatants), Louisiana, MC; Kate D. Foster Diary, September 20, 1863, DUKE. On patriotism as another form of honor see Ash, *When the Yankees Came*, 45.

36. Stone, *Brokenburn*, 185, 122-23. See also 137, 169, 179, 184.

37. Trotter memoir, Ida Barlow Trotter Papers, MDAH, 4; Dawson, ed., "Our Women in the War," 20; Elizabeth Christie Brown Diary, April 29, August 2, 1863, UM. See also Tompkins, "Women of the Sixties," 283; Irion-Neilson diary, April 1865, Irion-Neilson Family Papers, MDAH; Grace Lea Hunt to cousin, [undated] 1862, in Grace Lea Hunt Letters, TU; Irion-Neilson, *Lucy's Journal*, 46-47; Brickell diary, April 6, 1863, Edward Fontaine Papers, MSU; Douglas diary, May 1, August 2, 1863, Emily Caroline Douglas Papers, LSU; Sophie Collins to E. J. Stone, June 9, 1863, in Emmett Lloyd Ross Papers, MSU.

38. Worthington diary, April 23, 24, 1863, Amanda Dougherty Worthington Papers, UNC; Crutcher-Shannon sisters to [unknown], June/July 1863, in Crutcher-Shannon Family Papers, MDAH. There are many similar accounts left by young women in Mississippi and Louisiana. See Mitchell diary, August 4, 1864, (Lise) Elizabeth Mitchell Papers, TU; Jacobs manuscript, Annie E. Clark Jacobs Papers, MDAH, 103; Scales, "Notes and Documents," 175-77; Trotter memoir, Ida Barlow Trotter Papers, MDAH, 1-4; Louisa Russell Conner Memoirs, MDAH, 12; Morgan, *Civil War Diary*, 233-35, 239-40, 249; Mrs. S. G. McLain, "Some Incidents and a Skirmish Witnessed during the Civil War in My Home Town," MC; Miller memoir, Letitia Dabney Miller Papers, UNC, 10; Elizabeth Christie Brown Diary, July 14, 15, 1863, UM; Stone, *Brokenburn*, 243; "Caroline" to Sophie Collins, November 13, 1864, in Emmett Lloyd Ross Papers, MSU; Sidney Harding Diary, July 1863, LSU; Ellen Louise Power Diary, June 23, 1863, UNC.

39. Elizabeth Christie Brown Diary, August 1, 10, 1863, UM. See also July 14, 15, 1863.

40. Morgan, *Civil War Diary*, 238-39.

41. Worthington diary, July 25, April 20, 1863, Amanda Dougherty Worthington Papers, UNC.

42. Scales, "Notes and Documents," 179, 176. On the importance of controlling one's temper in the antebellum South see Clinton, *The Plantation Mistress*, 96-97; Wyatt-Brown, *Southern Honor*, 227; Nancy M. Theriot, *Mothers and Daughters in Nineteenth-Century America: The Biosocial Construction of Femininity*, 22; "Good Temper," *Godey's Lady's Book*, April 1864, 382. Young ladies often reprimanded themselves for exercising their temper. See, for example, Elizabeth Christie Brown Diary, April 14, 1863, UM; Sidney Harding Diary, August 15, 26, October 26, 1863, LSU; Wadley diary, February 6, 1861, Sarah Lois Wadley Papers, UNC; Maria Dyer Davies Diary, November 27, 1850, October 13, 1853, January 24, 1855, DUKE. See also Rable, *Civil Wars*, 157.

43. Stone, *Brokenburn*, 19, 182-83.

44. Trotter memoir, Ida Barlow Trotter Papers, MDAH, 4. See also Walton diary, Walton-Glenny Family Papers, WRC; Dawson, ed., "Our Women in the War," 20.

45. Morgan, *Civil War Diary*, 68-69, 111-12, 236. See also 109, 145; Randall C. Jimerson, *The Private Civil War: Popular Thought during the Sectional Conflict*, 150-58.

46. Harper, *Annie Harper's Journal*, 20. In her memoir, Harper assessed every general who was in command of Natchez during the war. See 20-22.

47. Elizabeth Christie Brown Diary, August 3, 20, September 27, 1863, UM; Kate D. Foster Diary, September 20, 1863, DUKE. See also July 17, August 16, 1863.

48. Scales, "Notes and Documents," 179; Morgan, *Civil War Diary*, 73. See also Stone, *Brokenburn*, 124, 181; Solomon, *Diary of Clara Solomon*, 356-57, 412; Belle Strickland Diary, August 5, 6, 1864, UM; Brickell diary, June 11, 1864, Edward Fontaine Papers, MSU; Wadley diary, January 7, April 16, August 31, 1863, Sarah Lois Wadley Papers, UNC.

CHAPTER SEVEN

"Our Slaves Are Gone"

1. Worthington diary, April 23, 1863, Amanda Dougherty Worthington Papers, UNC. Most historians argue that slavery shaped the identities of all Southerners, black and white. See Fox-Genovese, *Within the Plantation Household*, 29; Wayne, *The Reshaping of Plantation Society*, 15; Weiner, *Mistresses and Slaves*, 1.

2. On the challenge of the absent master's authority by his slaves see Faust, *Mothers of Invention*, 53-79; Mohr, *On The Threshold of Freedom*, 221, 223; Johnston-Miller, "Heirs to Paternalism," 168; Litwack, *Been in the Storm So Long*, 4, 11-12. On the legal position of the slave see, for example, Stampp, *The Peculiar Institution*, 197-98, 206-17; Stanley M. Elkins, *Slavery: A Problem in American Institutional and Intellectual Life*, 56-60; Wayne, *The Reshaping of Plantation Society*, 16; Roark, *Masters without Slaves*, 69; Edwards, *Scarlett Doesn't Live Here Anymore*, 48-52.

3. Wadley diary, April 15, 1864, Sarah Lois Wadley Papers, UNC; Stone, *Brokenburn*, 173, 176.

4. This part of my analysis examines the power relations as expressed through the plantation setting. While many of the elite women in this study lived on plantations, some did not. Still, as I will argue, young ladies in both urban and rural locations understood slavery predominantly through their experiences in the household. Further, the ideology of the master class governed relations among the master, mistress, and slave on plantations and in urban households.

5. On exercising power through the Southern landscape see Edwards, *Gendered Strife and Confusion*, 27.

6. Jacobs manuscript, Annie E. Clark Jacobs Papers, MDAH, 17. See also Scarborough, "So It Was when Her Life Began," 428, 430; Carmouche memoir, Annie Jeter Carmouche Papers, TU, 16. On childhood friendships between black and white children see Fox-Genovese, *Within the Plantation Household*, 155; Stevenson, *Life in Black and White*, 112-13, 137. On elite parents' concern over the influence of slaves on their children see Fox-Genovese, *Within the Plantation Household*, 111-12; Stevenson, *Life in Black and White*, 137; Clinton, *The Plantation Mistress*, 49; Wyatt-Brown, *Southern Honor*, 153; Farnham, *The Education of the Southern Belle*, 123.

7. A master drew upon his "dual power" to assert his dominance. This power found expression in his "control of state power" and his individual control over his slaves. See Genovese, *Roll, Jordan, Roll*, 46; Elkins, *Slavery*, 103-15. Elkins describes this power as absolute and likens the "closed system" of Southern slavery to the Nazi concentration camp.

8. See Stone, *Brokenburn*, 11, 13, 21, 29, 43, 46, 63; Solomon, *Diary of Clara Solomon*, 82, 171, 193, 359; Maria Dyer Davies Diary, November 8, 1855, DUKE; Ellen Louise Power Diary, March 9, December 26, 1862, UNC; Morgan, *Civil War Diary*, 17, 33, 42, 132; Brickell diary, January 22, 1860, Edward Fontaine Papers, MSU; Esther G. Wright Boyd Memoir, TSL, 8; Weiner, *Mistresses and Slaves*, 89, 92; Rable, *Civil Wars*, 32. Fox-Genovese, *Within the Plantation Household*, 197. I have chosen to use some references from the early years of the war. Young women's perception of slavery did not profoundly alter until slaves began to run away.

9. See Wadley diary, December 26, 1862, July 14, December 31, 1861, Sarah Lois Wadley Papers, UNC; Esther G. Wright Boyd Memoir, TSL, 8; Jacobs manuscript, Annie E. Clark Jacobs Papers, MDAH, 16; Ellen Louise Power Diary, April 19, 20, 1862, UNC. See also Harper, *Annie Harper's Journal*, 35-36. Hester Rabb drew upon similar images of slavery when writing to her daughter away at school. See Hester Rabb to Matilda Rabb, October 8, 1851, in Matilda C. Rabb Letters, MDAH. See also Sudie Duncan Sides, "Women and Slaves: An Interpretation Based on the Writings of Southern Women," 18; May, "Southern Elite Women," 259. In his most famous work, Stanley Elkins examined the "Sambo" image and argues that it was the result of "infantilization" of slaves, which was a repercussion of the closed system of Southern slavery. See *Slavery*. His thesis generated considerable debate among historians. See Anne J. Lane, ed., *The Debate over Slavery: Stanley Elkins and His Critics*. More recently, Wyatt-Brown critiqued Elkins's argument. See *The Shaping of Southern Culture*, 3-30. Fox-Genovese has identified four racial stereotypes (including "Sambo") used to classify slaves. See *Within the Plantation Household*, 291-92.

10. By centering their analysis on the wartime struggles between mistress and slaves, historians have not addressed the identity crisis that confronted young ladies within this same wartime landscape. See, for example, Faust, *Mothers of Invention*, 53-79; Weiner, *Mistresses and Slaves*, 157-84; Rable, *Civil Wars*, 112-21; Faust, "Trying To Do a Man's Business."

11. Stone, *Brokenburn*, 128, 173. See also 127, 170-72; Ellen Louise Power Diary, June 27, 1863, UNC; Wadley diary, April 11, 12, 15, October 27, 1864, Sarah Lois Wadley Papers, UNC; Sophie Collins to E. J. Stone, September 30, 1863, in Emmett Lloyd Ross Papers, MSU; Solomon, *Diary of Clara Solomon*, 384.

The extent to which slaves were able to run away varied in each region of the Confederacy. See Ash, *When the Yankees Came*, 160-69. The ability of slaves to run away was also influenced by gender. Drew Gilpin Faust, George Rable, and Thavolia Glymph argue that many slave women found it exceedingly difficult to run away and to maintain their freedom. They argue that slave women were often returned to their owners, or raped and beaten by Union soldiers. They also found it difficult to obtain food, shelter, and employment and were often perceived by Union soldiers as a "nuisance and dangerous to troop discipline." See Faust, Glymph, and Rable, "A Woman's War: Southern Women in the Civil War," 16, 23; Thavolia Glymph, "This Species of Property: Female Slave Contrabands in the Civil War"; Weiner, *Mistresses and Slaves*, 186; White, *Ar'n't I a Woman?* 164.

12. Solomon, *Diary of Clara Solomon*, 384; Kate D. Foster Diary, July 16, 30, August 23, 1863, DUKE; Douglas diary, August 2, 1863, Emily Caroline Douglas Papers, LSU. See also McRae diary, May 30, June 3, 1862, Sallie B. McRae Papers, MSU.

13. Wadley diary, October 27, 1864, Sarah Lois Wadley Papers, UNC; Elizabeth Christie Brown Diary, July 14, 1863, UM; Brickell diary, March 6, 1864, Edward

Fontaine Papers, MSU. See also Kate D. Foster Diary, July 28, 1863, DUKE; Solomon, *Diary of Clara Solomon*, 384. See also Genovese, *Roll, Jordan, Roll*, 98-99; Rable, *Civil Wars*, 118; Jimerson, *The Private Civil War*, 68-70. Deborah White argues that "Mammy" leaving was "shattering" to slaveholders, particularly masters, whose honor was bound up in the submission of women and slaves. See *Ar'n't I a Woman?* 167-68.

14. Worthington diary, April 24, May 4, 1863, Amanda Dougherty Worthington Papers, UNC.

15. Stone, *Brokenburn*, 172; Emma Walton to James Walton, June 26, 1864, in Walton-Glenny Family Papers, WRC; Solomon, *Diary of Clara Solomon*, 384. See also Belle Strickland Diary, August 8, 1864, UM.

16. Wyatt-Brown, *Southern Honor*, 363. Wyatt-Brown argues the "ethic" of honor required the willing submission of all slaves to their master and "the unfeigned willingness of slaves to bestow honor on all whites." Any hint of "grudging submission" on the part of slaves would "dissolve" the "essence of honor." Thus masters needed to believe in the innate contentment of their slaves in order to legitimate their honor.

17. Morgan, *Civil War Diary*, 213, 215; McRae diary, January 12, 1862, Sallie B. McRae Papers, MSU.

18. Kate D. Foster Diary, July 16, 25, 28, 30, 1863, DUKE.

19. Ibid., July 25, August 23, 1863.

20. Ibid., July 28, 1863.

21. Elizabeth Christie Brown Diary, August 9, 15, 12, 13, 12, 1863, UM. On women's use of the physical boundaries of the household or plantation to define slave loyalty and disloyalty see Whites, *The Civil War as a Crisis in Gender*, 121-22.

22. Elizabeth Christie Brown Diary, August 10, February 11, 1863, UM. See also George Fredrickson, *The Black Image in the White Mind: The Debate on Afro-American Character and Destiny, 1817-1914*, 52-55. Fredrickson argues that there were "ambiguities" in this theory. First, it never addressed whether the "savage" qualities in the Negro would disappear over time. Second, it did not address whether the ideal "domestication" of the Negro on the Southern plantation was in the context of economics or paternalism. See 55-56.

23. Elizabeth Christie Brown Diary, August 12, 1863, UM.

24. Weiner, *Mistresses and Slaves*, 176-77. Weiner argues that many slave women stayed with their mistresses because of their "feelings about a particular individual," yet planter women were unable to recognize the distinction between individual loyalty and loyalty to slavery.

25. Morgan, *Civil War Diary*, 234-35.

26. Ibid., 250. Sarah recorded other instances of slave loyalty to her family. See 91-93, 150.

27. Irion-Neilson, *Lucy's Journal*, 22; Douglas diary, May 1, 1863, Emily Caroline Douglas Papers, LSU; Emma Walton to James Walton, June 26, 1864, in Walton-Glenny Family Papers, WRC; Stone, *Brokenburn*, 298, 183, 200, 365-66. See also Wadley diary, August 29, 1863, Sarah Lois Wadley Papers, UNC; Miller memoir, Letitia Dabney Miller Papers, UNC, 11, 14, 15; Harper, *Annie Harper's Journal*, 13.

28. Solomon, *Diary of Clara Solomon*, 144, 101; Stone, *Brokenburn*, 53, 33. See also 35, 37, 39, 175, 185; Wadley diary, September 23, 1863, Sarah Lois Wadley Papers, UNC. On the ways in which slaves challenged their position in wartime

see Ash, *When the Yankees Came,* 153-54; Clinton, *Tara Revisited,* 74; Kolchin, *American Slavery,* 204; Litwack, *Been in the Storm So Long,* 143; White, *Ar'n't I a Woman?* 165.

29. Worthington diary, June 10, 1863, Amanda Dougherty Worthington Papers, UNC; McRae diary, June 5, 1862, Sallie B. McRae Papers, MSU; Kate D. Foster Diary, July 30, 1863, DUKE; Elizabeth Christie Brown Diary, January 19, 1863, UM.

30. Esther G. Wright Boyd Memoir, TSL, 7. See also Maria Dyer Davies Diary, December 3, 1850, DUKE. On fears of insurrection see, for example, David M. Potter, *The Impending Crisis, 1848-1861,* 452-54; Roark, *Masters without Slaves,* 74; Clinton, *The Plantation Mistress,* 193-95; Faust, *Mothers of Invention,* 59; Bercaw, "Politics of Household," 49; Edwards, *Scarlett Doesn't Live Here Anymore,* 79.

31. Stone, *Brokenburn,* 170-71. Sometimes these fears had some foundation, as Winthrop D. Jordan's examination of a slave conspiracy in Adams County, Mississippi, in 1861 has illustrated. See *Tumult and Silence at Second Creek: An Inquiry into a Civil War Slave Conspiracy.* On wartime insurrectionary activity see Litwack, *Been in the Storm So Long,* 45-49.

32. Stone, *Brokenburn,* 170-71, 298.

33. Solomon, *Diary of Clara Solomon,* 355. See also 57; Morgan, *Civil War Diary,* 184.

34. Ash, *When the Yankees Came,* 159; Worthington diary, April 20, 1863, Amanda Dougherty Worthington Papers, UNC; Ellen Louise Power Diary, August 2, 3, 1863, UNC; Elizabeth Christie Brown Diary, August 14, 12, 1863, UM. See also Brickell diary, March 6, 1864, Edward Fontaine Papers, MSU; Belle Strickland Diary, August 5, 1864, UM; Stone, *Brokenburn,* 208-9. See also Litwack, *Been in the Storm So Long,* 96-97. While the young women in this study mentioned black Yankees, they remained silent on the debate over the Confederacy arming its slaves to fight for the cause.

35. Stone, *Brokenburn,* 195-98, 184. See also 169, 202, 297.

36. Ibid., 297.

Epilogue

The Confederate Belle in Defeat, 1865-1870

1. Lou E. Thompson Diary, USM.

2. Ibid., January 15, 1870.

3. Stone, *Brokenburn,* 340, 355; Irion-Neilson diary, June 1865, Irion-Neilson Family Papers, MDAH.

4. Morgan, *Civil War Diary,* 610-12.

5. Kate D. Foster Diary, July 18, November 26, 1865, DUKE. On defeat see Brickell diary, May 13, 1865, Edward Fontaine Papers, MSU; Wadley diary, April 20, 1865, Sarah Lois Wadley Papers, UNC; Worthington diary, July 31, 1865, Amanda Dougherty Worthington Papers, UNC. Wyatt-Brown argues there were three "levels of response to failure in war": "first the initial shock when confronting the hopelessness of further action; second, the discovery of home conditions upon return; and third, the long-term problems of readjustment." See *The Shaping of Southern Culture,* 230-69. On defeat (general) see Dan T. Carter, *When the War Was*

Over: The Failure of Self-Reconstruction in the South, 1865-1867; Nancy Kondert, "The Romance and Reality of Defeat: Southern Women in 1865."

6. Statistics taken from the United States Census for 1860 and 1870, *United States Historical Census Data Browser.*

7. James Morgan to Francis Warrington Dawson, March 31, 1874, in Francis Warrington Dawson I & II Papers, DUKE.

8. Schuler, "Women in Public Affairs," 687. Rable argues that "poverty shaped daily life and became the war's most enduring legacy." See *Civil Wars,* 240, 247; Massey, *Bonnet Brigades,* 325; Kondert, "Romance and Reality of Defeat," 147; Wayne, *The Reshaping of Plantation Society,* 37. Yet, as Laura Edwards notes, "downward mobility was not the same thing as abject or permanent impoverishment." Some women, she argues, defined themselves as poor, not because they were, but because they had "less than they did before the war" and were now forced to undertake housework and wage work. See *Scarlett Doesn't Live Here Anymore,* 178.

9. Dawson, ed., *"Our Women in the War,"* 21; Jacobs manuscript, Annie E. Clark Jacobs Papers, MDAH, 170. See also Margaret Gooch Memoir, TSL, 7. This material reflects the conditions in Mississippi and Louisiana immediately after the war. Wayne argues that an analysis of the tax rolls for Mississippi and Louisiana indicates that despite their decrease in economic status, elite Southerners were able to hold onto their land. He contends that war and the depression of the 1870s did little to "diminish the relative economic position of the old elite." See *Reshaping of Plantation Society,* 86.

10. Stone, *Brokenburn,* 364, 362, 369, 375, 377. See also Anna Shaw to M. E. Lawson, January 20, 1867, in Bertie Shaw Rollins Papers, MSU.

11. Mary C. Wright diary, March 5, 1867, Wright-Boyd Family Papers, LSU; Worthington diary, October 8, 1865, Amanda Dougherty Worthington Papers, UNC. See also Wadley diary, October 10, 1865, Sarah Lois Wadley Papers, UNC; Anna Shaw to M. E. Lawson, January 15, 1866, in Bertie Shaw Rollins Papers, MSU; Irion-Neilson, *Lucy's Journal,* 68; Mary Ann Irvine Papers, MDAH.

12. Wadley diary, March 2, 1862, April 20, 1865, Sarah Lois Wadley Papers, UNC.

13. See Kolchin, *American Slavery,* 210-11; Rable, *Civil Wars,* 235. For an examination of these aspects of Reconstruction see Eric Foner, *Reconstruction: America's Unfinished Revolution, 1863-1877,* 228-80.

14. Stone, *Brokenburn,* 362. Foner's study on Reconstruction remains the most valuable overview of this period. For an examination of Reconstruction in Louisiana see Ted Tunnell, *Crucible of Reconstruction: War, Radicalism, and Race in Louisiana, 1862-1877.* For an examination of Reconstruction in Mississippi see William C. Harris, *Presidential Reconstruction In Mississippi;* William C. Harris, *The Day of the Carpetbagger: Republican Reconstruction in Mississippi.* For an analysis of the postwar relationship between planters and freedpeople see Edwards, *Gendered Strife and Confusion,* 118; Johnston-Miller, "Heirs to Paternalism," 244-311; Foner, *Reconstruction,* 136; Edwards, *Scarlett Doesn't Live Here Anymore,* 173-76. While young women in plantation households or urban locations often completed similar domestic tasks, Weiner notes that the role of the plantation mistress was transformed in a different way from her urban social counterpart in the postwar period. See *Mistresses and Slaves,* 212-13. Unfortunately, no young lady in this study reflected on the changed status of African Americans or the altered state of race relations in the postwar South in their diaries or letters. Annie Harper, however, detailed her thoughts on Reconstruction in her memoir. See *Annie Harper's Journal,* 41-42.

15. Worthington diary, August 7, 1865, Amanda Dougherty Worthington Papers, UNC.

16. Ibid., September 25, October 6, July 31, 1865; Morgan, *Civil War Diary*, 611.

17. Stone, *Brokenburn*, 364, 352. Southern women's lack of interest in politics seems to have been common across the postwar South. Rable argues that the "desperate plight of many families" took priority over public matters and women "took only a desultory interest in politics." See *Civil Wars*, 221; Roark, *Masters without Slaves*, 180. Varina Davis's recollections of Southern women's role in the defeated South also emphasizes "private concerns." See "Our Southern Women in War Times: Vivid Reminiscences by Mrs. V. Jefferson Davis," *Confederate Veteran* 1 (May 1893): 149. Young women also remained silent on their reaction to Federal troops, who occupied Mississippi and Louisiana sporadically after the war. Young women also failed to comment on their use of religion to sustain them in the postwar period. There is evidence to suggest that some Southerners renounced their faith, while for others, defeat strengthened their belief in God. See Carter, *When the War Was Over*, 89-90, 269; Faust, *Mothers of Invention*, 194-95. I do not wish to suggest that young women's silence on spirituality points to a lack of faith. Rather, I think it reflects a lack of time to devote to diary writing (or their choice not to spend their time in this way) in the immediate postwar period.

18. Edwards, *Gendered Strife and Confusion*, 107-44; Edwards, *Scarlett Doesn't Live Here Anymore*, 182. In her analysis of the postwar experiences of elite women in North Carolina, Jane Turner Censer found that the young woman's experience in the wartime household helped her to adapt to the conditions of postwar domesticity. See "A Changing World of Work."

19. Kate D. Foster Diary, November 26, 1865, March 12, 1868, DUKE; Mary C. Wright diary, January 20, 1866, June 3, 1865, Wright-Boyd Family Papers, LSU. See also Wadley diary, November 26, 1865, Sarah Lois Wadley Papers, UNC; Lou D. Thompson Diary, January 15, 1870, USM; Eliza Lucy Irion to Elizabeth C. Irion, November 23, 1867, in Irion-Neilson Family Papers, MDAH. The absence of leisure time perhaps explains the scarcity of young women's diaries in Mississippi and Louisiana during Reconstruction. In her study of Australian women diarists, Katie Holmes argues that a woman's economic position influenced her ability to make time for diary writing. See *Spaces in Her Day: Australian Women's Diaries, 1920s–1930s*, xiv. Rable also notes that primary material "becomes thinner in both quality and quantity" for the Reconstruction period. See *Civil Wars*, xi.

20. Wadley diary, September 26, October 10, November 8, 1865, Sarah Lois Wadley Papers, UNC; Stone, *Brokenburn*, 367, 364. See also Morgan, *Civil War Diary*, 605; Worthington diary, August 12, 1865, Amanda Dougherty Worthington Papers, UNC.

21. Eliza Lucy Irion to Elizabeth C. Irion, December 14, 1867, in Irion-Neilson diary, Irion-Neilson Family Papers, MDAH. Eliza frequently commented on the domestic tasks completed by herself and her sister. See, for example, Eliza Lucy Irion to Elizabeth C. Irion, February 23, May 4, November 23, 1867, July 5, 1868, Eliza Lucy Irion to Cordele Irion, December 16, 1867. For other examples of young ladies' role in the postwar household see Mary Ann Irvine Papers, MDAH; Carrie Nutt to Julia Nutt, October 16, 1865, in Nutt Family Papers, MDAH; Worthington diary, July 19, 28, September 11, 1865, Amanda Dougherty Worthington Papers, UNC; John D. Barnhart, ed., "Reconstruction on the Lower Mississippi," 391-92.

22. See Rable, *Civil Wars*, 283-84. Because a central component of Southern honor was the public assessment of self worth, paid employment undertaken with-

in the confines of the home minimized the loss of honor and the questioning of elite masculinity because it did not represent women's public physical shift into the world of employment. Instead, it provided a façade that maintained traditional representations of femininity. Schuler notes that women in Louisiana often took in sewing at home, and also became dressmakers, milliners, housemaids, cooks, and governesses. See "Women in Public Affairs," 672, 692-723. Yeoman or poor white women probably filled many of these positions. The socialization of elite women restricted their respectable employment opportunities to baking or sewing at home and teaching.

23. Morgan, *Civil War Diary*, 153.

24. Lou E. Thompson Diary, January 11, February 11, 12, March 20, April 28, 1869, USM.

25. Kate D. Foster Diary, November 26, 1865, February 5, 1872, DUKE.

26. O'Brien, ed., *An Evening when Alone*, 371, 373. In Britain, A. James Hammerton argues that gentlewomen suffered "downward social mobility" when they entered the ranks of paid employment. See *Emigrant Gentlewomen: Genteel Poverty and Female Emigration, 1830-1914*, 32; Davidoff, *Worlds Between: Historical Perspectives on Gender and Class*, 78. Faust argues this was also the case in the antebellum South. See *Mothers of Invention*, 81; Rable, *Civil Wars*, 279.

27. Stone, *Brokenburn*, 365; Mary C. Wright diary, June 3, 1865, Wright-Boyd Family Papers, LSU; Kate D. Foster Diary, March 12, 1868, DUKE; Worthington diary, August 12, September 29, 1865, Amanda Dougherty Worthington Papers, UNC. See also Medora Roxana Byers diary, Byers Family Papers, MDAH. This was a component of genteel poverty. See Florence Elliott Cook, "Growing Up White, Genteel, and Female in a Changing South, 1865 to 1915," 40.

28. Worthington diary, October 12, August 12, 1865, Amanda Dougherty Worthington Papers, UNC.

29. Kate D. Foster Diary, November 26, 1865, DUKE; Wadley diary, November 8, 1865, Sarah Lois Wadley Papers, UNC.

30. Sarah Morgan diary, September 6, 1866, Francis Warrington Dawson I & II Papers, DUKE; Worthington diary, September 20, 1865, Amanda Dougherty Worthington Papers, UNC; Mary C. Wright diary, July 7, 13, 1865, Wright-Boyd Family Papers, LSU; Kate D. Foster Diary, September 16, 1866, December 7, 1871, DUKE; Stone, *Brokenburn*, 369; Anna Shaw to M. E. Lawson, January 20, 1867, in Bertie Shaw Rollins Papers, MSU. See also Irion-Neilson diary, June 1865, Irion-Neilson Family Papers, MDAH.

31. Rable, *Civil Wars*, 270.

32. Kate D. Foster Diary, November 26, 1865, December 7, 1871, DUKE.

33. Mary C. Wright diary, September 7, 1865, Wright-Boyd Family Papers, LSU.

34. Eleanor Coleman Garrett and Rebecca Hood-Adams, eds., *Pocock Pickle: Louisa's 1863 Journal with Recipes and Household Hints*, 41; Stone, *Brokenburn*, 367. Southern men's marriage prospects were also constrained by their economic position. Kate Stone commented on the plight of her brother and his fiancée, Carrie, who were unable to wed because of her brother's limited financial resources. See 371. It is likely that conservative models of Southern womanhood became dominant in the postwar period, in part because of elite Southerners' use of domesticity as a site to resurrect their status. See Edwards, *Gendered Strife and Confusion*.

35. Anna Shaw to M. E. Lawson, January 15, 1866, in Bertie Shaw Rollins Papers, MSU; Solomon, *Diary of Clara Solomon*, 443.

Bibliography

MANUSCRIPTS

BATON ROUGE, LOUISIANA

Louisiana and Lower Mississippi Valley Collections, Hill Memorial Library, Louisiana State University

Emily Caroline Douglas Papers.
Sidney Harding Diary.
Eliza L. Magruder Diary.
Mary Estelle Rountree Letters.
Wright-Boyd Family Papers.
Carrie Zacharie Composition Book.

CHAPEL HILL, NORTH CAROLINA

Southern Historical Collection, University of North Carolina Library

Edwina Burnley Memoir.
Gibson and Humphreys Family Papers.
Chiliab Smith Howe Papers.
Letitia Dabney Miller Papers.
Ellen Louise Power Diary.
Quitman Family Papers.
Randolph and Yates Family Papers.
Frank Liddell Richardson Papers.
Richardson and Farrar Family Papers.
Roach and Eggleston Family Papers.
Louisa Campbell Sheppard Recollections.
Sarah Lois Wadley Papers.
Trist Wood Papers.
Amanda Dougherty Worthington Papers.

CLEVELAND, MISSISSIPPI

Charles W. Capps Jr. Archives and Museum Building, Delta State University

Mary Carson Warfield Papers.

DURHAM, NORTH CAROLINA

Rare Book, Manuscript, and Special Collections Library, Duke University

Maria Dyer Davies Diary.
Francis Warrington Dawson I & II Papers.
Kate D. Foster Diary.
John Knight Papers.

HATTIESBURG, MISSISSIPPI

William D. McCain Library and Archives, University of Southern Mississippi

Lou E. Thompson Diary/Attala County Records.

JACKSON, MISSISSIPPI

Mississippi Department of Archives and History

Bisland-Shields Family Papers.
Maud Morrow Brown Papers.
Byers Family Papers.
Chapman Family Papers.
Louisa Russell Conner Memoirs.
Crutcher-Shannon Family Papers.
Davenport Family Letters.
Mary Bertron Hughes Letters.
Irion-Neilson Family Papers.
Mary Ann Irvine Papers.
Annie E. Clark Jacobs Papers.
Nutt Family Papers.
Warren C. Ogden Miscellaneous Civil War Letters.
John Logan Power and Family Papers.
Matilda C. Rabb Letters.
Cordelia Lewis Scales Papers.
Mary E. Wilkes Shell Papers.
John Snodgrass and Family Papers.

Eunice J. Stockwell Papers.
Alcinda Timberlake Papers.
Ida Barlow Trotter Papers.

MACON, GEORGIA

Middle Georgia Archives

Wadley Family Papers.

MISSISSIPPI STATE, MISSISSIPPI

Mitchell Memorial Library, Mississippi State University

Effie Robinson Drane Papers.
Edward Fontaine Papers.
B. T. Hobbs Papers.
Malloy Papers.
Sallie B. McRae Papers.
Bertie Shaw Rollins Papers.
Emmett Lloyd Ross Papers.
Rufus Ward Papers.

NASHVILLE, TENNESSEE

Tennessee State Library and Archives

Margaret Gooch Memoir.
Esther G. Wright Boyd Memoir.

NEW ORLEANS, LOUISIANA

Manuscripts, Rare Books, and University Archives, Howard-Tilton Memorial Library, Tulane University

Annie Jeter Carmouche Papers.
Mathilda Todd DeVan Memorial Volume.
Grace Lea Hunt Letters.
(Lise) Elizabeth Mitchell Papers.

Williams Research Center

Laura Hyde Moss Journal.
Walton-Glenny Family Papers.
Wilkinson/Stark Family Papers.

RICHMOND, VIRGINIA

Eleanor S. Brockenbrough Library, Museum of the Confederacy

Soldiers' Letters (Civilians to Combatants), 1861-1865.
   Letters from unmarried girls in Louisiana.
   Letters from unmarried girls in Mississippi.
Southern Women's Collection.
   S. G. McLain, "Some Incidents and a Skirmish Witnessed during the Civil War in My Home Town."

UNIVERSITY, MISSISSIPPI

John Davis Williams Library, University of Mississippi

Elizabeth Christie Brown Diary.
Belle Strickland Diary.

NEWSPAPERS AND MAGAZINES

Confederate Veteran, 1893, 1903.
Godey's Lady's Book, 1861-1864.

CENSUS

Federal Census for 1860. *United States Historical Census Data Browser.*
   http://fisher.lib.virginia.edu/census/

PUBLISHED PRIMARY SOURCES, PUBLISHED AND UNPUBLISHED SECONDARY SOURCES

Abzug, Robert H., and Stephen E. Maizlish, eds. *New Perspectives on Race and Slavery in America: Essays in Honor of Kenneth M. Stampp.* Lexington: University Press of Kentucky, 1986.
Allport, Gordon W. *The Use of Personal Documents in Psychological Science, Prepared for the Committee on Appraisal of Research.* New York: Social Science Research Council, 1942.
Ash, Stephen V. *When the Yankees Came: Conflict and Chaos in the Occupied South, 1861-1865.* Chapel Hill: University of North Carolina Press, 1995.
Atkinson, Maxine P., and Jacqueline Boles. "The Shaky Pedestal:

Southern Ladies Yesterday and Today." *Southern Studies* 24 (winter 1985): 398-406.

Ayers, Edward L. "Honor." In *Encyclopedia of Southern Culture*, edited by Charles Wilson Reagan and William Ferris, 1483-84. Chapel Hill: University of North Carolina Press, 1989.

————— . *The Promise of the New South: Life after Reconstruction.* New York: Oxford University Press, 1992.

————— . *Vengeance and Justice: Crime and Punishment in the 19th-Century American South.* New York: Oxford University Press, 1984.

Baldwin, Christina. *One to One: Self-Understanding through Journal Writing.* New York: M. Evans and Co., 1977.

Barney, William L. *The Secessionist Impulse: Alabama and Mississippi in 1860.* Princeton, N.J.: Princeton University Press, 1974.

Barnhart, John D., ed. "Reconstruction on the Lower Mississippi." *Mississippi Valley Historical Review* 21 (December 1934): 387-96.

Bartley, Numan V., ed. *The Evolution of Southern Culture.* Athens: University of Georgia Press, 1988.

Begos, Jane Dupree. "Diaries and Journals." *Women's Diaries* 1 (spring 1983): 2-4.

Bercaw, Nancy Dunlap. "Politics of Household during the Transition from Slavery to Freedom in the Yazoo-Mississippi Delta, 1861-1876." Ph.D. diss., University of Pennsylvania, 1996.

Berg, Barbara J. *The Remembered Gate: Origins of American Feminism: The Woman and the City, 1800-1860.* New York: Oxford University Press, 1978.

Beringer, Richard E., Herman Hattaway, Archer Jones, and William N. Still Jr., eds. *Why the South Lost the Civil War.* Athens: University of Georgia Press, 1986.

Bernhard, Virginia, Betty Brandon, Elizabeth Fox-Genovese, and Theda Perdue, eds. *Southern Women: Histories and Identities.* Columbia: University of Missouri Press, 1992.

Berry, Trey. "A History of Women's Higher Education in Mississippi, 1819-1882." *Journal of Mississippi History* 53 (November 1991): 303-20.

Bertelson, David. *The Lazy South.* New York: Oxford University Press, 1967.

Blassingame, John W. *The Slave Community: Plantation Life in the Antebellum South.* New York: Oxford University Press, 1972.

Bleser, Carol, ed. *In Joy and Sorrow: Women, Family, and Marriage in the Victorian South, 1830-1900.* New York: Oxford University Press, 1991.

Boles, John B., and Evelyn Thomas Nolen, eds. *Interpreting Southern History: Historiographical Essays in Honor of Sanford W. Higginbotham*. Baton Rouge: Louisiana State University Press, 1987.

Bond, Bradley G. *Political Culture in the Nineteenth-Century South: Mississippi, 1830-1900*. Baton Rouge: Louisiana State University Press, 1995.

Boylan, Anne M. "Evangelical Womanhood in the Nineteenth Century: The Role of Women in Sunday Schools." *Feminist Studies* 4 (October 1978): 62-80.

Broussard, Joyce Linda. "Female Solitaires: Women Alone on the Lifeworld of Mid-Nineteenth Century Natchez, Mississippi, 1850-1880." Ph.D. diss., University of Southern California, 1998.

Brownmiller, Susan. *Against Our Will: Men, Women, and Rape*. Harmondsworth: Penguin Books, 1976.

Bunch, Clea Lutz. "Confederate Women of Arkansas Face the 'Fiends in Human Shape.'" *Military History of the West* 27 (fall 1997): 173-87.

Bunkers, Suzanne L., and Cynthia A. Huff, eds. *Inscribing the Daily: Critical Essays on Women's Diaries*. Amherst: University of Massachusetts Press, 1996.

Burton, Orville Vernon. *In My Father's House Are Many Mansions: Family and Community in Edgefield, South Carolina*. Chapel Hill: University of North Carolina Press, 1985.

Bynum, Victoria E. *Unruly Women: The Politics of Social and Sexual Control in the Old South*. Chapel Hill: University of North Carolina Press, 1992.

Campbell, Edward D. C. Jr., and Kym S. Rice, eds. *A Woman's War: Southern Women, Civil War, and the Confederate Legacy*. Richmond and Charlottesville: Museum of the Confederacy and the University Press of Virginia, 1996.

Carrigan, Jo Ann. "Nineteenth-Century Rural Self-Sufficiency: A Planter's and Housewife's 'Do-It-Yourself' Encyclopedia." *Arkansas Historical Quarterly* 21 (summer 1962): 132-45.

Carter, Dan T. *When the War Was Over: The Failure of Self-Reconstruction in the South, 1865-1867*. Baton Rouge: Louisiana State University Press, 1985.

Cashin, Joan E. *A Family Venture: Men and Women on the Southern Frontier*. New York: Oxford University Press, 1991.

————. "Into the Trackless Wilderness: The Refugee Experience in the Civil War." In *A Woman's War: Southern Women, Civil War, and the Confederate Legacy*, edited by Edward D. C. Campbell Jr.

and Kym S. Rice, 29-53. Richmond and Charlottesville: Museum of the Confederacy and the University Press of Virginia, 1996.

——— . "The Structure of Antebellum Planter Families: 'The Ties That Bound Us Was Strong.'" *Journal of Southern History* 56 (February 1990): 55-70.

——— , ed. *Our Common Affairs: Texts from Women in the Old South.* Baltimore: Johns Hopkins University Press, 1996.

Censer, Jane Turner. "A Changing World of Work: North Carolina Elite Women, 1865-1895." *North Carolina Historical Review* 1 (January 1996): 28-55.

——— . *North Carolina Planters and Their Children, 1800-1860.* Baton Rouge: Louisiana State University Press, 1984.

Chambers-Schiller, Lee Virginia. *Liberty, A Better Husband: Single Women in America: The Generations of 1780-1840.* New Haven: Yale University Press, 1984.

Clark, E. Culpepper. "Sarah Morgan and Francis Dawson: Raising the Woman Question in Reconstruction South Carolina." *South Carolina Historical Magazine* 81 (January 1980): 8-23.

Clark, Thomas D., and John D. W. Guice. *Frontiers in Conflict: The Old Southwest, 1795-1830.* Albuquerque: University of New Mexico Press, 1989.

Clinton, Catherine. *The Plantation Mistress: Women's World in the Old South.* New York: Pantheon Books, 1982.

——— . "'Southern Dishonor': Flesh, Blood, Race, and Bondage." In *In Joy and Sorrow: Women, Family, and Marriage in the Victorian South, 1830-1900,* edited by Carol Bleser, 52-68. New York: Oxford University Press, 1991.

——— . *Tara Revisited: Women, War, and the Plantation Legend.* New York: Abbeville Press, 1995.

Clinton, Catherine, and Nina Silber, eds. *Divided Houses: Gender and the Civil War.* New York: Oxford University Press, 1992.

Cobb, James C. *The Most Southern Place on Earth: The Mississippi Delta and the Roots of Regional Identity.* New York: Oxford University Press, 1992.

Columbus Chapter UDC, eds. *War Reminiscences of Columbus, Mississippi, and Elsewhere, 1861-1865.* Columbus, Miss.: United Daughters of the Confederacy, Columbus Chapter, 1961.

Cook, Florence Elliott. "Growing up White, Genteel, and Female in a Changing South, 1865 to 1915." Ph.D. diss., University of California, 1992.

Culley, Margo, ed. *A Day at a Time: The Diary Literature of American Women from 1764 to the Present*. New York: Feminist Press at the City University of New York, 1985.

Culpepper, Marilyn Mayer. *Trials and Triumphs: Women of the American Civil War*. East Lansing: Michigan State University Press, 1991.

Current, Richard N., ed. *Encyclopaedia of the Confederacy*. Vol. 2. New York: Simon and Schuster, 1993.

Currie, James T. *Enclave: Vicksburg and Her Plantations, 1863-1870*. Jackson: University Press of Mississippi, 1980.

Daniel, Lizzie Cary, ed. *Confederate Scrap Book Copied from a Scrap-book Kept by a Young Girl during and Immediately after the War, with Additions from War Copies of the "Southern Literary Messenger" and "Illustrated News" Loaned by Friends and Other Sections as Accredited. Published for the Benefit of the Memorial Bazaar, Held in Richmond, April 11, 1893*. Richmond, Va.: J.H. Hill, 1893.

Davidoff, Leonore. *The Best Circles: Society, Etiquette, and the Season*. London: Croom Helm, 1973.

——— . *Worlds Between: Historical Perspectives on Gender and Class*. Cambridge: Polity Press, 1995.

Dawson, Francis Warrington, ed. *"Our Women in the War": The Lives They Lived, the Deaths They Died*. Charleston, S.C.: News and Courier Book Presses, 1885.

Delamont, Sara. "The Contradictions in Ladies' Education." In *The Nineteenth Century Woman: Her Cultural and Physical World*, edited by Sara Delamont and Lorna Duffin, 134-63. London: Croom Helm, 1978.

D'Emilio, John, and Estelle Freedman. *Intimate Matters: A History of Sexuality in America*. New York: Harper and Row, 1988.

Dillman, Caroline Matheny, ed. *Southern Women*. New York: Hemisphere Publishing Corp., 1988.

Doyle, Elizabeth Joan. "Civilian Life in Occupied New Orleans." Ph.D. diss., Louisiana State University, 1955.

Dufour, Charles, L. *The Night the War Was Lost*. Lincoln: University of Nebraska Press, 1990.

——— . *Ten Flags in the Wind: The Story of Louisiana*. New York: Harper and Row, 1967.

Dumond, Dwight Lowell, ed. *Southern Editorials on Secession*. New York: Century, 1931.

Dyhouse, Carol. *Girls Growing Up in Late Victorian and Edwardian England*. London: Routledge and Kegan Paul, 1981.

Eaton, Clement. *The Growth of Southern Civilization, 1790-1860*. New York: Harper and Row, 1961.

Edwards, Laura F. *Gendered Strife and Confusion: The Political Culture of Reconstruction*. Urbana: University of Illinois Press, 1997.

————. *Scarlett Doesn't Live Here Anymore: Southern Women in the Civil War Era*. Urbana: University of Illinois Press, 2000.

Edwards, Madaline Selima Cage Elliott. *Madaline: Love and Survival in Antebellum New Orleans: The Private Writings of a Kept Woman*. Edited by Dell Upton. Athens: University of Georgia Press, 1996.

Elkins, Stanley M. *Slavery: A Problem in American Institutional and Intellectual Life*. Chicago: University of Chicago Press, 1959.

Escott, Paul D. *After Secession: Jefferson Davis and the Failure of Confederate Nationalism*. Baton Rouge: Louisiana State University Press, 1978.

————. "The Cry of the Sufferers: The Problem of Welfare in the Confederacy." *Civil War History* 23 (September 1977): 228-40.

Ewin, Margaret Johnson. *Like Some Green Laurel: Letters of Margaret Johnson Erwin, 1821-1863*. Edited by Erwin John Seymour. Baton Rouge: Louisiana State University Press, 1981.

Farnham, Christie Anne. *The Education of the Southern Belle: Higher Education and Student Socialization in the Antebellum South*. New York: New York University Press, 1994.

Faust, Drew Gilpin. "Altars of Sacrifice: Confederate Women and the Narratives of War." *Journal of American History* 76 (March 1990): 1200-28.

————. *The Creation of Confederate Nationalism: Ideology and Identity in the Civil War South*. Baton Rouge: Louisiana State University Press, 1988.

————. "Culture Conflict, and Community: The Meaning of Power on an Ante-Bellum Plantation," *Journal of Social History* 14 (fall 1980): 83-98.

————. *Mothers of Invention: Women of the Slaveholding South in the American Civil War*. Chapel Hill: University of North Carolina Press, 1996.

————. *Southern Stories: Slaveholders in Peace and War*. Columbia: University of Missouri Press, 1992.

————. "Trying To Do a Man's Business: Slavery, Violence, and Gender in the American Civil War." *Gender and History* 4 (summer 1992): 197-214.

Faust, Drew Gilpin, Thavolia Glymph, and George C. Rable. "A

Woman's War: Southern Women in the Civil War." In *A Woman's War: Southern Women, Civil War, and the Confederate Legacy*, edited by Edward D. C. Campbell Jr. and Kym S. Rice, 1-28. Richmond and Charlottesville: Museum of the Confederacy and the University Press of Virginia, 1996.

Faust, Drew Gilpin, Patricia Yaeger, Anne Goodwyn Jones, and Jacquelyn Dowd Hall. "Coming to Terms with Scarlett: A Southern Cultures Forum." *Southern Cultures* 5, no. 1 (1999): 1-48.

Fellman, Michael. *Inside War: The Guerrilla Conflict in Missouri during the American Civil War*. New York: Oxford University Press, 1989.

Finley, Emma. *Our Pen Is Time: The Diary of Emma Finley*. Edited by Robert Milton Winter. Lafayette, Calif.: Thomas Berryhill Press, 1999.

Foner, Eric. *Politics and Ideology in the Age of the Civil War*. New York: Oxford University Press, 1980.

———. *Reconstruction: America's Unfinished Revolution, 1863-1877*. New York: Harper and Row, 1988.

Forster, Stig, and Jörg Nagler, eds. *On the Road to Total War: The American Civil War and the German Wars of Unification, 1861-1871*. Cambridge: Cambridge University Press, 1997.

Foster, Gaines M. *Ghosts of the Confederacy: Defeat, the Lost Cause, and the Emergence of the New South, 1865 to 1913*. New York: Oxford University Press, 1987.

Fox, Tryphena Blanche Holder. *A Northern Woman in the Plantation South: Letters of Tryphena Blanche Holder Fox, 1856-1876*. Edited by Wilma King. Columbia: University of South Carolina Press, 1993.

Fox-Genovese, Elizabeth. "Scarlett O'Hara: The Southern Lady as New Woman." *American Quarterly* 33 (fall 1981): 391-411.

———. *"To Be Worthy of God's Favor": Southern Women's Defense and Critique of Slavery*. Gettysburg: 32d Annual Robert Fortenbaugh Memorial Lecture, 1993.

———. *Within the Plantation Household: Black and White Women of the Old South*. Chapel Hill: University of North Carolina Press, 1988.

Franklin, Penelope. *Private Pages: Diaries of American Women, 1830s–1970s*. New York: Ballantine Books, 1986.

Fraser, Walter J., Jr., and Winifred B. Moore, eds. *From the Old South to the New: Essays on the Transitional South*. Westport, Conn.: Greenwood Press, 1981.

Fraser, Walter J., Jr., R. Frank Saunders, and Jon L. Wakelyn, eds. *The

Web of Southern Social Relations: Women, Family, and Education. Athens: University of Georgia Press, 1985.

Fredrickson, George M. *The Black Image in the White Mind: The Debate on Afro-American Character and Destiny, 1817-1914.* Hanover, N.H.: Wesleyan University Press, 1987.

Freehling, William W. *The Road to Disunion.* Vol. 1, *Secessionists at Bay, 1776-1854.* New York: Oxford University Press, 1990.

Freeman, Douglas Southall. *The South to Posterity: An Introduction to the Writing of Confederate History.* Wendell, N.C.: Broadfords, 1983.

Frevert, Ute. *Men of Honour: A Social and Cultural History of the Duel.* Translated by Anthony Williams. Cambridge: Polity Press, 1995.

Friedman, Jean E. *The Enclosed Garden: Women and Community in the Evangelical South, 1830-1900.* Chapel Hill: University of North Carolina Press, 1985.

Gallagher, Gary W. *The Confederate War.* Cambridge: Harvard University Press, 1997.

Gannett, Cinthia. *Gender and the Journal: Diaries and Academic Discourse.* Albany: State University of New York Press, 1992.

Garcia, Céline Frémaux. *Céline: Remembering Louisiana, 1850-1871.* Edited by Patrick Geary. Athens: University of Georgia Press, 1987.

Gardner, Sarah Elizabeth. "Blood and Irony: Southern Women's Narratives of the Civil War, 1861-1915." Ph.D. diss., Emory University, 1996.

Garrett, Eleanor Coleman, and Rebecca Hood-Adams, eds. *Pocock Pickle: Louisa's 1863 Journal with Recipes and Household Hints.* Bolivar, Miss.: Bolivar County Historical Society, 1986.

Genovese, Eugene D. *The Political Economy of Slavery: Studies in the Economy and Society of the Slave South.* New York: Pantheon Books, 1965.

——— . *Roll, Jordon, Roll: The World the Slaves Made.* New York: Pantheon Books, 1974.

——— . "Toward a Kinder and Gentler America: The Southern Lady in the Greening of the Politics of the Old South." In *In Joy and Sorrow: Women, Family, and Marriage in the Victorian South, 1830-1900,* edited by Carol Bleser, 125-34. New York: Oxford University Press, 1991.

Ginzberg, Lori D. *Women and the Work of Benevolence: Morality, Politics, and Class in the Nineteenth-Century United States.* New Haven: Yale University Press, 1990.

Glatthaar, Joseph T. *The March to the Sea and Beyond: Sherman's Troops in the Savannah and Carolinas Campaigns*. New York: New York University Press, 1986.

Glymph, Thavolia. "This Species of Property: Female Slave Contrabands in the Civil War." In *A Woman's War: Southern Women, Civil War, and the Confederate Legacy*, edited by Edward D. C. Campbell Jr. and Kym S. Rice, 55-71. Richmond and Charlottesville: Museum of the Confederacy and the University Press of Virginia, 1996.

Gorham, Deborah. *The Victorian Girl and the Feminine Ideal*. London: Croom Helm, 1982.

Gray, Ricky Harold. "Corona Female College (1857-1864)." *Journal of Mississippi History* 42 (May 1980): 129-34.

Greenberg, Kenneth S. *Honor and Slavery: Lies, Duels, Noses, Masks, Dressing as a Woman, Gifts, Strangers, Humanitarianism, Death, Slave Rebellions, the Proslavery Argument, Baseball, Hunting, and Gambling in the Old South*. Princeton: Princeton University Press, 1996.

——— . *Masters and Statesmen: The Political Culture of American Slavery*. Baltimore: Johns Hopkins University Press, 1985.

Haites, Erik F., James Mak, and Gary M. Walton. *Western River Transportation: The Era of Early Internal Development, 1810-1860*. Baltimore: Johns Hopkins University Press, 1975.

Hammerton, A. James. *Emigrant Gentlewomen: Genteel Poverty and Female Emigration, 1830-1914*. London: Croom Helm, 1979.

Hampsten, Elizabeth. *Read This Only to Yourself: The Private Writings of Midwestern Women, 1880-1910*. Bloomington: Indiana University Press, 1982.

Harper, Annie. *Annie Harper's Journal: A Southern Mother's Legacy*. Edited by Jeannie Marie Deen. Corinth, Miss.: General Store, 1992.

Harris, William C. *The Day of the Carpetbagger: Republican Reconstruction in Mississippi*. Baton Rouge: Louisiana State University Press, 1979.

——— . *Presidential Reconstruction in Mississippi*. Baton Rouge: Louisiana State University Press, 1967.

Harwell, Richard B., ed. *The Confederate Reader: How the South Saw the War*. New York: Barnes and Noble, 1992.

Hawks, Joanne V., and Shelia L. Skemp, eds. *Sex, Race, and the Role of Women in the South: Essays*. Jackson: University Press of Mississippi, 1983.

Hewitt, Lawrence Lee, and Arthur W. Bergeron Jr., eds. *Louisianians in the Civil War*. Columbia: University of Missouri Press, 2002.

Hoffschwelle, Mary S. "Women's Sphere and the Creation of Female Community in the Antebellum South: Three Tennessee Slave-holding Women." *Tennessee Historical Quarterly* 50 (summer 1991): 80-89.

Holmes, Katie. *Spaces in Her Day: Australian Women's Diaries, 1920s–1930s.* St. Leonards, N.S.W.: Allen and Unwin, 1995.

Hospodor, Gregory S. "'Bound by all the Ties of Honor': Southern Honor, the Mississippians, and the Mexican War." *Journal of Mississippi History* 61 (spring 1999): 1-28.

Hunter, Jane H. "Inscribing the Self in the Heart of the Family: Diaries and Girlhood in Late-Victorian America." *American Quarterly* 44 (March 1992): 51-81.

Irion-Neilson, Eliza Lucy. *Lucy's Journal.* Greenwood, Miss.: Baff, 1967.

Jabour, Anya. "'Grown Girls, Highly Cultivated': Female Education in an Antebellum Southern Family." *Journal of Southern History* 64 (February 1998): 23-64.

Jackson, Joy J. "Keeping Law and Order in New Orleans under General Butler, 1862." In *Louisianians in the Civil War,* edited by Lawrence Lee Hewitt and Arthur W. Bergeron Jr., 22-36. Columbia: University of Missouri Press, 2002.

Jimerson, Randall C. *The Private Civil War: Popular Thought during the Sectional Conflict.* Baton Rouge: Louisiana State University Press, 1988.

Johnson, Michael P. "Planters and Patriarchy: Charleston, 1800-1860." *Journal of Southern History* 46 (February 1980): 45-72.

Johnston-Miller, Mary. "Heirs to Paternalism: Elite Women and Their Servants in Alabama and Georgia, 1861-1874." Ph.D. diss., Emory University, 1994.

Jones, Katherine M., ed. *Heroines of Dixie: Confederate Women Tell Their Story of the War.* Indianapolis: Bobbs-Merrill, 1955.

Jordan, Winthrop D. *Tumult and Silence at Second Creek: An Inquiry into a Civil War Slave Conspiracy.* Baton Rouge: Louisiana State University Press, 1993.

Joyner, Charles W. *Down By the Riverside: A South Carolina Slave Community.* Urbana: University of Illinois Press, 1984.

Kaufman, Janet E. "'Under the Petticoat Flag': Women in the Confederate Army." *Southern Studies* 23 (winter 1984): 363-75.

Kerber, Linda K. *Women of the Republic: Intellect and Ideology in Revolutionary America.* Chapel Hill: University of North Carolina Press, 1980.

Kimmel, Michael S. *Manhood in America: A Cultural History*. New York: Free Press, 1996.

Kolchin, Peter. *American Slavery, 1619-1877*. New York: Penguin Books, 1993.

Kondert, Nancy T. "The Romance and Reality of Defeat: Southern Women in 1865." *Journal of Mississippi History* 35 (May 1978): 141-52.

Laas, Virginia Jeans. *Love and Power in the Nineteenth Century: The Marriage of Violet Blair*. Fayetteville: University of Arkansas Press, 1998.

Lane, Anne J., ed. *The Debate over Slavery: Stanley Elkins and His Critics*. Urbana: University of Illinois Press, 1971.

Lebsock, Suzanne. *The Free Women of Petersburg: Status and Culture in a Southern Town, 1784-1860*. New York: Norton, 1984.

LeGrand, Julia. *The Journal of Julia LeGrand, New Orleans, 1862-1863*. Edited by Kate Mason Rowland and Mrs. Morris L. Croxall. Richmond, Va.: Everett Waddey Company, 1911.

Litwack, Leon F. *Been in the Storm So Long: The Aftermath of Slavery*. New York: Knopf, 1979.

Lohrenz, Mary Edna, and Anita Miller Stamper. *Mississippi Homespun: Nineteenth-Century Textiles and the Women Who Made Them*. Jackson: Mississippi Department of Archives and History, 1989.

Loughborough, Mary Webster. *My Cave Life in Vicksburg*. 1864. Reprint, Vicksburg, Miss.: Vicksburg and Warren County Historical Society, 1990.

Loughridge, Patricia R., and Edward D. C. Campbell Jr. *Women in Mourning: A Catalog of the Museum of the Confederacy's Corollary Exhibition Held November 14, 1984, through January 6, 1986*. Richmond, Va.: Museum of the Confederacy, 1985.

Malone, Ann Patton. *Sweet Chariot: Slave Family and Household Structure in Nineteenth-Century Louisiana*. Chapel Hill: University of North Carolina Press, 1992.

Massey, Mary Elizabeth. *Bonnet Brigades*. New York: Knopf, 1966.

——— . *Ersatz in the Confederacy: Shortages and Substitutions on the Southern Homefront*. Columbia: University of South Carolina Press, 1952.

——— . *Refugee Life in the Confederacy*. Baton Rouge: Louisiana State University Press, 1964.

Mathews, Donald G. *Religion in the Old South*. Chicago: University of Chicago Press, 1977.

May, Robert E. "Southern Elite Women, Sectional Extremism, and the Male Political Sphere: The Case of John A. Quitman's Wife and Female Descendants, 1847-1931." *Journal of Mississippi History* 50 (November 1988): 251-85.

McCardell, John. *The Idea of a Southern Nation: Southern Nationalists and Southern Nationalism, 1830-1860.* New York: Norton, 1979.

McDonald, Roderick A. *The Economy and Material Culture of Slaves: Goods and Chattels on the Sugar Plantations of Jamaica and Louisiana.* Baton Rouge: Louisiana State University Press, 1993.

McKinley, Emilie Riley. *From the Pen of a She-Rebel: The Civil War Diary of Emilie Riley McKinley.* Edited by Gordan A. Cotton. Columbia: University of South Carolina Press, 2001.

McMillen, Sally G. *Motherhood in the Old South: Pregnancy, Childbirth, and Infant Rearing.* Baton Rouge: Louisiana State University Press, 1990.

——— . *Southern Women: Black and White in the Old South.* Arlington Heights, Ill.: Harlan Davidson, 1992.

McPherson, James M. *Battle Cry of Freedom: The American Civil War.* New York: Penguin Books, 1990.

——— . *For Cause and Comrades: Why Men Fought in the Civil War.* New York: Oxford University Press, 1997.

Miller, James David. "South by Southwest: Planter Emigration and Elite Ideology in the Deep South, 1815-1861." Ph.D. diss., Emory University, 1996.

Miller, Mary Carol. *Lost Mansions of Mississippi.* Jackson: University Press of Mississippi, 1996.

Mitchell, Margaret. *Gone with the Wind.* London: Macmillan, 1936.

Mitchell, Reid. *The Vacant Chair: The Northern Soldier Leaves Home.* New York: Oxford University Press, 1993.

Mohr, Clarence L. *On the Threshold of Freedom: Masters and Slaves in Civil War Georgia.* Athens: University of Georgia Press, 1986.

Moody, V. Alton. *Slavery on Louisiana Sugar Plantations.* New York: AMS Press, 1976.

Moore, Albert Burton. *Conscription and Conflict in the Confederacy.* New York: Macmillan, 1924.

Moore, John Hebron. *The Emergence of the Cotton Kingdom in the Old Southwest: Mississippi, 1770-1860.* Baton Rouge: Louisiana State University Press, 1988.

Morgan, Sarah. *Sarah Morgan: The Civil War Diary of a Southern Woman.* Edited by Charles East. New York: Simon and Schuster, 1992.

Morris, Christopher. *Becoming Southern: The Evolution of a Way of Life, Warren County and Vicksburg, Mississippi, 1770-1860.* New York: Oxford University Press, 1994.

Morton, Patricia, ed. *Discovering the Women in Slavery: Emancipating Perspectives on the American Past.* Athens: University of Georgia Press, 1996.

Murray, Gail S. "Charity within the Bounds of Race and Class: Female Benevolence in the Old South." *South Carolina Historical Magazine* 96 (January 1995): 54-73.

Nagler, Jörg. "Loyalty and Dissent: The Home Front in the American Civil War." In *On the Road to Total War: The American Civil War and the German Wars of Unification, 1861-1871,* edited by Stig Forster and Jörg Nagler, 329-55. Cambridge: Cambridge University Press, 1997.

Nguyen, Julia Huston. "The Value of Learning: Education and Class in Antebellum Natchez." *Journal of Mississippi History* 61 (fall 1999): 237-64.

Nix, Elizabeth Morrow. "An Exuberant Flow of Spirits: Antebellum Adolescent Girls in the Writing of Southern Women." Ph.D. diss., Boston University, 1996.

Nolan, Dick. *Benjamin Franklin Butler: The Damnedest Yankee.* Novato, Calif.: Presidio, 1991.

Norse, Clifford C. "School Life of Amanda Worthington of Washington County, 1857-1862." *Journal of Mississippi History* 34 (May 1972): 107-16.

North, Douglas C. *The Economic Growth of the United States, 1790-1860.* Englewood Cliffs, N.J.: Prentice Hall, 1961.

Norton, Mary Beth. *Liberty's Daughters: The Revolutionary Experience of American Women, 1750-1800.* Boston: Little, Brown, 1980.

Oakes, James. *The Ruling Race: A History of American Slaveholders.* New York: Knopf, 1982.

O'Brien, Michael, ed. *An Evening When Alone: Four Journals of Single Women in the South, 1827-67.* Charlottesville: University Press of Virginia for the Southern Texts Society, 1993.

O'Connor, Rachel. *Mistress of Evergreen Plantation: Rachel O'Connor's Legacy of Letters, 1823-1845.* Edited by Allie Bayne Windham Webb. Albany: State University of New York Press, 1983.

Olsen, Christopher J. *Political Culture of Secession in Mississippi: Masculinity, Honor, and the Antiparty Tradition, 1830-1860.* New York: Oxford University Press, 2000.

——— . "Respecting 'The Wise Allotment of Our Sphere': White Women and Politics in Mississippi, 1840-1860." *Journal of Women's History* 11 (fall 1999): 104-25.

Olwell, Robert. *Masters, Slaves, and Subjects: The Culture of Power in the South Carolina Low Country, 1740-1790.* Ithaca: Cornell University Press, 1998.

Osterweis, Rollin G. *The Myth of the Lost Cause, 1865-1900.* Hamden, Conn.: Archon Books, 1973.

——— . *Romanticism and Nationalism in the Old South.* Baton Rouge: Louisiana State University Press, 1967.

Painter, Nell Irvin. *Southern History across the Color Line.* Chapel Hill: University of North Carolina Press, 2002.

Peristiany, John G., ed. *Honour and Shame: The Values of Mediterranean Society.* London: Weidenfeld and Nicolson, 1965.

Peristiany, John G., and Julian Pitt-Rivers, eds. *Honour and Grace in Anthropology.* Cambridge: Cambridge University Press, 1992.

Peterson, M. J. *Family, Love, and Work in the Lives of Victorian Gentlewomen.* Bloomington: Indiana University Press, 1989.

Phillips, Ulrich Bonnell. *Life and Labor in the Old South.* Boston: Little, Brown, 1929.

Pitt-Rivers, Julian. "Honour." In *International Encyclopedia of the Social Sciences,* edited by David Sills, 6:503-10. New York: Macmillan and Free Press, 1968.

——— . "Honour and Social Status." In *Honour and Shame: The Values of Mediterranean Society,* edited by John G. Peristiany, 19-77. London: Weidenfeld and Nicolson, 1965.

Ponsonby, Arthur M. *English Diaries: A Review of English Diaries from the Sixteenth to the Twentieth Century with an Introduction on Diary Writing.* Ann Arbor, Mich.: Gryphon Books, 1971.

Potter, David M. *The Impending Crisis, 1848-1861.* New York: Harper and Row, 1976.

——— . *The South and the Sectional Conflict.* Baton Rouge: Louisiana State University Press, 1968.

Rable, George C. *Civil Wars: Women and the Crisis of Southern Nationalism.* Urbana: University of Illinois Press, 1989.

——— . "Missing in Action: Women of the Confederacy." In *Divided Houses: Gender and the Civil War,* edited by Catherine Clinton and Nina Silber, 134-46. New York: Oxford University Press, 1992.

Rikard, Marlene Hunt, and Elizabeth Crabtree Wells. "'From It Begins a New Era': Women and the Civil War." *Baptist History and*

Heritage 32 (July/October 1997): 59-74.

Riley, Franklin L., ed. *Publications of the Mississippi Historical Society.* Vol. 4. Oxford: Mississippi Historical Society, 1901.

Ripley, C. Peter. *Slaves and Freedmen in Civil War Louisiana.* Baton Rouge: Louisiana State University Press, 1976.

Roark, James L. *Masters without Slaves: Southern Planters in the Civil War and Reconstruction.* New York: Norton, 1977.

Robinson, Armstead Louis. "Day of Jubilo: Civil War and the Demise of Slavery in the Mississippi Valley, 1861-1865." Ph.D. diss., University of Rochester, 1977.

Rothman, Ellen K. *Hands and Hearts: A History of Courtship in America.* New York: Basic Books, 1984.

Rotundo, Anthony E. *American Manhood: Transformations in Masculinity from the Revolution to the Modern Era.* New York: Basic Books, 1993.

Ryan, Mary P. *Womanhood in America: From Colonial Times to the Present.* New York: New Viewpoints, 1975.

———. *Women in Public: Between Banners and Ballots, 1825-1880.* Baltimore: Johns Hopkins University Press, 1990.

Sacher, John M. "'The Ladies Are Moving Everywhere': Louisiana Women and Antebellum Politics." *Louisiana History* 42 (fall 2001): 439-57.

Scales, Cordelia Lewis. "Notes and Documents: The Civil War Letters of Cordelia Scales." Edited by Percy L. Rainwater. *Journal of Mississippi History* 1 (July 1939): 169-81.

Scarborough, Lucy Paxton. "So It Was when Her Life Began: Reminiscences of a Louisiana Girlhood." *Louisiana Historical Quarterly* 13 (July 1930): 428-44.

Schuler, Kathryn Reinhart. "Women in Public Affairs in Louisiana during Reconstruction." *Louisiana Historical Quarterly* 19 (July 1936): 668-750.

Scott, Anne Firor. *The Southern Lady: From Pedestal to Politics, 1830-1930.* Chicago: University of Chicago Press, 1970.

Seabury, Caroline. *The Diary of Caroline Seabury, 1854-1863.* Edited by Suzanne L. Bunkers. Madison, Wis.: University of Wisconsin Press, 1991.

Severo, Richard, and Lewis Milford. *The Wages of War: When America's Soldiers Came Home—from Valley Forge to Vietnam.* New York: Simon and Schuster, 1989.

Sides, Sudie Duncan. "Women and Slaves: An Interpretation Based on the Writings of Southern Women." Ph.D. diss., University of North Carolina, 1969.

Siedel, Kathryn Lee. *The Southern Belle in the American Novel.* Tampa: University of South Florida Press, 1985.

Silber, Nina. *The Romance of Reunion: Northerners and the South, 1865-1900.* Chapel Hill: University of North Carolina Press, 1993.

Sills, David, ed. *International Encyclopedia of the Social Sciences.* New York: Macmillan and Free Press, 1968.

Silver, James, ed. *Mississippi in the Confederacy: As Seen in Retrospect.* Baton Rouge: Louisiana State University Press, 1961.

Simkins, Francis Butler, and James Welch Patton. *The Women of the Confederacy.* Richmond, N.Y.: Garrett and Massie, 1936.

Smith-Rosenberg, Carroll. *Disorderly Conduct: Visions of Gender in Victorian America.* New York: Oxford University Press, 1985.

————. "The Female World of Love and Ritual: Relations between Women in Nineteenth-Century America." *Signs: A Journal of Women in Culture and Society* 1 (autumn 1975): 1-29.

Solomon, Clara. *The Civil War Diary of Clara Solomon: Growing Up in New Orleans, 1861-1862.* Edited by Elliott Ashkenazi. Baton Rouge: Louisiana State University Press, 1995.

Stampp, Kenneth M. *The Imperiled Union: Essays on the Background of the Civil War.* New York: Oxford University Press, 1980.

————. *The Peculiar Institution: Slavery in the Ante-Bellum South.* New York: Knopf, 1956.

————, ed. *The Causes of the Civil War.* New York: Simon and Schuster, 1991.

Sterkx, H. E. *Partners in Rebellion: Alabama Women in the Civil War.* Rutherford: Fairleigh Dickinson University Press, 1970.

Sternberg, Mary Ann. *Along the River Road: Past and Present on Louisiana's Historic Byway.* Baton Rouge: Louisiana State University Press, 2001.

Stevenson, Brenda E. *Life in Black and White: Family and Community in the Slave South.* New York: Oxford University Press, 1996.

Stone, Kate. *Brokenburn: The Journal of Kate Stone, 1861-1868.* Edited by John Q. Anderson. Baton Rouge: Louisiana State University Press, 1995.

Stowe, Steven M. "Growing Up Female in the Planter Class." *Helicon Nine: A Journal of Women's Arts and Letters* 17/18 (spring 1987): 194-205.

————. *Intimacy and Power in the Old South: Ritual in the Lives of the*

Planters. Baltimore: Johns Hopkins University Press, 1987.

Sydnor, Charles S. *Slavery in Mississippi*. Baton Rouge: Louisiana State University Press, 1966.

Taylor, Joe Gray. *Louisiana: A Bicentennial History*. New York: Norton, 1976.

Theriot, Nancy M. *Mothers and Daughters in Nineteenth-Century America: The Biosocial Construction of Femininity*. Lexington: University Press of Kentucky, 1996.

Thomas, Emory M. *The Confederate Nation, 1861-1865*. New York: Harper and Row, 1979.

Tompkins, Florence Cooney. "Women of the Sixties." *Louisiana Historical Quarterly* 2 (July 1919): 282-85.

Tunnell, Ted. *Crucible of Reconstruction: War, Radicalism, and Race in Louisiana, 1862-1877*. Baton Rouge: Louisiana State University Press, 1984.

Underwood, J. L., ed. *The Women of the Confederacy*. New York: The Neale Publishing Company, 1906.

Varon, Elizabeth R. "Tippecanoe and the Ladies, Too: White Women and Party Politics in Antebellum Virginia." *Journal of American History* 82 (September 1995): 494-521.

Vexler, Robert I., and William F. Swindler, eds. *Chronology and Documentary Handbook of the State of Mississippi*. Dobbs Ferry, N.Y.: Oceana Publications, 1978.

Walker, Peter F. *Vicksburg: A People at War, 1860-1865*. Chapel Hill: University of North Carolina Press, 1960.

Wayne, Michael. *The Reshaping of Plantation Society: The Natchez District, 1860-1880*. Baton Rouge: Louisiana State University Press, 1983.

Weiner, Marli F. *Mistresses and Slaves: Plantation Women in South Carolina, 1830-1880*. Urbana: University of Illinois Press, 1998.

Wheeler, Richard. *Voices of the Civil War*. New York: Thomas Y. Crowell, 1976.

White, Deborah Gray. *Ar'n't I a Woman?: Female Slaves in the Plantation South*. Rev. ed. New York: Norton, 1999.

Whites, Lee Ann. *The Civil War as a Crisis in Gender: Augusta, Georgia, 1860-1890*. Athens: University of Georgia Press, 1995.

Wiley, Bell Irvin. *The Life of Billy Yank: The Common Soldier of the Union*. Indianapolis: Bobbs-Merrill, 1962.

———. *The Life of Johnny Reb: The Common Soldier of the Confederacy*. 1943. Reprint, Baton Rouge: Louisiana State University Press, 1992.

Wilson, Charles Reagan. *Baptized in Blood: The Religion of the Lost Cause, 1865-1920.* Athens: University of Georgia Press, 1980.

Wilson, Charles Reagan, and William Ferris, eds. *Encyclopedia of Southern Culture.* Chapel Hill: University of North Carolina Press, 1989.

Wilson, Edmund. *Patriotic Gore: Studies in the Literature of the American Civil War.* London: Deutsch, 1962.

Wink, Amy L. *She Left Nothing in Particular: The Autobiographical Legacy of Nineteenth-Century Women's Diaries.* Knoxville: University of Tennessee Press, 2001.

Winschel, Terrence J. *Alice Shirley and the Story of Wexford Lodge.* Vicksburg, Miss.: Eastern National Park Association, 1993.

Winters, John D. *The Civil War in Louisiana.* Baton Rouge: Louisiana State University Press, 1963.

Wyatt-Brown, Bertram. *The Shaping of Southern Culture: Honor, Grace, and War, 1760s–1880s.* Chapel Hill: University of North Carolina Press, 2001.

——— . *Southern Honor: Ethics and Behavior in the Old South.* New York: Oxford University Press, 1982.

Zornow, William Frank. "State Aid for Indigent Soldiers and Their Families in Louisiana, 1861-1865." *Louisiana Historical Quarterly* 39 (July 1956): 375-80.

Index

173, 177, 178; and religious nationalism, 41; sewing for soldiers, 49, 84; on single life, 91; and slaves, 149, 151, 153; and substitution, 46–47; and Union raids, 129; and Union soldiers, 131, 139, 140; view of on cause, 40, 117; view of on war, 112, 115, 123, 124

Wadley, William (brother), 46–47

Wadley, William Morrill (father), 44, 112

Walton, Emma, 76–78, 87, 90, 93, 123, 130, 131, 154, 160

Walton, James B. (father), 76–78

Walton Bend plantation, 178

Warfield, Mary Carson, 28–29

War news: censorship of, 115; lack and unreliability of, 109, 114–115

Washington, George, 8

Wayside plantation (Worthington), 40, 70, 89, 115, 127, 128, 143, 148, 178

Weiner, Marli, 1

Whitley, Mollie, 39

Women (elite white): and Confederate soldiers, 130; employment of, in antebellum South, 17–18; employment of, in postwar South, 174–76; ideal of, 21–22; moral superiority of, 20–21; and patriotic feminine ideal, 5, 43, 78, 87; and politics, 39; position of in social hierarchy, 7, 20, 21; and postwar identity, 172; and reciprocity, 20; as refugees, 63–64; and religion, 20–21; role of in

antebellum household, 28; role of in Confederate household, 55–58; and slavery, 28, 150; view of on war, 130. *See also* Belle ideal; Belles; Mistresses

Worthington, Amanda: and black soldiers, 163; and brothers' bravery, 116–17; and Confederate soldiers, 89, 116, 130; and death of soldiers, 119–20; desire of to fight, 134; on employment, 91; and housework, 66, 70–71; postwar life of, 170, 171–72, 176, 177, 178; and slaves, 148–49, 153–54, 161; and Union raids, 127–28, 142, 143–44; and Union soldiers, 139; view of on cause, 40; view of on war, 111, 113, 115, 121, 122; and wartime fundraising, 52

Worthington, Bert (brother), 116, 119, 128

Worthington, Samuel (father), 148

Worthington, William (brother), 116, 117

Wright, Esther (sister). *See* Boyd, Esther Wright

Wright, Mary: and death of soldiers, 87–88; depression of, 86; and fasting, 41; postwar life of, 169–70, 173, 177, 178; sewing for soldiers, 49, 50, 84; and shortages, 59

Wyatt-Brown, Bertram, 3, 4

Yeoman farmers, 3, 7, 8, 37

Yerger, Louise, 87